CULINARY SECRETS
of Great Virginia Chefs

CULINARY SECRETS
of Great Virginia Chefs

❧ ELEGANT DINING ☙
from Colonial Williamsburg to Historic Richmond

By the
VIRGINIA CHEFS ASSOCIATION
and
MARTHA HOLLIS ROBINSON

RUTLEDGE HILL PRESS
Nashville, Tennessee

The Brunswick Stew recipes on page 116 are from Marion Cabell Tyree, ed.,
Housekeeping in Old Virginia (Louisville, Ky.: John P. Morton and Co., 1879), 212.
The recipe for Old Virginia Catsup on page 199 is from Maud C. Cooke,
The Colorado Cook Book or What to Eat and How to Prepare It (Victor, Colo.:
Colorado Book Co., 1901), 322–23.

Published in Nashville, Tennessee, by Rutledge Hill Press,
211 Seventh Avenue North, Nashville, Tennessee 37219

Typography by D&T/Bailey Typesetting, Inc., Nashville, Tennessee
Design by Gore Studio, Inc., Nashville, Tennessee
Instructional illustrations by Jan Ledbetter Studio, Williamsburg, Virginia

Library of Congress Cataloging-in-Publication Data

Culinary secrets of great Virginia chefs : elegant dining from colonial Williamsburg
    to historic Richmond / by the Virginia Chefs Association and Martha Hollis
    Robinson.
        p.   cm.
    Includes index.
    ISBN 1-55853-335-4
    1. Cookery, American—Southern style. 2. Cookery—Virginia.
    I. Robinson, Martha Hollis. II. Virginia Chefs Association.
    TX715.2.S68C84 1995
    641.59755—dc20
                                                                                    95–15890
                                                                                    CIP

Printed in the United States of America.

1 2 3 4 5 6 7 8 9 — 99 98 97 96 95

CONTENTS

ACKNOWLEDGMENTS

So MANY people contributed in developing this haute cuisine of Virginia. First, the chefs graciously shared their recipes, tips, and worked hard on the manuscript. Each magnificent chef deserves my thanks for their generosity, enthusiasm, and patience. In the two years since this book began I have received a million-dollar education in the culinary arts. With every recipe and every chef's meeting, there was always new information, new learning, and insight from these authorities on Virginia cuisine. Their kitchens were always opened to me, even with their hectic schedules. And it was so rewarding spending time with people passionate about their profession.

Particularly instrumental was Chef Robert Corliss, the cookbook liaison, who encouraged chefs to complete their recipes. He was always ready with culinary advice and suggestions. His patient, unrelenting efforts brought this book to completion with his excellent writing of recipes and tips and careful reading of drafts. As editor of *The Stockpot,* the VCA newsletter, he researched a substantial amount of the chefs' profile section. Chef Corliss is an outstanding young chef with a brilliant career ahead.

David Bruce Clarke led the early contributors and researched early Virginia ways. Anthony Conte painstakingly read through early drafts, making helpful hints. Otto Bernet generously gave of his energies in converting professional baking ingredients to home scale. John Marlowe inspired us to keep going with his creative hardware hints.

William F. Fulton magnanimously shared "Tremendous Trifles," his collection of personal touches and success secrets of individuals in the food service field—a piece used for many years in his teaching of new chefs.

Manfred Roehr, the careful treasurer, regularly paid all the bills and supplied encouragement, his good humor, and his recipes. Mark Kimmel, Mike Vosburg, Brad Ozerdem, and Winslow Goodier, busy executive chefs, kept the recipes pouring in. Rolf Herion, over a glorious lunch at the Golden Horseshoe golf course restaurant, gave insight into the life of a professional baker along with a tour of the course. Ted Kristensen, prompt with recipes, over lunch in his former restaurant in the Williamsburg Lodge, told stories of his career cheffing all over the world. Chef Jeff Bland led the pack with cooking tips. Marcel Desaulniers, David Barrish, and Karen Sherwood made extra efforts in finding a publisher.

Atlantic Seafood, through the vivacious Jo Olson, graciously supplied seafood for testing. I gained great insights from the food show sponsored by Pocahontas Foods and their representative Colby Fitzhugh. Baker Brothers Produce and Nesson Meats, through demonstrations at monthly chefs' meetings, were helpful. The Virginia Institute of Marine Science, through its annual chef seafood seminar, taught us the latest in seafood safety while providing a forum for chefs to display their skills.

Cuisinart supplied both mechanical and electronic scales and their conversion chart for weights and measurements. Bendes supplied their ultimate nonstick pan and high-tech pan along with baking equipment.

The American Culinary Federation, of which the Virginia Chefs Association is a regional chapter, supplied information on the professional role of a chef, their professional code of ethics, and certification. The ACF directs the Horizons 2000 project aimed at increasing the chefs' knowledge so they may better serve the public.

As my job was to convert recipes for the consumer, I am grateful to many who opened their kitchens and mouths to our testings. Libba and Julian Fields, Mary and Tom Inman, Patsy and Bob Fulmer, Lois and Carl Polifka shared dishes at their parties. Ethel and Phil Goodman cheerfully lent me their Palm Springs kitchen for testing. Elizabeth and John L. Hollis ate many, many creations while their children Caroline, Lydia, and John provided a totally honest "kids' perspective." And the ladies of my literary group nibbled many items before feeding my cultural soul with literary knowledge, while those in my water aerobics class kept me in touch with local chef gossip and healthy eating.

A trained chef in his own right, Richard Walker spent an enormous amount of time testing some of the bread recipes. His insights enriched this book. Fabulous gourmet cooks and friends who shared insight include Emily McCardle, Annabelle Goodman, Susie Williamson, and Elaine

Nalls Bell. Susan Hailey's comments on the weighing of ingredients, particularly flour, were invaluable.

My parents, Louise and John M. Hollis, who love anything I make, kept loving them and faithfully saved their local newspaper food sections for my further enlightenment.

My husband Neal Robinson enjoyed the testings, but rarely had a complete dinner since I tended to test mostly by available ingredients. One night would be all crab dishes, one night everything was eggplant, one night soups, another night desserts or potatoes. He was always available for technological support, with gifts of a new computer, fax, enlarged monitors, and a ready answer to all those nasty computer questions. His underwriting the overhead of the test kitchen is equally appreciated. But more importantly, he kept the encouragement coming while jokingly complaining that he never got to eat his favorite items twice.

Larry Stone, president and publisher of Rutledge Hill Press, decided to produce this book after an inspired trip through our beloved Virginia. Special thanks also go to illustrator Jan Ledbetter, whose pen-and-ink drawings illustrate the chefs' techniques and plate layouts. Bill Boxer did a wonderful job photographing the chefs' creations and the picture on the cover.

And finally my thanks to Chef Hans Schadler who conceived the idea of this book and included me in the project. He constantly managed to be available and creatively helped to bring the project to completion.

MARTHA HOLLIS ROBINSON

PREFACE

CULINARY SECRETS is for everyone sharing our cooking enthusiasm—serious home cooks, weekend dabblers, novices, gourmets, culinary students, and professional chefs. It is a working tool belonging in the kitchen—not a coffee table book. We trust it will become worn with use. We've tried to share innovative ideas and unusual approaches. Not solely a cookbook, it is a book of information, history, and culinary expertise.

We are very excited to showcase our Virginia Chefs Association members and their enormous talents. Since our first unique collection of recipes, *Great Chefs of Virginia*, we have expanded to over 150 active members. Our cookbook was forgotten by us, except for its periodic royalty check.

But time has passed, and our second book reflects our growth in size, prowess, ideas, and knowledge of nutrition and health. Continually our members receive recognition from their restaurants and institutions, celebrity dinners, and charity events through their wealth of beautiful and creative dishes. With this book, we hope to reach more lovers of fine cuisine. Its contents reflect a myriad of styles and personalities as diverse and ingenious as our membership.

Book proceeds are partially dedicated to the chapter's quality culinary education and the Horizons 2000 project of the American Culinary Federation (ACF). The ACF (see appendix) is the national professional organization responsible for certifying chefs and assisting with their continuing education. For initial certification, the chef must past rigorous examinations on nutrition, sanitation, and supervisory management in addition to those on culinary knowledge. It also sponsors ACFEI (ACF Educational Institution) programs for a two-year college degree in the culinary arts. Associated with such education is an intensive hands-on working apprenticeship.

Before dining in any establishment, ask the question, are the chefs trained and certified to cook for me? Remember, your dining pleasure and health are at stake.

With advancements in food science, nutritional research, and technology, chefs must continue to learn. The more informed a chef, the better he or she can serve the public.

Through the nationwide network of local chapters, expert knowledge through videotapes is being shared. The USA culinary team's series on cooking around the world took every chef on an armchair learning discovery. Videos prepared by the Beef and Lamb councils are teaching us about the butchering, preparation, and safe handling of product.

Horizons 2000 aims to eventually build its own studio kitchen at ACF headquarters in Saint Augustine, Florida. In addition, experts on various topics will also be sent to lecture at chapter meetings to further our knowledge base.

We all will benefit from the continuing education of chefs. It promises to enhance dining experiences for our customers.

HANS SCHADLER, CEC, AAC
Executive Chef, Director of Food Operations, The Williamsburg Inn and Williamsburg Lodge and Conference Center
Chairman, Virginia Chefs Association, ACF

INTRODUCTION

TODAY'S COMPOSITION of Virginia Chefs mirrors three hundred years of immigrants improving and changing our stockpots and culinary stylings: from Europe, Africa, Asia, and South America. Men and women employed in restaurants, resorts, private clubs, and hospitals as well as purveyors of product each have valued contributions and varying notions about today's exciting Virginia cuisines.

Each has contributed an important piece of today's Virginia cuisine—a cuisine steeped in historic tradition and grounded in impeccably delicious tastes. This is not a melting-pot cuisine. It is the carefully crafted integration over centuries of the finest gastronomic concepts, homespun ways, and professional skills which have been tested, enhanced, and loved by all who call Virginia their home.

In this unique cookbook we have carefully selected a rich variety of recipes requiring all levels of cooking skills. Each recipe is rated according to the degree of difficulty. If a recipe has five stars, be prepared to work hard. An example is the Tuxedo Truffle Torte by 1993 Perrier Jouet Chef and award-winning cookbook author Marcel Desaulniers. But also be prepared to establish yourself as a well-accomplished cook. A one-star recipe, such as the Dried Cherry and Cranberry Fruit Compote, is fast, easy, and guaranteed to be good. These too will establish your reputation.

Many ingredients featured are seasonally fresh in Virginia—asparagus, snap beans, strawberries, sweet corn, peaches, tomatoes, cantaloupes, and watermelons. Others we import from other parts of the world. Locally we find crabs, oysters, fishes, and scallops. Along with our famous Virginia country-cured hams, our recipes promote our bounty.

Chef's Notes, included with each recipe, are tantamount to having a chef in your kitchen whispering tested secrets to improve your culinary skills. Here you will find secrets on many fascinating topics—equipment, ingredients, stylings, substitutions, variations, tricks. These represent millions of dollars' worth of cooking lessons and practical experience.

Scientific evidence clearly links eating and health. Our chefs accepted this challenge and created elegant heart-healthy • entrées: Shrimp with Angel Hair Pasta, Mexican Chicken, and Breast of Chicken on a Roasted Red Pepper Sauce with Red Onion Marmalade and Spinach Fettuccine.

Lower-fat recipe versions that do not sacrifice taste appear in many of the notes. These are the result of hours of experimentation and testing. Nothing will ever duplicate the rich mouth-feel of heavy cream, but that sensation is not needed everyday. Be sure to try the skim milk "cream" soups.

Many fruit- and vegetable-based sauces and chutneys emphasize new, healthier cooking styles and bolster the count towards consuming more of these vitamin- and fiber-rich foods. Try Black-eyed Pea Salsa, Bing Cherry Chutney, or Chinese Brown Sauce. In fact, only 10 percent of the recipes in chapter 8 (Condiments, Chutneys, and Other Tempters) contain added fats.

Basic techniques—French and rye bread, Italian sausage, fresh pastas, homemade ice cream, pastry meringues, and breakfast egg cookery—carefully reveal new additions for your repertoire.

Also look for cost-effective methods of food preparation, storage tips, beautiful presentation and garnishing insights, and creative substitution ideas. These secrets are as diverse as the chefs and their cuisines.

Mise en place (have all ingredients and equipment ready to use) is a motto of professional chefs. And the most important culinary secret. By reading the entire recipe ahead of time and arranging your ingredients and equipment, the cooking progress becomes smoother and easier.

Brad Ozerdem, executive chef of the Hyatt Richmond, encourages our readers: "Remember, cooking is a creative process that should give pleasure to the eye, nose, mouth, and especially the spirit. You should feel free to change ingredients to your fancy. Please ask yourself 'what if?' when cooking. Do not judge your ideas until you've tried them. Above all, enjoy your experience with food."

VIRGINIA CUISINE THROUGH TIME

NO DOUBT the tired settlers on three tiny ships landing on Jamestown Island in 1607 would have enthusiastically greeted the Virginia Chefs Association cuisine of the twentieth century. No Epicurean delights did they enjoy along the way. The cruise on the *Godspeed*, the *Susan Constant*, and the *Discovery* is better defined as an unplanned weight loss sailing.

Hunger was a powerful motivator for jumping right into the native foods of fish and shellfish, game, poultry, and vegetation. Adapt the newcomers did—their fragile lives were at stake. Along with the primarily agrarian Algonquin Indian tribes, these settlers, employees of the venture capitalist London Company, were early players in an evolutionary cuisine. During the winter of 1607 Chief Powhatan's men both provided foods while sharing their agriculture and fishing techniques.

Maize (or corn) cultivated by the native Indians became a staple as well as a profitable export item to Europe. Over the years it has been found in corn bread, corn cakes, the sensual spoon bread, hush puppies, grits—just to mention a few cornerstones of the Virginia regional cuisine. Even though some Virginia cooks claim that only white cornmeal is suitable, others prefer the golden yellow cornmeal.

With no walk-in refrigeration, salt preservation techniques safely created a meat supply. Today's Virginia country hams (originally peanut-fed) are prized for their complex flavors. Virginians eat such in paper-thin portions frequently teamed with oysters, eggs, biscuits, or chicken. The chefs favor these hams, bacon, and Surry sausages as regional signature products.

Women emigrating to Virginia brought European seeds and cooking styles. Rare was a family without a kitchen garden including fresh herbs for seasonings and medicines and tender vegetables. Plenty of rain pounded the rich soils, bringing forth bountiful produce.

To manage the evolving plantation structure or large self-sufficient dwelling centers, the first slaves arrived in 1619 bringing along the glorious peanut (originally carried from South America by the Portuguese). Today's chefs enhance these for Virginia favorites—

sweet peanut pie, cream of peanut soup, and even for their peanut butter sandwiches. Also of African origin are watermelons, black-eyed peas, and okra. Some Africans came by way of Caribbean slavery, bringing more spices and varied food stylings.

The Colonial era's foodways are well-documented thanks to our nation's largest living historic museum under the Colonial Williamsburg Foundation. The food historians' and archaeologists' research are instrumental in recreating the food program. Demonstrations at the Governor's palace detail the hearthside cooking techniques of the eighteenth century. Similar work on the seventeenth century is demonstrated at the Jamestown Settlement park operated by the state of Virginia.

Thomas Jefferson, our first governor during the American Revolution, was the first farmer to grow potatoes and tomatoes in Virginia soil. He also introduced the forerunners of two important gadgets: the waffle iron and pasta maker. Dazzled by French cuisine, he brought the first French chef to the area.

Measuring Amounts

Our home testers very positively responded to the use of scales for measuring items. "How easy it makes cooking!" "Why have I not used these all along?" exclaimed many of our testers.

Professional chefs weigh many dry items—liquids are measured by volume. A professional recipe formula would call for "4 ounces of flour" not "1 cup sifted flour" as in most home recipes.

Weighing is precise. The cup for non-liquid items is not. More than 4 ounces may be in the cup of flour depending on how packed is the flour, the humidity, and the angle of cook's eyes looking at the cup.

By using weights we have simplified both shopping and preparation. How many pounds of carrots would one purchase to create 2 cups of grated carrots? Do the size of the holes make a difference? By specifying the number of ounces needed, these questions become irrelevant.

The number of cooking steps is simplified when weighing. Suppose a recipe in which the cheese is to be melted calls for ½ cup grated cheese. Usually, the only reason to undertake the time-consuming and messy job of grating is to measure the amount. With scaling, cut off the required ounces. Weigh. Simple.

We recommend a small home scale that may be purchased for less than thirty dollars. We tested these from numerous manufacturers and suggest Cuisinart's precision scale. Their electronic scale, while more expensive, is an excellent investment as a container's weight can be subtracted and each successive ingredient's weight accumulated—the perfect instrument for baking measurements.

All recipes provide both the traditional home cup measurement system and the professional weighing system. Thus, the user can select either measuring system and experiment with a more accurate approach.

By sharing the experience of the Virginia chefs we hope to meet our goal of making your cooking a more creative and rewarding experience.

Recipe Complexity and Yields

Each recipe is rated for difficulty using a scale of one to five stars. Easiest recipes have one star. The more difficult, the more stars. A five-star recipe will be both difficult and time consuming. There are several recipes with this rating, but if you follow the directions and allow plenty of time, the results should be good.

Standard restaurant servings provide information about a recipe's yield. To be more precise, frequently the serving size is stipulated, such as 4 8-ounce servings. As an example, the rating for Chicken Provençale with Saffron Linguine (page 108) is:

Complexity ✪ Yield: 2 servings

The dish is easy to make and will provide two adult servings.

THE MAKING OF A CHEF: TWO PERSPECTIVES

THE CHEF's profession is rigorous and demanding—one of constant pressure and little glamour. It is a life without a traditional social life as most chefs work when the majority of the world is at its partying best. It is a life requiring good shoes to support feet that are always in use, well-developed upper body strength to lift heavy pots, and dexterity and artistry to create the finer points of exceptional cuisine. The work environment is not a luxury. There are no chairs in kitchens, no air conditioning, and often cramped work spaces. The pace is unrelenting during peak periods. It is a life without regular meals—no eating is permitted in kitchens. Staff meals are held in-between traditional dining hours, and the food is usually pedestrian, saving the finest ingredients for the patrons. Executive chefs have the luxury of chairs in their offices, but they are little used except to check supplies, review personnel, and requisite management tasks.

Despite the rigors of the profession, there are many rewards. The primary one is bringing pleasure, intrigue, and excitement to diners. Two chefs offer brief essays below on their perspective on the profession. The first is from a seasoned executive chef, honored as a member of the prestigious American Academy of Chefs. The second is from a rising star who is most ambitious about the profession.

NOT ALWAYS does a good cook make a chef. Without good cooks, there would be no great chefs.

The young boy or girl first asking their mother in the kitchen at home: "How do you do this? Could I try it?" is the beginning of this wonderful sense called curiosity which is the first requirement; the next is devotion and commitment to an industry where only the best succeed. When you are committed, eager, and full of ideas, and have applied to culinary college or an apprentice program in a hotel or restaurant for the next few years, you will find the word "Chef" stands for educator, instructor, drill sergeant, confessor, and mentor.

If all goes well, now you are entitled to be called "Cook." Thus begins special training over a wide spectrum: entremetier, saucier, chef du parti, garde manger, sous chef, executive sous chef, working chef, executive chef, master chef.* In that same light and format bakers and pastry chefs are also created.

The road of ten to twelve years can be long and arduous, but then the first of many rewards comes when you hear from your audience "Thank you, chef, for a wonderful meal." When accepted, your peers in the culinary world also call you "Chef."

You now, as other respected professionals, have earned an office and a code to live by. The code of the American Culinary Federation says:

> I pledge my professional knowledge and skill to the advancement of our profession

---

* The kitchen brigade was established by Maitre Auguste Escoffier at the turn of the twentieth century, providing organization for restaurant and hotel kitchens. Escoffier detailed the classical management team of an executive chef (chief-executive officer) and sous chef (second chef, in charge of production) with the division of labor (chefs de partie): saucier (sauces, stocks, hot hors d'oeuvres), potager (soups and chowders), poissoner (fish dishes), entremetier (vegetables, starches, and eggs), rotisseur (roasted meats and gravies), grillardin (broiled and fried items), garde manger (cold foods), patissier (pastries and desserts), baker (breads and rolls), and tournant (relief cook).

and to pass on to those that are to follow. I shall foster a spirit of courteous consideration and fraternal cooperation within our profession.

I trust that the members of the Virginia Chefs Association have conscientiously and faithfully fulfilled the promises of the title of this work. We look with pleasure on our book, however defective, and deliver it to the world with the spirit of a profession that has endeavored well.

TED KRISTENSEN, CEC, AAC
The Willows Bed and Breakfast
Glouchester

"WHAT DO I have to offer to the culinary art? What does it have to offer to me?" ultimately brought me to a position as a culinary apprentice.

I want to be a chef in order to satisfy my life-long artistic aspirations while using my business savvy. The culinary arts are indeed an art form, but every kitchen's mere existence is dependent upon the restaurant's financial success. The balance between art and business with relation to past tradition and future trends forms a challenging matrix which I find captivating.

I have been involved in the restaurant industry for more than ten years in one fashion or another. Upon graduating from college I was employed in restaurant management for three years, after which I created The Blue Ridge Brewing Company, a restaurant and brew-pub in Charlottesville, Virginia, with two childhood friends. To this day I am a stockholder in this highly successful operation.

The culinary profession is an extremely demanding one. It is often criticized for its long hours, strenuously fast pace, staff shortages, odd work schedules, and minuscule pay at the lower levels. These are not unjus-

tified criticisms, but they help to characterize the uniqueness of the business.

Cheffing is a fast-paced business, constantly changing and evolving. Interpretations of the past traditions provide impetus for cutting-edge trends that drive us into the future. Because of these trends the business as a whole tends to be very spirited and youthful. Menu and recipe creation, along with culinary competition, are among the most rewarding aspects of the profession. They provide constant gratification if the proper amount of work and knowledge are applied.

The public's perception of the culinary art is one of respect. Peer recognition is very important, especially if many personal sacrifices are made in order to fulfill occupational demands. The public perception of a chef is one of creative talent and mystical knowledge.

Cheffing is the perfect outlet for artistic aspiration. The variety of media is unlimited. Fruits, vegetables, starches, meats, fish, sauces, and soups all provide endless combination potential. It not only has to look appealing, but also has to taste delectable.

As in any art form, there is the potential for expressing one's personality through style. Culinary creations are a parade ground for stimulated expression. The bright yellow of a saffron sauce may reflect a light cheery mood, whereas the red of a cabernet sauce may reflect a more earthen, wintry mood.

The passionate side of cooking is in its artistic influence, the realistic side is in the demand for financial success. Food cost control, labor force and payroll, overhead costs, and advertising are a restaurant's life line. The bottom line is that a restaurant has to keep all these elements in perspective in order for it to survive and be successful.

ANTHONY CONTE, CC
The Country Club of Virginia
Richmond

CHAPTER 1
Sumptuous Starters

Seasoning a skillet properly is important so that food will not stick. To a very hot pan add a couple of tablespoons of oil. Tilt so entire bottom is coated. Pour out any excess oil and reserve. Pour in a half cup of salt (or less for a small pan). Do not worry: salt is cheap. Rub in with a rag. Remove salt, wipe again with oil. Keep warm if there is waiting period before using. Do not use this technique for a nonstick, coated pan.—*Chef Conte*

When working with bacon or pancetta, if very thin or fine dice is needed, freeze it first. Because of the high fat content it will cut easily while frozen.—*Chef Conte*

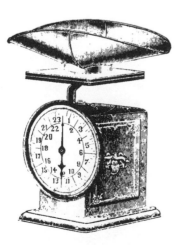

To mince garlic easily, first mash with the back edge of a chef's knife (opposite the cutting edge). When finely mashed, it can now be chopped in a fraction of the normal chopping time.—*Chef Conte*

To store fresh herbs, place in a plastic bag with a damp paper towel. Exhale into the bag with air and seal. Store in the refrigerator. Herbs thrive on carbon dioxide.
　　　　　　　　　　　　　—*Chef Conte*

Fresh basil is very inexpensive late in the summer. Purée in a food processor with a bit of olive oil. Roll in film wrap like a large cigar. Then cover with foil and twist ends to tightly seal. Store in the freezer. As needed, cut off a section. Enjoy the sensational taste of basil all year long. Do not forget to label everything before placing in the freezer.—*Chef Conte*

Utilize fresh herbs whenever possible for seasoning and garnishing. Add fresh herbs at the end of a cooking process to ensure maximum flavor. Before chopping fresh herbs remove as much of the stems as possible. Crush or rub gently between the hands to bring out the essential oils.
　　　　　　　　　　　　　—*Chef Bland*

A sure way to tell if fish is fresh is by the smell. Freshly caught fish have little smell. As fish age, they smell stronger.

—Chef Bland

If you store fish on ice beware of the melted water. It takes away the color and flavor of the fish along with valuable nutrients and oils. Change the ice often. If possible, use a perforated pan insert that will permit the water to drain.—*Chef Bland*

With crabmeat less seasoning is more. Lemon juice, white wine, Tabasco or hot sauce mask and cover up the wonderful, delicate flavor of crab.—*Chef Bland*

Do not be afraid to substitute one protein for another. Try cod in place of salmon, or swordfish or shark in a recipe for tuna. Use judgment and imagination. Dare to be different, and try chicken or pork for beef or veal.—*Chef Bland*

The FDA consumer seafood hot line at (800) FDA-4010, has recorded safety, cooking, and storage information on finfish and shellfish.

Grilled Scallops on a Rosemary Stem with Sautéed Shiitake Mushrooms

JEFF BLAND
EXECUTIVE CHEF
Buckhead Steak House, Richmond
CHEF-INSTRUCTOR
J. Sargeant Reynolds Community College

Run out to the garden and harvest a bit of rosemary. This woody herb grows well in an indoor sunny location during the winter months. The fresh sea scallops are glorious with the subtly imparted herb flavor matched with the woodsy taste of shiitakes.

Complexity ✪✪✪   Yield: 4 servings

16 medium sea scallops
 4 medium rosemary stems with leaves intact
   salt and pepper to taste
12 large shiitake mushrooms
 2 cloves garlic, minced
   juice of 1 lemon
 ¼ cup (2 ounces) butter
   chopped parsley

Skewer 4 scallops on each rosemary stem. Season with salt and pepper. Remove stems from mushrooms and julienne tops very fine. Sauté in a hot skillet with a small amount of butter. Add minced garlic. Cook for 1 minute. Stir in lemon juice. Remove from heat. Swirl in butter. Spray scallops and grill with nonstick coating. Grill approximately 2 minutes on each side or until just cooked through. Arrange mushrooms on center of each plate. Carefully place scallops on top. Sprinkle with parsley.

Chef's Notes
* *Save the woody mushroom stems for making stock. Fresh shiitakes are available in selected markets. Both fresh and dried ones are available from Woodland Farm, 100 Woodland Road, Williamsburg, VA 23188, (804) 566-3346 or (800) 296-8530.*
* *The dried ones must first be soaked.*
* *Both the rosemary and scallops are delicate. Use care when inserting stems so as not to lose many leaves nor to tear the scallops.*
* *Use the hottest part of the grill to prevent scallops from sticking.*

Baby Green Beans with Grilled Scallops

BRAD OZERDEM

EXECUTIVE CHEF

Hyatt Richmond at Brookfield, Richmond

Chef's Notes

- *Pink scallops, the female during certain cycles, are edible, as is the scallop roe. Chefs are beginning to use more of the delicate roes even though most are exported to Europe and Asia. Scallops are shucked on deep sea dredges and stored under carefully controlled conditions to ensure safety and quality.*
- *In the market, make scallops the last item to go into the cart so they can remain refrigerated. Or take a small six-pack cooler. Add a little ice, which a fishmonger gladly gives customers who care enough to transfer products correctly. Place scallops in wrapper on ice. Do not place directly on ice as they will absorb water.*
- *Wash scallops before cooking.*
- *Store scallops in refrigerator at 33° to 36°. They will deteriorate rapidly at higher temperatures.*
- *Marinate only under refrigeration.*
- *If a grill is not handy, broil or sauté the scallops.*
- *For two, this recipe makes the perfect entrée.*

Serve the scallops just warm from the grill when the translucency is nearly gone. Just at this point they are cooked and exceptionally tender, moist, and succulent. Slice open one scallop to test for doneness—an appropriate "sacrifice" for the cook. Since scallops cook quickly, start testing even before you think they are done. Yes, more sacrifices. Scallop shells, as Greek legends tell, carried Aphrodite, the goddess of love, over the Aegean Sea.

Complexity ❁❁❁   Yield: 4 servings

SALAD

½ **pound baby green beans (haricots verts), stems removed**
1 **medium yellow bell pepper, sliced into very fine strips**
1 **medium red bell pepper, sliced into very fine strips**
¾ **pound sea scallops**

MARINADE

2 **tablespoons (1 ounce) extra-virgin olive oil**
1 **tablespoon (½ ounce) dry white wine or dry sherry**
1 **tablespoon (½ ounce) fresh lemon juice (or juice of ½ large lemon)**
   freshly ground black pepper to taste

DRESSING

1 **medium shallot, peeled and minced**
⅓ **cup (2½ ounces) canola oil**
2 **tablespoons (1 ounce) walnut oil**
3 **tablespoons (1½ ounces) Spanish sherry vinegar**
   salt to taste
   freshly ground black pepper to taste

Bring 2 quarts of water to boil in a 3-quart pan. Cook beans 3 minutes. Drain. Plunge into icy water to stop cooking. Drain well. Mix marinade ingredients. Marinate scallops for 30 minutes. Mix dressing ingredients. Grill scallops. Toss beans and peppers in three-fourths of the dressing. Place on platter. Toss scallops with remaining dressing. Arrange on top of vegetables.

Oysters with Diced Peaches and Curry Sabayon

DOMINADOR VALEROS

SUPERVISOR LEAD CHEF, C.C.

Shields Tavern, Colonial Williamsburg, Williamsburg

A trip to the docks where the oystermen come in with the catch is the best place to find fresh oysters. Flash-cooked oysters are returned to their cleaned shell base, sweetened with fresh, fragrant pieces of peach, then covered with a lightly curry-scented sabayon sauce. Finish under the broiler and serve 6 to each connoisseur, who will probably begin negotiations with the other diners for some of their portions.

Complexity ✪✪✪   **Yield: 4 servings**

24 *Chesapeake Bay oysters, brushed and cleaned*
 2 *handfuls fresh seaweed or 4½ pounds rock salt*
 2 *teaspoons curry powder*
 1 *teaspoon unsalted butter*
 6 *tablespoons (3 ounces) oyster juice*
 3 *egg yolks*
 5 *tablespoons (2½ ounces) unsalted butter, melted*
    pinch cayenne pepper
    salt to taste
 ¼ *cup (2 ounces) heavy cream, whipped to soft peaks*
    squeeze of fresh lemon
 2 *ripe peaches (8 ounces), peeled, diced, and refrigerated*

oyster preparation

Shuck oysters, saving juices. Place the shucked oysters in juice and refrigerate. Discard flat top shell. Wash curved bottom shell and save. Wash seaweed. Blanch 1 minute. Refresh in ice water. Arrange seaweed (or rock salt) on 4 plates. Arrange 6 curved shells on each plate.

curry sabayon

In a large nonstick fry pan, cook curry powder in 1 teaspoon of butter over high heat for 3 minutes or until it begins to release its fragrance. Reserve half in nonstick pan for cooking oysters. In a double boiler over simmering water add the remaining half to oyster juice and egg yolks. Whisk until tripled in volume. Whisk in melted butter (and one more tablespoon of oyster juice if too thick). Add cayenne pepper and salt, if needed. Whisk in whipped cream. Remove from heat.

Chef's Notes
- *Fresh oysters are available year-round and are excellent to eat even if "r" is not in the name of the month. Fresh oysters are alive with a tightly closed shell. Any that do not close the shell when tapped must be discarded. When shucked, these oysters should be plump with a creamy color and a clear or opalescent liquid.*
- *Add a squeeze of fresh lemon to the oysters before refrigeration to prevent browning.*

cooking oysters

Flash-sauté oysters in fry pan with reserved curry for 10 seconds to firm up. Remove from heat. Add squeeze of lemon. Let sit 1 minute. Drain off remaining juices.

assembly

Garnish each oyster shell with a teaspoon of diced peaches. Top with oyster. Mask with curry sabayon. Place under broiler until sauce begins to brown. Serve immediately.

Crabmeat Randolph

HANS SCHADLER
Executive Chef, C.E.C., A.A.C.

The Williamsburg Inn, Colonial Williamsburg, Williamsburg

This recipe is based on an eighteenth-century recipe found in the papers of Mrs. John Randolph by Rosemary Brandau, the excellent Foodways director for the Colonial Williamsburg Foundation. It originally called for a velouté sauce with local rockfish and Virginia hams.

Lumps of sweet, silky crabmeat matched with the fine-grained, salty Smithfield or Surry Virginia ham regally sit on puff pastry croutons. Then, reminiscent of the royal cuisine served in Chef Schadler's five-star Williamsburg Inn, the starter receives a golden crown of sensual, tangy Hollandaise sauce. To complete the royal theme, serve on your finest bone china and savor with a silver fork.

Chef's Notes
- *Do not egg wash pastry.*
- *Save trimmed puff pastry sides for a delicate, crunchy soup garnish.*
- *For appetizers, use 1½-inch diameter puff pastry rounds. Assemble immediately before serving.*
- *Richard Grausman's* At Home with the French Classics *(New York: Workman, 1988) has one of the best written and fail-proof recipes for Hollandaise sauce.*

Complexity ❸❸❸   **Yield: 4 servings**

- 4 **shells frozen puff pastry**
- ½ **pound backfin crabmeat, picked over**
  juice of half a fresh lemon
- 2 **tablespoons (1 ounce) butter**
- 1 **shallot, minced**
- ¾ **cup (6 ounces) Hollandaise sauce**
- 2 **teaspoons Dijon mustard**
- 2 **small (2 ounces), paper-thin slices Smithfield or Surry Virginia ham**

Place puff pastry shells upside-down on an ungreased baking sheet in a 450° oven. Reduce heat to 400°. Bake for 18 to 20 minutes or until golden brown. Cut each shell in half, forming two round pieces. Trim sides off to leave a flat crouton. Toss crabmeat gently with lemon juice. Melt butter in small skillet. Add shallot and sauté over medium heat until soft. Do not brown. Add crabmeat and gently toss over low heat for 2 minutes so crabmeat is well-coated with butter. Combine Hollandaise and mustard. Place 2 croutons on each of 4 warmed plates. Top each with a slice of ham, followed by crabmeat. Crown with sauce. Serve immediately.

Crab and Roasted Red Pepper Cheesecake

JO OLSON
ACCOUNT EXECUTIVE
Atlantic Food Services, Inc., Richmond

Chef's Notes
- *Red peppers can be roasted under the broiler. Turn frequently until peppers are charred on all sides. Place in plastic bag for 10 minutes. Then pull off charred exterior. They can be rinsed; however, purists claim that process washes away critical flavors.*
- *Substitute lobster or shrimp for the crab.*

Baking in a slow, slow oven allows this appetizer cheesecake to gently set up. Because it is extravagantly rich, it will feed a crowd. Serve with slices of fresh baguette and crisp Granny Smith apples. Freeze any leftovers for partying at a later time.

Complexity ❸❸❸   Yield: 16 to 20 servings

⅓ cup fine breadcrumbs (from 1 slice fresh bread)
¼ cup grated fresh Parmesan cheese
1 medium (4 ounces) onion, diced
2 small cloves garlic, minced
2 pounds cream cheese
¼ cup (2 ounces) all-purpose flour
5 eggs
3 egg yolks
⅓ cup (3 ounces) heavy cream
3 cups grated (12 ounces) sharp Cheddar cheese
1 pound red bell peppers, roasted and chopped
1 pound lump crabmeat, picked over

Butter a 10-inch springform pan. Combine breadcrumbs and Parmesan cheese. Sprinkle over bottom of pan. In a small pan sauté onions and garlic in a small amount of butter until limp. Using an electric mixer, beat together the cream cheese, flour, eggs, and cream. Fold in onions, garlic, Cheddar, roasted red peppers, and crab. Place pan in a water bath filled with 2 inches of boiling water. Bake at 250° for 1 hour and 40 minutes. Turn off heat. Leave in oven 1 hour. Remove. Let cool for 2 hours before unmolding.

Crab Balls

JOHN LONG
ROUNDS CHEF, C.C.

The Williamsburg Inn, Colonial Williamsburg, Williamsburg

One bite into these crab balls is the only reminder needed to double the recipe next time. Serve while still hot. They go quite well with Bloody Marys.

Complexity ✪   **Yield: 8 servings**

1	pound crabmeat, picked over
2½	tablespoons mayonnaise
2	tablespoons (1 ounce) prepared mustard
1	egg
1	tablespoon seafood seasoning (Old Bay)
12	crackers, crushed

Mix. Form into walnut-size balls and deep-fry until golden brown. Serve immediately.

Chef's Notes
• *Use a small scoop to speed the preparation time immensely. Similar to an ice cream scoop, these are available in many sizes in restaurant supply stores and well worth the investment.*

Smithfield Crab Fritters

RICHARD H. GOODWIN
CHEF-OWNER
Delaney's Cafe and Grill, Richmond

Chef's Notes
• *Blue crab is abundant in Virginia's waters. Commercially, crab is available fresh, frozen, and canned. While any form may be used, fresh is best. Spread out crabmeat on plastic wrap or on plate. Carefully run fingers through to remove stray bits of cartilage and shell.*

Merging two wildly popular Virginia products—blue crab and Smithfield ham—yields an irresistible starter.

Complexity ✪✪   Yield: 6 servings

2¼ cups (10 ounces) all-purpose flour
1½ cups warm water
¼ cup (2 ounces) vegetable oil
1 teaspoon garlic powder
½ teaspoon salt
½ teaspoon black pepper
2 tablespoons Old Bay seasoning
½ pound backfin crabmeat, picked over
½ cup chopped scallions
½ cup (3 ounces) diced Smithfield ham
3 egg whites, whipped to stiff peaks
   peanut oil for frying, heated to 350°
   cocktail sauce

In a small bowl combine flour, water, and oil with a wire whip. Combine with garlic powder, salt, pepper, and Old Bay seasoning. Gently add crab, scallions, and ham and mix with a spoon. Fold in egg whites. Drop by large spoonfuls into peanut oil. Fry until firm or when a toothpick inserted in the center comes out dry. Drain. Serve immediately with cocktail sauce.

Hot Crab Dip

JOHN LONG

ROUNDS CHEF, C.C.

The Williamsburg Inn, Colonial Williamsburg, Williamsburg

On a chilly fall afternoon as the ball players charge onto the field and the at-home critics have almost made the first down into the kitchen, it is time to bring out this crab dip. It will create more excitement than a touchdown in the final seconds of play.

Complexity ✪   Yield: 6 servings

8 ounces cream cheese
½ pound crabmeat
¼ cup (2 ounces) mayonnaise
1 teaspoon dry mustard
1 teaspoon confectioners' sugar
1 clove garlic, minced
1 tablespoon minced onion

Combine all ingredients together in a small ovenproof 1-quart dish. Heat at 350° for 15 to 20 minutes or until it starts to bubble and the edges brown. Serve on crackers or slices of warm baguette.

Chef's Notes
- *Use the less expensive "special" crabmeat for this dip. And use the cartilage removal tip on page 26.*
- *Two teaspoons of prepared Dijon mustard can be substituted for dry mustard.*
- *The dip can be made with nonfat cream cheese and mayonnaise; however, the seasonings should be increased. Experiment by doubling the quantity of onion and adding freshly chopped herbs.*

Warm Smoked Salmon in Puff Pastry with Sautéed Cucumber and Dill Sauce

EDWARD DAGGERS

EXECUTIVE CHEF, C.E.C.

Country Club, Memphis, Tennessee

Chef's Notes

- *Frozen puff pastry can be found in most grocery stores. Thaw according to package directions.*
- *Use a very sharp knife for cutting pastry to ensure proper rising. Guide rings are helpful or use a jar lid. Do not use a cookie or biscuit cutter.*
- *Bake any extra pieces for garnishing soups or salads. These garnishes can be frozen after baking.*
- *If pastry must be held for any time, quickly refresh bottoms and salmon for 1 minute under broiler.*
- *For an elegant presentation place ½ cup sour cream in pastry bag. Pipe rosettes around plate and garnish with fresh dill sprigs and American caviar.*
- *For a healthier version substitute ⅔ cup plain yogurt in place of heavy cream.*

The delicate taste of Norwegian salmon will be greatly appreciated when most graciously served in a shell of puff pastry over a creamy shallot-dill sauce topped with fresh cucumber moons.

Complexity ❶❷❸   **Yield: 4 servings**

1   sheet puff pastry
1   egg
1   tablespoon (½ ounce) cream
1   shallot, peeled and minced
1   tablespoon (½ ounce) butter
¼   cup (2 ounces) white wine
½   teaspoon cracked pepper
2   tablespoons fresh dill, chopped
1   cup (8 ounces) heavy cream
2   cucumbers, peeled, seeded, and cut into ½-inch slices
1   tablespoon (½ ounce) butter
12 ounces Norwegian smoked salmon, thinly sliced

Cut 3½-inch circles of puff pastry. Arrange on baking sheet. With paring knife, cut diamond pattern on top being careful not to cut through pastry. Combine egg and cream to make wash. Brush wash on top of pastry (keeping it off sides). Bake at 350° for about 12 minutes or until nicely browned. Remove from oven. Horizontally split in half. Remove and save tops.

In a saucepan sauté shallot in butter. Add white wine and pepper. Over a low fire, reduce by two-thirds. Add dill. Remove from heat. Cool slightly and stir in heavy cream.

In another small pan, sauté cucumber moons in butter until just soft.

To assemble, spoon sauce on 4 serving plates. On plates place pastry bottoms with salmon slices in a shingled pattern. Place tops on halfway. Arrange cucumber slices around sides.

Gravad Läx

TED KRISTENSEN
CHEF-OWNER, C.E.C., A.A.C.
The Willows Bed and Breakfast, Gloucester

Chef's Notes
- *An impeccably fresh salmon guarantees the success of this appetizer. Have the fishmonger fillet the fish. With tweezers remove any remaining bones found by running hand over surface.*
- *A large turkey roaster is the perfect size for marinating the salmon.*
- *Serve with Danish pumpernickel, cream cheese, capers, and finely chopped Bermuda onion.*
- *Gravad läx can be refrigerated for several weeks.*

The Danish relish the cured salmon or smoked fish-herring, mackerel, and eel—with the proper accompaniments of schnapps and dark bread. Cured fish has been part of the cuisine of Northern Europe from the time of the Vikings.

Complexity ✪✪   Yield: 8 to 12 servings

1	fillet North Pacific or North Atlantic fresh pink salmon
2	tablespoons finely chopped fresh dill
1	tablespoon finely chopped fennel
1	tablespoon coarse salt
1	teaspoon crushed black pepper
1	quart (32 ounces) vegetable oil
½	cup (4 ounces) wine vinegar
¼	cup (2 ounces) Pernod (for aniseed flavors)

Place salmon in a shallow aluminum foil pan. Rub both sides of salmon with dill, fennel, salt, and pepper. Blend remaining ingredients and pour over salmon. Cover with foil. Place a large pan filled with water on top of foil to allow the marinade to penetrate the salmon. Refrigerate at 38° (bottom shelf of refrigerator) for 48 hours. Drain marinade. Slice thinly.

Chicken Galantine with Pesto Farce

STEPHEN PERKINS
CHEF GARDE MANGER
The Williamsburg Inn, Colonial Williamsburg, Williamsburg

In 1992 the Virginia Chefs Association, using delicate quail meat, served this as the appetizer to rave reviews at their highly successful Horizons 2000 benefit dinner. For practicality we've substituted chicken breast stuffed with a chicken-and-pesto farce which is cooked by gentle poaching. Serve with Red Onion Confit (page 205) and Dried Cherry and Cranberry Fruit Compote (page 196).

Complexity ✪✪   Yield: 8 servings

CHICKEN

4 chicken breasts (about 1 pound), skinless
   salt and white pepper to taste

FARCE

1½ teaspoons salt
¼ teaspoon white pepper
2 chicken breasts (½ pound), skin and tissue removed, cut into cubes
¼ cup ice water
¾ cup (6 ounces) cream
¼ cup (2 ounces) pesto

chicken
Pound chicken breasts to a uniform ¼-inch thickness. Season with salt and pepper and reserve.

farce
In a cold food processor, purée the seasoned meat with ice water until it reaches a gummy consistency. Add cold cream and incorporate. Add pesto. Place in freezer for 10 to 15 minutes.

assembly
Arrange chicken breasts end to end, slightly overlapping.

Chef's Notes
- *Ground chicken is available now and will save preparation time and create a smoother farce.*
- *Chill food processor and blade in refrigerator before beginning.*
- *Put a tablespoon of farce mixture on spatula. If it clings when turned over, the mixture is gummy enough.*
- *When poaching be sure water does not boil. Boiling water will toughen the meat.*

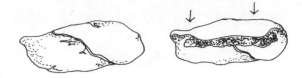

With a spatula spread with farce to ⅛ inch of edges. Roll each breast in plastic film. Tie ends with string.

Poach in water just under the boiling point until cooked or to an internal temperature of 140°. Slice into ½-inch thick pieces.

Brandied Chopped Chicken Livers

MANFRED E. ROEHR
C.E.C., A.A.C.

**Chowning's and Christiana Campbell's Taverns,
Colonial Williamsburg, Williamsburg**

The complex sweetness of brandy tempers the chicken livers. Their fine texture combined with hard-cooked eggs and onion makes an excellent starter. Serve on a bed of lettuce garnished with parsley and tomato wedges.

Complexity ✪✪   **Yield: 6 to 8 servings**

1 *pound chicken livers*
¼ *teaspoon salt*
1 *medium (4 ounces) onion, chopped*
3 *eggs, hard boiled*
1½ *teaspoons salt*
¼ *teaspoon black pepper*
½ *cup (4 ounces) brandy*
1 *to 2 (½ to 1 ounce) tablespoons butter*
   lettuce leaves
⅛ *cup chopped fresh parsley*
1 *tomato, cut into wedges*

Score chicken livers with a sharp knife. Wash, drain, and sprinkle lightly with ¼ teaspoon salt. Broil for 3 to 5 minutes or until done. Finely chop onions, eggs, and livers or put through a grinder. Stir in salt, pepper, and brandy. Add enough butter to make the mixture smooth to the consistency of mashed potatoes. Serve on a bed of lettuce. Sprinkle with parsley and side with tomato wedges.

Chef's Notes
- *Pass with toast points.*
- *The dish may be made ahead and refrigerated until service time.*
- *Chopping may be done in a food processor. Use short pulses so as not to overprocess and ruin the texture.*
- *Any leftovers are superb with bagel slices.*

Turkey Pot Stickers

DAVID BRUCE CLARKE
CHEF-INSTRUCTOR
J. Sargeant Reynolds Community College, Richmond

Chef's Notes
- *The dough resting time permits the gluten strands to relax making it easy to roll.*
- *To test filling seasonings, sauté a teaspoonful of filling. Adjust if necessary. Do not taste raw.*
- *Dry sherry may be substituted for the Shao Hsing wine.*
- *Light sesame oil can be used; however, the dark oil is made from roasted and more flavorful seeds.*
- *Canola oil may be substituted for the peanut oil, but it has significantly less flavor.*
- *Use a good quality chicken stock for best results.*
- *Serve family style or arrange five dumplings straight in a row for individual service.*
- *Try adding a small amount of grated ginger for a variation on the dipping sauce. A specialized ginger grater is excellent as the ginger needs no peeling and all the juices are saved. Find these graters, often fish shaped, in gourmet specialty shops or Asian markets.*
- *This recipe can also be used for preparing steamed dumplings. An important difference is that the filling must be sautéed in a large pan with both the peanut oil and stock. Let filling cool. Form dumplings in the same fashion. Place in bamboo steamers on a piece of cheesecloth over a pan or wok of boiling water. Bamboo steamers can be stacked. Steam for about 15 minutes or until the wrapper is*

Kwo-tieh (pronounced Ko-t-eh) are healthy dumplings stuffed with fresh ground turkey meat and vegetables, with spicy garlic and ginger. The dipping sauce is tantalizing with a tamari base, Shao Hsing rice wine with just a touch of scallions and sesame oil. The wrappers take a bit of time, but commercial ones are also available—but certainly not as good.

Complexity ❶❶❶

Yield: approximately 20 pieces, or appetizers for 4

DOUGH WRAPPERS
4 cups (1 pound) all-purpose flour
  pinch salt
2 cups water at 190°

FILLING
10 ounces fresh ground turkey
½ pound Chinese cabbage, minced fine
1 clove fresh garlic, puréed
1 teaspoon freshly grated ginger
1 teaspoon tamari soy sauce
1 teaspoon Shao Hsing wine
1 teaspoon sesame oil
½ egg white, beaten
  salt and pepper to taste

DIPPING SAUCE
½ cup (4 ounces) tamari sauce
2 tablespoons (1 ounce) Shao Hsing wine
¼ cup water
1 tablespoon finely chopped scallions
1½ teaspoons dark sesame oil

COOKING DUMPLINGS
2½ teaspoons peanut oil
¼ cup (2 ounces) chicken stock

dough wrappers
Sift flour. Add salt. Stir in simmering water. Mix well using a wooden spoon. Let stand 30 minutes. Roll into long French bread shape. Divide in half. Cover and refrigerate one half. With a sharp knife cut off into ½ ounce (about tablespoon-size) pieces. Roll each into a thin 3-inch circle. Place on waxed paper. Cover with plastic wrap and refrigerate. Repeat until all dough is rolled.

filling
Combine all ingredients, blending well.

assembly
Place 1 tablespoon filling slightly off center of each wrapper. Fold wrapper around the filling. Pleat one side, pressing against the unpleated side to seal. Form into a crescent shape. Repeat until all dumplings are filled.

dipping sauce
Combine all ingredients, mixing well.

cooking dumplings
Heat a large flat-bottomed pan. Add the peanut oil. Arrange dumplings around pan in a clock-wise position. Start second row and continue until the pan is full. They should touch side to side, but not point to point.

   Sauté over high heat. Drain oil. Add chicken stock. Reduce heat and cover. Continue to cook until most of the stock is gone or for approximately 4 to 5 minutes. By this time the dumplings will be stuck together. Drain off excess stock. Bounce pan on sturdy surface to carefully dislodge the stuck dumplings. Serve with dipping sauce.

completely cooked. Serve with dipping sauce.
• *Won ton wrappers can be found in the fresh produce section of many grocery stores. Since these are square the finished dumplings will have a different shape.*

Swiss Ham Croissants

OTTO J. BERNET

DIRECTOR OF EUROPEAN SPECIALTIES, C.M.P.C., A.A.C.

Ukrop's Supermarket, Richmond

The airy, flaky layers of puff pastry almost melt in your mouth while the ham provides salty flavors. These can be baked ahead, frozen, and refreshed just before serving for seemingly effortless entertaining.

Chef's Notes
- *Make smaller triangles for cocktail parties. These may be baked ahead of time and refreshed at 350° for 7 minutes.*
- *If pastry becomes warm during cutting, return to refrigerator for about 20 minutes.*
- *Frozen, prerolled puff pastry is readily available in supermarkets. Thaw for 20 minutes in the refrigerator before using.*
- *Substitute Virginia country ham and delete mustard for a traditional starter.*

Complexity ✪✪   Yield: 10 servings (2 per serving)

1 cup (6 ounces) lean, cooked, finely minced ham
1 teaspoon country-style mustard
1 teaspoon unsalted butter, softened
1 pound puff pastry dough
1 egg mixed with 1 teaspoon water

Combine ham, mustard, and butter. On a large floured board, roll out puff pastry into an 18x7-inch rectangle. With a sharp knife divide into 2 rows of 10 triangles, each about 3½ inches. Place a tablespoon of filling on each triangle. Spread. Roll, pulling top sides out slightly and stretching point into a croissant. Curve slightly and place with final point tucked under on ungreased baking sheet. Brush with egg and water mixture. Bake at 420° for 10 to 12 minutes or until golden brown. Serve either hot or cold.

1
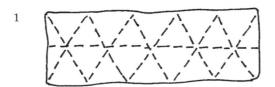

3

2
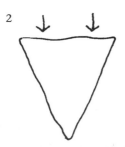

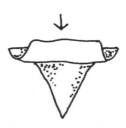

4
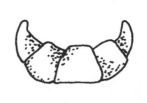

Marinated Mushrooms

JO OLSON

ACCOUNT EXECUTIVE

Atlantic Food Services, Inc., Richmond

The perfectly fresh, small button mushrooms are just right for popping in one's mouth. Present either solo or with an antipasto selection.

Complexity ✪   Yield: 8 servings

½ cup (4 ounces) balsamic vinegar
½ cup (4 ounces) vegetable oil
1 tablespoon dried basil leaves
1 teaspoon dried oregano leaves
1 teaspoon dried thyme leaves
1 large (8 ounces) red onion, thinly sliced
1 tablespoon cracked black pepper
1½ teaspoons salt
4 large cloves garlic, minced
1½ pounds fresh button mushrooms

Place all ingredients except mushrooms in a 4-quart saucepan. Bring to a boil. Add mushrooms and stir. Remove from heat. Let sit for 3 hours. Pour into glass jars and seal. Store in refrigerator until needed.

Chef's Notes
- *To speed-clean mushrooms, place in a plastic bag. Add 1 teaspoon salt and fill with cool water. Shake the bag for a minute. Drain.*
- *The oil may be completely eliminated from this recipe, if desired.*

Cheese Balls: Orange or Pineapple

JOHN LONG
ROUNDS CHEF, C.C.

The Williamsburg Inn, Colonial Williamsburg, Williamsburg

Chef's Notes
• *Make these three days ahead so that the flavors can marry.*

Fast, easy, and healthy when using fat-free cream cheese. Serve with crackers or slices of fresh baguette.

Complexity ✪   Yield: 6 servings per cheese ball

ORANGE CHEESE BALL

1 pound cream cheese
2 tablespoons orange-flavored drink powder
⅓ cup chopped walnuts

Combine cheese with orange-flavored drink powder. Form into a ball. Roll in chopped walnuts. Refrigerate.

PINEAPPLE CHEESE BALL

1 pound cream cheese
1 6-ounce can crushed pineapple, drained
1 tablespoon finely chopped onion
1 teaspoon seasoned salt
¼ cup finely chopped green bell pepper

Combine all ingredients. Form into a ball. Refrigerate.

Wild Mushroom Strudel

STUART DEUTSCH

EXECUTIVE CHEF

The American Tobacco Company, Chester

The mushroom essence made from the wild stems and white mushrooms is the reduction of the mushroom stock and the cornerstone of the wild, permeating flavors of this dish. The filling of heavy cream, butter, and mushrooms is wonderfully rich, creating an exotic starter. In a burst of reckless abandon we tried this sauce on fresh fettuccine (of course skipping the phyllo and breadcrumbs); totally awesome.

Complexity ✪✪✪✪   **Yield: 12 pastries**

1 pound shiitake mushrooms
1 pound oyster mushrooms
½ pound white mushrooms
2 cups water
2 cups (17 ounces) heavy cream
1 shallot, finely diced
5 ounces Boursin cheese
½ cup (4 ounces) butter, melted
½ pound phyllo dough sheets
    fresh breadcrumbs from 1 slice white bread

mushroom essence and cream
Remove stems from mushrooms. Set tops aside for strudel. Place stems in large stock pot with white mushrooms and 2 cups water to make stock. Cook over medium-low heat for 1 hour. Strain liquid to remove mushroom pieces and reduce to 2/3 cup. Set aside mushroom essence. Reduce heavy cream by half. Combine reduced cream with mushroom essence.

strudel
Chop shiitake and oyster mushroom tops coarsely. Sauté with shallots. Add to essence and cream mixture. Add Boursin cheese. Combine well and cool completely. Brush phyllo dough sheets with butter and lightly sprinkle with breadcrumbs. Sheets should be 3 layers in thickness. Cut 3-layer sheets into 3 equal strips vertically. Place 2 ounces mushroom mixture on end of strip closest to you and fold into triangles.

Brush filled pastries with more butter. Place on baking sheet.
Bake at 400° for 15 minutes or until the dough is golden brown.
Serve immediately.

Chef's Notes
- *If the reduced cream with mushrooms is not a thick, sauce consistency, it may be adjusted with a small amount of roux.*
- *Phyllo dough dries out quite quickly. Keep it covered at all times with waxed paper or a slightly damp dish cloth.*
- *Nonstick vegetable spray can be used in the place of butter for coating the phyllo dough.*
- *Boursin cheese flavored with garlic and herbs is suggested.*

CHAPTER 2
Sublime Soups

THE SECRET IS IN THE STOCK

QUALITY STOCKS are essential in the creation of quality cuisine. The flavorful liquids are the extraction of flavors from bones, trimmings, and aromatic vegetables. The new nutritional cooking techniques use such stocks and their reductions in the place of butter, cream, and thickened sauces of the past. Stocks are the beginning of soups and a primary ingredient in many side dishes such as rice, couscous, and vegetables.

Chef Schadler, a leader in healthy cuisine, often ladles rich stock reductions on julienned vegetables to accompany seared Scallops and Salmon (see page 71). No addition of butter or cream is needed for incredible taste; the secret is the intensity of well-selected and matched natural flavors. Either a white stock or a fish fumet might be used for this recipe. For more robust flavors with less delicate meats try brown stock, with its color from an initial browning of the bones before simmering.

Making stock is time-consuming, but it takes little work after preparing the ingredients and getting them into the stock pot. Little intervention is needed during the simmering.

A basic recipe producing about 6 quarts of white stock is to place 6 pounds of cut-up bones into a large, heavy-bottomed stock pot. Select chicken, beef, or veal bones cut into small pieces.

Cover with 8 quarts of cold water. Slowly bring to a boil and skim off the grayish protein coagulations that rise to the top. An easy method is to use a soup ladle. Stir the surface in center and the scum will move to the edges. Try to remove only the scum and not the liquid.

Aromatic flavors are added next with 1 large onion, 2 carrots, and 2 stalks of celery. One large leek will also enhance the stock. Roughly dice these vegetables. Precision cutting is not important as they will eventually be discarded. Sauté the vegetables in 2 tablespoons of butter or other fats, in a large skillet until just soft. Do not permit any browning of the vegetables. Add vegetables to stock pot.

Add a sachet bag with 1 bay leaf, ¼ teaspoon dried thyme, ¼ teaspoon peppercorns, and 2 whole cloves. The bag is made of 3 square inches of cheesecloth tied with kitchen string. Use fresh thyme if available. This is an excellent place to use the herb stems and save the tender leaves for more refined preparations. Some chefs prefer to stick the cloves in a small whole onion so they can be easily removed from the stock.

Salt is not included in stock. This seasoning should be added when using the stock in a recipe.

Slow simmering, about 5 hours for chicken and 8 hours for beef and veal, completes the flavor extraction process. The surface should be calm with gently surfacing bubbles. Lower the temperature if activity is greater.

Strain the liquid through a fine strainer or a "china cap" lined with several layers of cheesecloth. Quickly cool liquid. A fast way is to put the stock into smaller, fairly shallow containers. Cool briefly at room temperature, then refrigerate.

Any stock not to be used in one or two days should be frozen in small quantities. One-cup portions are very handy. Line a small rigid freezer container with a small freezer bag and fill. Seal bag, remove from rigid container, label, and date. Freeze until needed. Two-tablespoon (1-ounce) portions may be made in ice cube trays. After freezing, place in labeled freezer bags.

Brown stocks, using only veal or beef bones, have a slightly different procedure. The bones are roasted and browned in a 350° oven for about 1 hour. At that time the diced vegetables are placed over the bones and cooked for about 20 more minutes. Add ingredients to stock pot. Be sure to add a small amount of the water to the roasting pan and scrape up all the flavorful bits that stick. Add to stock pot. Add cold water. Bring to a boil. Reduce to a simmer. Skim off gray scum. Add herbs and spices. After skimming, ½ cup of tomato paste may be added if desired. Simmer stock for 8 hours. Strain. Cool. Pack in conveniently sized containers and label. Freeze.

Fish stocks require about 45 minutes of simmering. To make 1 quart of stock, start with 1 pound of fish bones and trimmings. Do not use a fatty fish. Use a lean fish such as flounder, sole, or a local whitefish. Clean bones, removing all skin. In a stock pot sauté 2 tablespoons onions, 1 tablespoon celery in a small amount of butter until soft. Add fish bones. Cover with 5 cups cold water. An optional flavor enhancer is ¼ cup of white wine. Add half a bay leaf and several thyme stems. Bring to a boil. Reduce to a simmer. Simmer for 45 minutes. Strain, cool, and label.

You have now added new meaning to the "well-stocked" freezer. Smile with contentment. Flavor secrets await your future creations.—*Chefs Schadler and Parziale*

MORE SECRETS

For a dark, rich beef, veal, or chicken stock, slow-roast the bones and vegetables for a long period of time, developing a robust flavor. Deglaze pan so as not to lose any flavor. Start stock in cold water.—*Chef Bland*

When making seafood bisque, break lobster shells with the back of a French knife. Sauté lobster and shrimp shells. First add mirepoix, then chop shells and vegetables even further in a food processor. Add back to the pot, cover with wine and water.
—*Chef Bland*

Cut vegetables for stock proportional to the amount of stock making and the length of time it will cook. For smaller amounts that will cook a shorter time use smaller vegetables. With large quantities with long cooking time, use larger cuts of vegetables.—*Chef Bland*

When preparing cream soups, substitute evaporated skim milk for fewer calories.
—*Chef Corliss*

Try floating a dab of whipped cream on top of tomato, cream of mushroom, cream of celery, or clear consommé—delicious!—*Chef Fulton*

This old saying is still true—Soup boiled is soup spoiled. Cook it gently and evenly.
—*Chef Fulton*

A bouquet garni (bunch of herbs) is the chef's secret to finer flavor in soups or stews. Tie the seasoning in cheesecloth. Discard prior to serving.—*Chef Fulton*

Too much salt in the soup—all is not lost. Add a teaspoon of sugar or cut a few pieces of raw turnip or grate a raw potato.—*Chef Fulton*

Add a little lemon and onion juice to your favorite canned soups before heating.
—*Chef Fulton*

Dress up soups with croutons, noodles, spaghetti, rice, barley, grated cheese, dumplings, sliced sausage, hard-cooked eggs or sieved egg yolk over a slice of lemon or melba toast.—*Chef Fulton*

The foundation of a well-prepared kitchen is an assortment of rich and flavorful stocks. Unfortunately, the time and effort required to properly make stocks is daunting to many individuals who retreat to bouillon cubes, sodium-laden bases, and other totally unacceptable substitutes.

The home cook may find it easier to make stocks by planning ahead, arranging for their grocer to special order bones, fish trimmings, crustacean shells, and other necessary ingredients, and then prepare the stock recipes in large (three to five gallon) quantities on a semiannual basis, reducing them to a highly concentrated syrup or glacé. After cooling, slice the gelatinous stock concentrates into 1- or 2-ounce portions that can be individually wrapped, labeled, and frozen for future use. When a stock is called for in a recipe, the portions can be added to water and diluted into a flavorful, genuine stock. Relatively little freezer space is needed, and the semi-annual stock-making ritual can be made the focus for a gathering of like-minded friends who will share in the bounties of the stock pot.—*D. Barrish*

Sweet Potato Soup with Toasted Almonds and Currants

ROBERT D. CORLISS
SOUS CHEF
The Williamsburg Inn, Colonial Williamsburg, Williamsburg

Chef's Notes
- *A lower-calorie soup can be made by substituting evaporated skim milk for the cream. Do not boil soup after its addition.*
- *Poultry seasoning mix, where thyme is the major ingredient, can be used in the place of ground thyme.*

Sweet potatoes are prolific in the Tidewater area of Virginia. Chef Corliss first sautés the potatoes in butter to enhance their robust flavor. A slow simmer melds the golden flavors. Serve this smooth, puréed soup garnished with toasted almonds and sweet currants.

Complexity ✪✪   Yield: 6 servings

2 *cups (1 pound) peeled and chopped sweet potatoes*
¼ *cup (1 ounce) peeled and chopped carrot*
½ *cup (3 ounces) peeled and chopped onion*
2 *tablespoons (1 ounce) butter*
1 *tablespoon (¼ ounce) all-purpose flour*
3 *tablespoons (1½ ounces) white wine*
¼ *teaspoon ground thyme*
1 *bay leaf*
1 *cup (8 ounces) heavy cream*
3 *cups (24 ounces) chicken stock*
   salt to taste
   pinch each of ground nutmeg, ground cinnamon, and white pepper
2 *tablespoons (1 ounce) toasted almond slivers*
1 *tablespoon currants*

In a 3-quart saucepan, sauté potatoes, carrot, and onion in butter for 5 minutes or until potatoes begin to soften. Dust with flour. Cook for 1 minute. Add wine, thyme, and bay leaf. Reduce slightly. Add cream and chicken stock. Simmer for 40 minutes. Purée in a blender or food processor until completely smooth. Strain through a fine sieve. Season and serve hot garnished with almond slivers and currants.

Chilled Carrot Soup

MARCEL DESAULNIERS
CHEF-OWNER, C.E.C., A.A.C.
The Trellis Restaurant, Williamsburg

The clean, refreshing, uncomplicated flavor makes this a favorite soup on humid days in Williamsburg. It is certainly nutritious as well as delicious. The texture of the purée is quite smooth and garnishes of diced fresh oranges continue the delicate orange coloring.

Complexity ✪✪   **Yield: 8 servings**

1 tablespoon (½ ounce) vegetable oil
1 tablespoon water
2 pounds carrots, peeled and chopped
2 stalks (5 ounces) celery, chopped
1 medium (4 ounces) onion, chopped
   salt and pepper
6 cups (48 ounces) chicken stock
7 tablespoons (3 1/2 ounces) unsalted butter
¾ cup (3 ounces) all-purpose flour
1 cup (8 ounces) half and half
1 large navel orange, peeled, sectioned, and cut into ¼-inch pieces

In a 5-quart saucepan over medium heat, combine the oil and water. Sauté chopped carrots, celery, onion, salt, and pepper for 10 minutes. Add stock and bring to a boil. Reduce heat and simmer slowly for 45 minutes or until carrots are thoroughly cooked. Simmer stock and vegetables very slowly to prevent evaporation of stock (resulting in reduced volume and soup that is too thick). While stock is simmering prepare a roux by melting butter in a 2½-quart saucepan over low heat. Add flour and stir constantly for 6 to 8 minutes or until the roux bubbles. Strain 4 cups simmering stock into the roux, whisking vigorously until smooth. Add this mixture to the 5-quart saucepan with remaining stock and vegetables. Whisk until well-combined. Simmer for 10 minutes. Remove from heat. Purée in a food processor fitted with a metal blade. Strain soup. Chill thoroughly. To serve, whisk in half and half. Adjust seasonings with salt and pepper. Portion soup into chilled soup plates. Garnish with orange pieces.

Chef's Notes
- *Carrots must be completely cooked so they will purée and strain easily—this ensures an intense, rather than an insipid, carrot flavor.*
- *Instead of using orange garnish, try a fine julienne of cantaloupe.*
- *For a lower-calorie version substitute nonfat plain yogurt for the half and half.*

Gingered Carrot and Fennel Soup with Vegetable Won Tons

ROBERT D. CORLISS
Sous Chef
The Williamsburg Inn, Colonial Williamsburg, Williamsburg

Chef's Notes

- *Fennel bulbs are large, pale green with feathery foliage and a celery-like texture. Cut off root end and foliage before slicing. The foliage can be used as an attractive garnish in the same manner as dill. The flavor sweetens when cooked. Use any extra raw in salads.*

- *For easy ginger preparation, cut off knobs. Peel with a vegetable peeler or scrape with a paring knife. Then chop with a French knife. Alternatively, shred on the small holes of a cheese grater.*

- *Sachet bags make it easy to infuse this soup with wonderful flavors without having herb pieces float in the finished soup. To make sachet, cut a 6-inch square of cheesecloth. Add fresh herbs. Bring up each corner. Twist together to hold ingredients. Tie with a 6-inch length of kitchen string. Remove bag before serving.*

- *Substitute evaporated milk for the cream for a lower-calorie version of this soup. As the milk will break during reduction, reduce before adding milk. Stir in milk and heat just before adding arrowroot thickening mixture. Do not boil.*

The won tons, easy to make with prepared Oriental wrappers, are filled with crunchy vegetables. Float these on the lustrous and intensely flavored soup made from puréed vegetables and fish stock.

Complexity ❋❋❋   **Yield: 4 servings**

SOUP

- 4 **carrots (8 ounces), peeled and diced**
- 1 **fennel bulb, diced**
- 1 **white onion, diced**
- 3 **tablespoons (3 ounces) fresh diced ginger**
- ¼ **cup (2 ounces) lightly salted butter**
- 1 **cup (8 ounces) sweet white wine**
- 2 **cups (16 ounces) fish stock**
- 1 **cup (8 ounces) heavy cream**
- 1 **tablespoon arrowroot powder**
- ¼ **cup cold water**
- 1 **tablespoon lemon juice**
  salt to taste
  dry ginger, white pepper, and red pepper for garnish

SACHET BAG

- 1 **bay leaf**
- 4 **sprigs fresh thyme**
- 2 **parsley stems**

VEGETABLE WON TONS

1 tablespoon diced red bell peppers
1 tablespoon diced yellow bell peppers
1 tablespoon diced cucumber
1 tablespoon small broccoli florets
1 tablespoon yellow corn kernels
2 tablespoons (1 ounce) butter
4 won ton wrappers

- *Fry won tons in 340° oil.*
- *Won tons can be steamed instead of fried. Won ton wrappers are readily available in the supermarket's fresh produce section.*
- *Steam a large batch of these won tons and serve with light soy sauce and fresh ginger as a delectable appetizer.*

Sauté carrots, fennel, onion, and ginger in butter in a 2-quart pot over medium heat until tender. Add white wine and fish stock and reduce by half. Add heavy cream and sachet bag. Simmer gently for 30 minutes. Stir arrowroot powder into cold water. Whisk into soup for thickening. Purée in a blender until smooth. Strain through a sieve to remove any pulp.

Sauté won ton vegetables in a large sauté pan until medium soft. Using fingers slightly moisten edges of won ton wrapper with cold water. Place 1 tablespoon filling in center of each wrapper. Fold in half to form a triangle. Fold the middle point to the center and overlap two remaining corners to connect to the center edge. Press gently to secure. Fry in hot oil until golden brown.

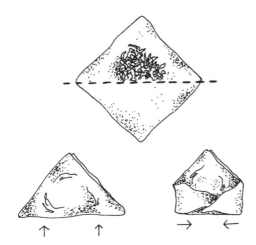

Finish soup with lemon juice, salt, and garnishes. Serve hot in a cream soup bowl with one won ton floating in each serving.

Broccoli Cheddar Soup

RICHARD IVEY

EXECUTIVE CHEF

ARAMARK, Campus Dining Services, Randolph Macon College, Ashland

Crunchy broccoli florets, cooked just before serving, swim in a silky cream sauce elegantly flavored with Cheddar cheese. Whipping soups continuously for at least 10 minutes after thickening with a roux can be the difference between a classical cream soup and a simple country one. After thickening, gently simmer.

Complexity ✪✪   Yield: 8 servings

- 1 **pound broccoli, stems removed to 1 inch from florets**
- 2 **teaspoons butter**
- ½ **cup (3 ounces) diced onions**
- 1 **tablespoon freshly chopped garlic**
- ½ **cup (4 ounces) white wine**
- 4 **cups (1 quart) chicken stock**
- ¼ **cup (1 ounce) all-purpose flour**
- ¼ **cup (2 ounces) butter**
- 1 **cup (8 ounces) heavy cream**
- ¼ **pound sharp Cheddar, cut into medium cubes**

Cut broccoli into bite-size florets. In a heavy-bottomed soup pot sauté onions and garlic in butter over medium heat for about 5 minutes or until slightly translucent. Add white wine and reduce by half over high heat. Add chicken stock. Bring to a boil. In a small pan make a roux using flour and butter. Using wire whip add roux to stock. Continue whisking for 10 minutes. Whip in cream. Reduce heat to medium. Add broccoli florets and cook for 3 minutes. Add Cheddar cubes. Stir until melted. Serve immediately.

Chef's Notes

- *Garnish soup with small croutons, grated Cheddar cheese, or paprika sprinkled on top.*
- *To prepare a roux heat clarified butter or margarine in a heavy-bottomed saucepan over moderate heat. Add the flour all at once. Stirring constantly, cook over low heat for approximately 8 minutes or until roux is very pale ivory. To avoid lumps, the roux must cool before being added to the boiling soup.*
- *When thickening with roux, the longer the mixture is whipped the silkier the sauce or soup becomes.*
- *Add a small amount of oil to the cutting board when chopping garlic to keep it from flying away.*
- *To make soup in advance, complete all steps before adding broccoli. Hold at a simmer. Just before service time bring soup to almost to a boil. Follow above directions.*
- *To increase the cheese's impact, grate and sprinkle on top after serving in bowls.*

Corn Chowder

MANFRED E. ROEHR
C.E.C., A.A.C.
**Chowning's and Christiana Campbell's Taverns,
Colonial Williamsburg, Williamsburg**

EDWARD SWAN
CHEF
Shields Tavern, Colonial Williamsburg, Williamsburg

Chowders and one-pot hearty fare were important meals in the Colonial times. Corn was abundant, as were pork products. Two centuries later, the convenience of bouillon, prepared mustard, and canned corn are welcomed time-savers to re-create such meals.

Complexity ✪✪   **Yield: 12 servings**

1 cup (7 ounces) diced raw bacon
1 tablespoon chicken bouillon granules
1 large (6 ounces) onion, minced
1 cup (4 ounces) minced celery
1 tablespoon minced garlic
3 tablespoons minced fresh thyme
½ cup (4 ounces) Grey Poupon country-style mustard
2 cups (1 pound) precooked, diced potatoes (still crunchy)
    pinch white pepper
2 cups cream-style corn
6 cups half and half

Sauté bacon on high heat for 5 minutes or until brown. Add bouillon, onions, celery, and garlic to bacon and stir. Add thyme and mustard and stir. Add potatoes, pepper, corn, and half and half. Bring to a boil on high heat, stirring continuously. Reduce heat and simmer for 20 to 30 minutes or until done. Serve hot.

Chef's Notes
- *Substitute lower-fat milks for half and half if desired.*
- *Save ½ cup of this chowder for the Chicken Breast in Two Sauces on page 100. Cool soup for this sauce.*

Roasted Chili Corn Bisque with Lump Crab Chesapeake

EDWARD DAGGERS

EXECUTIVE CHEF, C.E.C.

Country Club, Memphis, Tennessee

Chef's Notes
- *Treat the crab gently to keep the lumps intact.*
- *A less expensive version can be made substituting cooked and shredded chicken breast for the crab.*
- *Try lean turkey bacon cut into small slivers in place of pork bacon.*

Oven-roasting the corn and garlic starts the flavor-building process. Onions and jalapeño peppers add an aromatic and hot hit while the spices up the ante on flavor. The cream smoothes the consistency, providing just the right base for the delicate crab that finishes this bisque.

Complexity ✪✪   Yield: 4 servings

2 *cups (12 ounces) corn kernels (off the cob)*
3 *cloves garlic*
2 *tablespoons (1 ounce) olive oil*
1 *ounce bacon, diced*
¼ *cup (1½ ounces) diced onions*
1 *small jalapeño, seeded and minced*
½ *teaspoon ground cumin*
1 *tablespoon chili powder*
2 *tablespoons (½ ounce) all-purpose flour*
1 *cup (8 ounces) chicken stock*
¾ *cup (6 ounces) cream*
½ *pound lump crabmeat, cleaned, all cartilage removed*
   minced chives for garnish

In a heavy skillet, roast corn kernels and garlic in olive oil in a 375° oven for 10 minutes or until lightly browned. Remove from oven. In a 3-quart saucepan sauté bacon. Add onions and jalapeño. Sauté until onion is translucent. Add corn mixture, cumin, and chili. With a wooden spoon stir in flour to make a roux. Add stock and simmer 10 minutes on medium heat, stirring with a whip. Transfer to a food processor and purée until smooth. Return to pan. Add cream. Bring to a simmer. Place in soup bowls. Top with crabmeat. Sprinkle with chives and a touch of chili powder.

Virginia Peanut Soup, Chunky Style

Adapted from the U.S. Army Culinary Olympic Team, Fort Lee

A true Virginian reveres peanuts and will request the ground nut in place of the tree nuts, almonds, even when flying first class. Virginians will consume all the peanuts out of the mixed cocktail nuts. The fanatical Virginian eats the giant, No. 1 grade peanuts freshly roasted and sings paeans of praise to this native (since the seventeenth century) soup. While there are other peanut soup recipes, few approach the heights of this Culinary Olympics version—a classic stock chock full of vegetables with flavors enhanced by dark chicken meat and country ham. Egg whites form a raft floating on the surface to clarify the soup. Our version of Chunky Virginia Peanut Soup keeps all the goodness in the bowl. Try it both ways.

Complexity ✪✪✪   **Yield: 12 servings**

SOUP

1½ pounds chicken thighs
1 large (6 ounces) leek
2 carrots (about 6 ounces)
2 stalks celery (about 6 ounces)
1¼ cups (6 ounces) Virginia peanuts, roasted, unsalted
¾ cup (8 ounces) peanut butter (natural suggested)
1 cup (6 ounces) chopped Virginia country ham
3 quarts chicken stock
2 egg whites, lightly beaten (optional for raft)

GARNISH

5 ounces unsalted Virginia peanuts, roasted and coarsely chopped
1 ounce Virginia country ham, cut into slivers

Remove skin, all fat, and bones from chicken. In a food processor fitted with a metal blade, mince chicken. Place in a 5-quart stock pot. Coarsely pulse-chop vegetables and peanuts. Add all ingredients (and optional egg whites if a raft is desired for clarifying) to pot. Mix thoroughly. Bring to a boil, stirring occasionally. Reduce to a simmer. Stop stirring and permit raft to form. Cook for 1 hour. Strain, if desired. Ladle into bowls. Garnish with chopped peanuts and slivers of Virginia ham.

Chef's Notes
- *Add the chicken bones to the stock pot for extra flavor. Remove before serving.*
- *Water may be added if the soup becomes too thick.*
- *The Olympic version maintained elegance by preparing two-thirds of the vegetables as a paysanne garnish cooked separately in a small amount of soup. After cooking, the soup was strained through cheesecloth, removing the raft. The paysanne garnish was added to the smooth soup and garnished with peanuts.*
- *An excellent compilation of all recipes from the U.S. Teams is by Keith Keogh, CEC, AAC, Culinary Team USA, New Currents in American Cuisine: Cooking with Team USA, edited by Pamela Erickson Otto and Nancy Ross Ryan (Des Plaines, Ill.: Cahners Publishing Co., 1993).*
- *Reduce any leftover soup to a sauce consistency and use to top chicken breast.*
- *The Virginia Peanut Shop, Merchant's Square, Williamsburg, stocks a complete line of peanut products, including the No. 1 grade in the shell, raw, roasted, with and without salt, and the best peanut butter in the world. Call (800) PEANUTS for their catalog.*

Vegetable Soup with Virginia Ham and Crabmeat

LISA A. PITTMAN
CHEF-OWNER
Lisa's Elegant Edibles, Williamsburg

Chef's Notes

- *To cut ¼-inch zucchini dice, cut off top and bottom. Slice lengthwise into ¼-inch pieces. Lay on cut side and cut into ¼-inch strips. Cut across to make perfectly diced squares.*
- *Cut onion in half from top to root. Lay cut side down. Place hand on top round portion to hold in place. Do not cup hand. Lay flat. Cut onion horizontally ¼ inch above board almost to the edge. Repeat up ¼ inch, almost to the edge. Make a series of ¼-inch vertical cuts down toward the board. Turn onion on side holding with fingertips and slice across in ¼ inch to make perfectly consistent pieces. Chop any stray pieces.*
- *Try to keep crabmeat from shredding with gentle handling while removing any bits of shell and cartilage.*
- *A quick way to pick crabmeat is to spread it on a flat pan. Place the pan under a preheated broiler for 10 to 15 seconds. The shells will change from clear to white. Gently remove shells.*

The freshest of summer produce meets the sweet Chesapeake Bay crab touched with Virginia's signature country ham, creating this healthy, low-calorie soup.

Complexity ✪✪   **Yield: 12 to 16 servings**

½ cup (3 ounces) diced Virginia country ham
2 medium carrots (about 8 ounces), peeled
1 cup (4 ounces) diced celery
½ cup (3 ounces) diced onion
1 medium zucchini (about 5 ounces), diced
1 small (12 ounces) eggplant, diced
1 medium (5 ounces) yellow squash, peeled and diced
1 gallon chicken stock
1 bay leaf
½ teaspoon ground thyme
salt to taste
⅛ teaspoon ground black pepper
2 Roma tomatoes, diced
½ pound crabmeat, picked over
½ cup Parmesan cheese, garnish

Place diced ham into 8-quart soup pot over medium heat. Add carrots, celery, and onions. Cook for 5 minutes. Add zucchini, eggplant, and squash. Cook for 5 more minutes. Stir in stock, bay leaf, thyme, salt, and pepper. Bring to a simmer and cook over low heat for 40 minutes. Add diced tomato and crab 5 minutes before serving. Ladle into bowls. Top with Parmesan cheese.

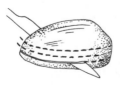

Summer Gazpacho with Lump Crabmeat and Crème Fraîche

HANS SCHADLER
EXECUTIVE CHEF, C.E.C., A.A.C.

The Williamsburg Inn, Colonial Williamsburg, Williamsburg

Gazpacho, the cold fresh tomato soup originating in the Andalusian region of Spain, is a must for a hot summer day. In the spirit of true international culinary unity, this German-born chef adds French crème fraîche, Greek olive oil, and Italian croutons to Virginia-grown produce and Chesapeake Bay crabmeat.

Chef's Notes
- *Crème fraîche can be approximated by adding two tablespoons of buttermilk to 1 cup of heavy cream in a glass jar. Permit to stand at room temperature for 1 or 2 days or until thick.*
- *Substitute sour cream or yogurt if crème fraîche is not available.*

Complexity ✪✪   Yield: 6 servings

4 large (1½ pounds) very ripe tomatoes, peeled and seeded
3 scallions (about 1 ounce), chopped
half a green bell pepper (about 3 ounces), seeded and chopped
half a cucumber (about 3 ounces), peeled, seeded, and chopped
one-quarter red onion (about 1 ounce), peeled and chopped
¼ cup chopped parsley
¼ cup chopped basil
2 tablespoons (1 ounce) red wine vinegar
2 tablespoons (1 ounce) olive oil
1 cup (8 ounces) tomato juice
1 teaspoon salt
¼ teaspoon freshly ground black pepper
¾ pound lump crabmeat, cleaned
¼ cup (2 ounces) crème fraîche
6 slices Italian bread, cubed and baked in oven until brown and crisp
    fresh basil leaves, garnish

Place vegetables and herbs in a food processor and process until almost smooth, but with some texture. Pour into a bowl. Add vinegar, oil, juice, salt, and pepper. Mix and refrigerate for several hours. Pour into bowls. Top with crabmeat, crème fraîche, crumbled croutons, and basil leaves.

Cold Yellow Soup with Fresh Basil

JOHN LONG
ROUNDS CHEF, C.C.

The Williamsburg Inn, Colonial Williamsburg, Williamsburg

Chef's Notes
- *Red tomatoes can be substituted, but it will reduce the soup's conversational novelty.*
- *Yellow tomatoes have less acid than red tomatoes.*

"What's this?" shouted the market checker as she held up our tester's tomatoes. With the entire market's attention, the other checker screamed, "Never saw them before." The tester informed all that it was a yellow tomato—a tangy variety for Chef Long's chilled soup. Within minutes the other customers scrambled for the rest of the yellow tomatoes and sped home to whip up batches of this highly conversational soup.

Complexity ✪✪✪   Yield: 6 servings

2 *medium onions (8 ounces), peeled and sliced*
4 *cloves garlic, sliced*
2 *tablespoons (1 ounce) extra-virgin olive oil*
9 *medium ripe yellow tomatoes (about 3 pounds), cored and quartered*
½ *bunch basil, chopped*
½ *to 1 cup (4 to 8 ounces) defatted chicken stock to adjust consistency*
   sea salt
   freshly ground black pepper
6 *basil leaves for garnish*

In a large nonstick skillet sauté onions and garlic in oil until translucent. Add tomatoes and basil. Cook over medium heat for 10 minutes. Place in a blender or food processor. Process until smooth. Strain. Add stock if purée is too thick. Season with salt and pepper. Chill. Serve in chilled bowls garnished with basil leaf.

Chilled Peach Soup

ANTHONY CONTE
PASTRY CHEF, C.C.
Country Club of Virginia, Richmond

Virginia's peaches hit the peak of their fragrance in early summer. Farmers markets or pick-your-own supply some of our best. They are low in calories and always a light way to start or finish a meal.

Complexity ✪   Yield: 8 servings (8-ounce portions)

 9 *peaches (about 2½ pounds)*
⅔ *cup (6 ounces) plain low-fat yogurt*
1¼ *cups (10 ounces) milk*
1⅔ *cups (13 ounces) orange juice*
 2 *tablespoons (1 ounce) peach schnapps*
¾ *cup water*
¼ *cup sugar*
¼ *teaspoon ground nutmeg*
¼ *teaspoon ground cinnamon*
    whipped cream, optional
    sprigs of fresh mint leaves, optional

Peel and remove pits from peaches. Combine all ingredients—except cream and mint—in a blender. Purée until smooth. Chill for several hours before serving. Place soup in a large-rimmed soup bowl. Pipe on a rosette of whipped cream and top with sprigs of fresh mint leaves, if desired.

Chef's Notes
- *While the blender creates a creamier consistency, a food processor may be used.*
- *When fresh peaches are unavailable substitute canned or frozen ones.*
- *A fresh peach is ripe when it has a slight resistance to the touch. It will continue to ripen at room temperature. Avoid placing in the refrigerator where it will become mushy.*

Chicken and Sausage Gumbo

STUART DEUTSCH

Executive Chef

The American Tobacco Company, Chester

Chef's Notes
- *Andouille sausage is a very spicy smoked Cajun sausage.*
- *A lower-fat version of this may be prepared by using spicy smoked turkey sausage.*
- *Gumbo filé powder, used as a thickener, is made from the dried, ground leaves of the sassafras tree. Add only in the last few minutes of cooking, otherwise the gumbo becomes quite stringy. When reheating, do not boil.*

Steaming bowls of thick, spicy stew, based on a rich brown roux, are thickened by fresh okra. The spicy sausage and pepper zip fresh vegetables into a beautiful blend of Cajun-inspired flavors. Serve this as an appetizer or in huge bowls with freshly baked bread as an entire meal.

Complexity ✪✪   **Yield: 8 servings (or 4 for entrée)**

¼ cup (2 ounces) vegetable oil or bacon fat
⅛ cup (1 ounce) all-purpose flour
1 large (6 ounces) onion, chopped
3 celery stalks (8 ounces), chopped
1 medium (6 ounces) green bell pepper, chopped
3 tablespoons chopped parsley
2 cloves garlic, minced
½ pound Andouille sausage
⅓ pound okra, tops removed
1 medium (4 ounces) tomato, chopped
5 cups chicken stock
3 tablespoons Worcestershire sauce
1 to 2 teaspoons Tabasco sauce
3 tablespoons ketchup
1 teaspoon salt
⅛ teaspoon cayenne pepper
  pinch dried thyme
  pinch dried rosemary
  pinch hot pepper flakes
1 bay leaf
1 pound cooked chicken meat
1 teaspoon gumbo filé powder

In heavy pot heat oil or fat over low heat. Stir in flour. Cook until browned or for about 30 minutes stirring continuously. Add onion, celery, bell pepper, parsley, and garlic to roux. Cook 30 minutes over medium heat. Stir often. Cut sausage into ½-inch slices. Sauté briefly in a fry pan to eliminate excess fat. Add sausage to vegetables along with okra, tomato, chicken stock, Worcestershire, Tabasco, ketchup, salt, cayenne pepper, thyme, rosemary, pepper flakes, and bay leaf. Simmer, stirring occasionally, for approximately 2 hours. Five minutes before serving add chicken meat and gumbo filé powder.

Chicken and Scallop Florentine Soup

REGINA LOWERY

CHEF APPRENTICE

The Tobacco Company Restaurant, Richmond

This classic treatment of a cream soup has a twist with scallops and fresh spinach. The texture is sublime and its creamy goodness tenaciously clings to the ingredients. Bay scallops, particularly the always available aquacultured product, can be used in place of the sea scallops.

Complexity ✪   Yield: 6 to 8 servings

1 large (⅛ pound) chicken breast, skinless and boneless
½ cup (4 ounces) butter
1 cup (4 ounces) all-purpose flour
⅓ cup (2 ounces) finely chopped onion
2 cloves minced garlic
4 cups chicken stock
⅛ cup (1 ounce) julienned spinach, packed
⅛ pound sea scallops, coarsely chopped
¼ cup (2½ ounces) white wine
¾ cup (6 ounces) cream
*   salt, white pepper, and paprika to taste*

In a small nonstick pan coated with vegetable spray, sauté chicken for 2 minutes on each side. Cut into ½-inch pieces and set aside. In a 3-quart pan, melt butter and add flour, onion, and garlic to make a roux. Cook for 10 minutes. Whisk in half the chicken stock. Simmer until it thickens, then add remaining stock, chicken, spinach, scallops, wine, cream, and seasonings. Simmer approximately 20 minutes until spinach is tender. Ladle into cream soup bowls.

Chef's Notes
- *Alternately, on a sheet pan bake chicken breasts at 350° for 15 minutes.*
- *A lower-calorie version of this soup can be prepared without the roux. Substitute milk for the cream and thicken the soup when spinach is tender with a mixture of 2 tablespoons of cornstarch mixed in ⅛ cup cold water. Bring soup to boil. Reduce heat, stirring until it is again clear (approximately 4 minutes).*

Leberknodelsuppe

MANFRED E. ROEHR
C.E.C., A.A.C.

**Chowning's and Christiana Campbell's Taverns,
Colonial Williamsburg, Williamsburg**

Chef's Notes
- *Calf's liver makes a more deli-cate meatball; however, it is more expensive.*
- *Soup should look like a con-sommé. Beef bouillon may be used in place of stock, but do not add extra salt.*
- *Serve from a grand soup tureen family style for a festive holi-day, Thanksgiving, or Christmas starter.*

For a true German dinner, start with this liver dumpling soup. Nothing is more heartwarming than a steaming crock of leber-knodelsuppe during the cold winter months. Using a food processor makes fast work of the meatballs.

Complexity ✪ 　　　　　　**Yield: 4 servings**

¼ *pound beef liver, membrane removed*
1 *egg*
2 *tablespoons (1 ounce) butter or margarine, melted*
¾ *cup (1 ounce) fresh fine breadcrumbs*
1 *teaspoon parsley flakes*
¼ *teaspoon dried marjoram*
¼ *teaspoon salt*
5 *cups beef stock*
1 *small (3 ounces) onion, finely chopped*
  fresh parsley, garnish

In a nonstick pan sprayed with vegetable spray sauté liver for 3 min-utes on each side. Mince finely in blender. Add egg, butter, crumbs, spices, and salt to blender. Process until mixed. Chill mixture 30 min-utes. In a 3-quart pan, bring stock with onion to a boil. Form meat mixture into 20 small meatballs. Place balls in soup. Cook 10 min-utes. Ladle soup into bowls each with 5 meatballs. Sprinkle with chopped parsley.

New England Clam Chowder

RAOUL B. HEBERT

EXECUTIVE CHEF

Bull and Bear Club, Richmond

The Bull and Bear has been serving this soup—a wonderful club tradition—for many, many years every Friday night.

Complexity ✪✪   **Yield: 8 servings**

```
 3  6½-ounce cans chopped clams
 4  ounces diced bacon
 ¼  cup (2 ounces) butter, melted
 ½  pound celery, small dice
 ½  pound onions, small dice
 ½  cup (2 ounces) all-purpose flour
10  ounces bottled clam juice
 ¾  pound potatoes, ¼-inch dice
 3  cups (24 ounces) milk
    salt to taste
    pepper to taste
    pinch of Old Bay seasoning
    thyme leaves, to taste
```

Strain clams. Reserve juice. Render bacon in 6-quart soup pot. Add butter, celery, and onion. Cook until translucent. Add flour to make a roux. Add bottled and reserved clam juices gradually. Simmer potatoes in juice until tender. Add milk to pot. Simmer for 10 minutes or until smooth. Add clams. Add seasonings to taste. When hot, ladle into bowls.

Chef's Notes
- *Fresh clams can easily be used. Rinse under cold water. Place on a pan in a 450° oven for about 2 or 3 minutes or until shells pop open. Drain off juices and reserve. Chop.*
- *Try turkey bacon or reduced-fat pork bacon in this recipe.*
- *New England chowder is white like snow while Manhattan is red like the Indians who origi-nally lived on the island.*

She Crab Soup

MARK KIMMEL
EXECUTIVE CHEF, C.E.C., A.A.C.
The Tobacco Company Restaurant, Richmond

This classic soup, thickened with both a roux and heavy cream, makes a perfect white sea for the succulent pieces of crab to swim. As it is rich, select other meal components that are considerably lighter.

Complexity ✪   **Yield: 8 to 10 servings**

6 tablespoons (3 ounces) butter
½ medium (2 ounces) onion, finely diced
1 crushed clove of garlic
¾ cup (3 ounces) all-purpose flour
1 bay leaf
1 teaspoon salt
1 teaspoon white pepper
6 cups seafood stock
2 tablespoons (1 ounce) diced pimientos
2 teaspoons Worcestershire sauce
½ cup (4 ounces) sherry
½ cup (4 ounces) heavy cream
½ pound crabmeat, all cartilage removed

In soup pot, melt butter. Add onion and garlic and cook until transparent. Add flour and cook over medium heat for 5 minutes. Add bay leaf, salt, pepper, and stock. Whip until smooth. Cook over low heat for 10 minutes or until thickened. Stir in pimientos, Worcestershire, sherry, and cream. When heated gently add crabmeat pieces. Mix gently and serve when heated.

Chef's Notes
• *If seafood stock is unavailable use chicken broth. If seafood bouillon is used, eliminate all other salt in the recipe.*
• *Use clam juice for half the seafood stock and water for the remaining liquid.*

CHAPTER 3
Elegant Entrées
Seafood and Vegetarian

PRESENTATION SECRETS

THE PLATE is a chef's blank canvas for creating sensual pleasures. Many claim that one eats first with the eyes. Others claim they have started long before seeing by smelling tempting aromas wafting from the kitchen.

On this three-dimensional plate, color, texture, shapes, and flavors meld producing an esthetic experience. Here originality and creativity reign supreme, of course, tempered with good taste. Many practical considerations limit the presentation—good nutrition, sensible portions, and ease of consumption.

Basic elements of design suggest attention to simple geometry. A single shape shows little imagination. The textbook example is round scallops, potatoes, and Brussels sprouts—often called the "marble meal." The "scoop meal" is equally as unimaginative—a scoop of chicken, egg, and tuna salad.

Food naturally comes in a rich variety of shapes and sizes. Some interesting ones are mushrooms, both whole and sliced, asparagus spears, and sliced tomatoes. As in flower arranging, odd numbers of repetitions are pleasing, such as five new potatoes or three small squash.

Several knife strokes transform foods into very pleasing shapes. A classic is the seven-sided tournéed potato. What can be more beautiful than a pork loin stuffed with fruit dressing, rolled, roasted, and carved into beautiful slices?

The effort is not only appreciated but celebrated.

Food as art is enjoyable on many levels. Granted the picture only lasts for the meal, but it gives an exciting enjoyment to the dinner. A series of plates may evoke more pleasure than many of the finest paintings as they are intensely experienced before eating.

Restaurant presentations are like a visit to a fine art gallery. One can return for some of the pieces but it really is a changing exhibit. Do look around at the fresh works of art coming from the kitchen. (Yes, the table by the kitchen door can be a bonus.) And the dessert cart may be an extra artful stimulation for the eyes in addition to the palate.

Surprise is an important element. Once a spun sugar sailing mass floated out from the kitchen anchored in a dense chocolate ganache. The mast, at least twelve inches tall, aimed the dessert toward the skies. Ecstasy.

Plate creation need not be difficult. Several basic elements are helpful for a starter. All items on the plate must be edible. Place the main item near the center of the plate with the most favorable side toward the diner. Match vegetables, starches, and sauces for flavor, color, and texture. Use sauces as a background by creating a pool on the plate, then placing the companion item on top. Perhaps drizzle a bit of sauce on top.

Another basic is to keep food off the plate's rim. The rim is like the picture's frame. Recently some experimentation with garnishes on the rim have resulted in plates where the diner touches the plate and soils his hands.

Our society is accustomed to selected food colors. I have made blue mashed potatoes and green rolls only to find they were not eaten except by the adventuresome. The Japanese adore blue and purple pickles, while we keep blue for berries and purple for plums, preferring not to see these in our meats and side dishes.

The "snow blizzard" plate is to be avoided—white fish fillet, mashed potatoes, white corn, and white rolls.

Mix up cooking techniques. An all-fried plate of fried chicken, French fries, and fried zucchini is a napkin manufacturer's dream. Try boiled new potatoes and sautéed zucchini with the chicken.

The textures, both visually and physically, benefit from contrast. Vary with soft, crunchy, crisp, hard, dry, wet. Now eating can be fun. People love to hear their food. Dining is a very sensual experience.

Flavor, one of the most important components, will distinguish excellent food from the ordinary. We subscribe to natural approaches particularly with complementary herbs. But repetition of the same herb in too many courses becomes monotonous. Use a sparing hand, allowing herbs to enhance not overpower.

Garnishes are not just an afterthought, like a sprig of parsley with a steak and baked potato. Garnishes are meant to be eaten and enjoyed. It would be much more fun to garnish the plate with a bit of red onion confit,

an introduction of both color and additional taste sensations.

The plate items are assumed to be eaten in combination with one another. There are the sequential eaters doomed to eating only one thing at a time, but the majority enjoy having a taste of this and a taste of that, marrying flavors, looking for contrasts, tweaking the sweet, salty, bitter centers of taste on the tongue and palate. The cook's ingredient and preparation selection now become the property of the diner to combine for their personal satisfaction. And what an adventure this can be.

This is dining, not eating. Savor every bite. Pay attention to this beautiful food. Appreciate the art, the freshness, the care, the entire experience.

View the entire dining room as part of the visual landscape for enhancing the experience. Select linens, plates, cutlery, glasses, candles, and table decorations to create the meal's backdrop. Change the scenery for different dinners to match the moods. Vary the places you serve meals.

Fish Secrets

With fish, serve fresh carrot purée jazzed with fresh chopped dill. Peel carrots, rough chop. Place in saucepan. Cover with water or chicken stock. Add diced white onion for flavor. Slow simmer until water has evaporated. Put on a baking sheet in a low oven, 250°, to dry out. Purée, then pipe onto plate.—*Chef Corliss*

Mix fresh lemon juice with egg wash for fish. Or try fish dipped into salted milk, then cornmeal for fried fish.—*Chef Fulton*

A little vinegar poured over fresh fish before broiling keeps it from breaking.
—*Chef Fulton*

Grilled Gulf Shrimp with Lobster Butter, Zucchini, and Red and Yellow Peppers

MARCEL DESAULNIERS

CHEF-OWNER, C.E.C., A.A.C.

The Trellis Restaurant, Williamsburg

The College of William and Mary's historic Wren Building, visible from The Trellis, is the starting point for graduating ceremonies. To celebrate such occasions properly, complimentary champagne is offered to dining graduates and their guests. A sip or two between bites of this large, succulent shrimp dripping with lobster butter made from an intensely flavorful reduction should impel the most reluctant graduate out into the world of earning.

Complexity ✪✪✪✪ Yield: 8 servings

1 2½- to 3-pound live lobster
1 teaspoon salt in 3 quarts water
1 pound unsalted butter, softened
   salt and pepper to taste
3 pounds jumbo shrimp (12 to 15 shrimp per pound), peeled and deveined
¼ cup (2 ounces) vegetable oil
4 medium (2 pounds) zucchini, peeled, cut into 2½x¼-inch sections, discarding the center section
2 tablespoons water
4 medium (1½ pounds) red bell peppers, cut into 1¼-inch thin strips
2 medium (¾ pound) yellow bell peppers, cut into 1¼-inch thin strips

lobster butter
Remove the tail and claws, reserving the body. Cook tail and claws for 10 minutes in 3 quarts boiling water with 1 teaspoon salt. Remove. Run under cool water. Remove meat. Cut meat into ¼-inch pieces. Refrigerate covered. Return shells to water along with uncooked lobster body cut into 1- to 1½-inch pieces. Simmer at medium for 3 hours. Strain liquid, pushing down on shells to extract as much liquid as possible. Place stock (about 3 cups) in saucepan. Simmer for 1 hour. Strain into nonstick sauté pan and reduce over low heat for about 20 minutes, or to 2 tablespoons. In a food processor fitted with a metal blade, process butter, lobster meat, and stock reduction until

Chef's Notes
- *Preparation of the lobster butter is time-consuming. It is recommended that the lobster butter be prepared at least 1 day in advance. It can be refrigerated for 3 to 4 days or frozen for several weeks. If frozen, defrost in refrigerator for 24 hours before using. This size lobster yields 12 to 16 ounces of cooked meat. Do not purchase cooked meat unless certain that lively lobsters were dropped into the cooking pot— some fish dealers selling cooked meat use it as a vehicle to part company with crustaceans in a state of imminent demise.*
- *This recipe calls for a generous amount of lobster butter. For economy, a smaller lobster could be used, resulting in less meat, yet still producing a flavorful butter. For even more economy the shrimp shells can be used to prepare a reduction instead of the lobster and made without the texture-providing lobster meat.*
- *Large shrimp are desirable for grilling. Smaller ones dry out quickly and become overcooked, sacrificing flavors.*

smooth. Season with salt and pepper. Combine thoroughly. Refrigerate covered until ready to use.

shrimp and vegetables
Skewer 5 shrimp on each of 8 skewers. Lightly brush with vegetable oil. Cover with plastic wrap and refrigerate until needed. Season shrimp with salt and pepper. Grill skewers over a medium charcoal or wood fire for 1½ minutes on each side. Transfer to a baking sheet. Baste with half the lobster butter. Hold in a preheated 225° oven. In a large nonstick sauté pan heat 2 tablespoons of lobster butter with 2 tablespoons water on high. When hot add pepper strips. Sauté for 2 minutes. Add zucchini and remaining lobster butter, seasoning to taste. Heat about 4 minutes or until hot. Portion the sautéed zucchini and peppers onto warm 10-inch plates. Unskewer shrimp onto vegetables and serve immediately.

Shrimp with Angel Hair Pasta

WINSLOW GOODIER
EXECUTIVE CHEF, C.E.C.
Hermitage Country Club, Richmond

We tested this on a California audience with a lemon picked just outside the test kitchen in Palm Springs. And after consuming these succulent shrimp in a light, basil-lemon-garlic-wine sauce on a bed of angel hair pasta surrounded by beautiful California vegetables, it was pronounced a definite winner. Subsequent tests found loyal fans in Virginia.

Complexity ✪   Yield: 2 servings

4 ounces angel hair pasta
4 teaspoons virgin olive oil
3 cloves garlic, chopped
half a yellow bell pepper (about 3 ounces), seeded and sliced
2 sun-dried tomatoes, chopped
1 cup (8 ounces) broccoli florets
6 ounces shrimp, peeled and deveined
¼ cup (2 ounces) white wine
2 tablespoons (1 ounce) fresh lemon juice
3 fresh basil leaves, chopped
   salt and pepper to taste

Cook angel hair pasta, rinse, and drain well. Set aside. Place olive oil in hot nonstick sauté pan. Add garlic, peppers, sun-dried tomatoes, and broccoli. Sauté approximately 4 minutes, then add shrimp. Continue sautéing for 2 to 3 minutes, then add white wine, lemon juice, and basil. When shrimp is cooked, add angel hair pasta and mix well. Add salt and pepper to taste.

Chef's Notes
- *Double or triple the quantities for more servings.*
- *To make chopping tomatoes quite easy try this trick. In a small glass dish place sun-dried tomatoes and ¼ cup water. Microwave for 1 minute. Drain. Now chop.*
- *Precooked shrimp may be used. Defrost by running under hot tap water for several minutes. Drain.*
- *The addition of red, green, and more yellow bell peppers adds very few calories, but lots more to eat.*

Macadamia-crusted Softshell Crabs with Crispy Asian Vegetable Slaw

EDWARD DAGGERS

EXECUTIVE CHEF, C.E.C.

Country Club, Memphis, Tennessee

Chef's Notes
- Garnish with sweet potato chips.
- If necessary, frozen softshell crabs, such as the high-quality ones cleaned and packaged at Tangier's Island, can be used.

Softshell crab season, the short period when crabs shed their shells, is celebrated by crab devotees. The entire crab is eaten. Here Chef Daggers adds a creative touch with a macadamia nut crust over a rich, eggy batter.

Complexity ✪✪   **Yield: 4 servings**

CRABS

- 8 jumbo (2 pounds) softshell crabs, cleaned
- ½ cup (2 ounces) all-purpose flour
- 3 eggs
- 3 tablespoons (1½ ounces) heavy cream
- 1 cup (5 ounces) chopped macadamia nuts
- ½ cup white breadcrumbs
-   sesame oil for sautéing
-   vegetable oil for sautéing

ASIAN SLAW

- 2 red bell peppers (12 ounces), julienned
- 1 yellow bell pepper (6 ounces), julienned
- half a medium (2 ounces) carrot, julienned
- 1 stalk (2 ounces) celery, julienned
- 1 green bell pepper (6 ounces), julienned
- ½ cup (1 ounce) bean sprouts
- ⅓ cup (1 ounce) finely shredded red cabbage
- 1 cup (8 ounces) mayonnaise
- ¼ cup (2 ounces) cider vinegar
- ¼ cup sugar
- ¼ cup (2 ounces) sesame oil, dark
- ¼ cup (2 ounces) soy sauce
- ¼ cup (1 ounce) sesame seeds

Clean crabs. Dredge in flour. Mix eggs and cream. Mix nuts and breadcrumbs. Dip crabs in eggs with cream. Coat with nut and crumb mixture. Place sesame and vegetable oil in heavy skillet about ½-inch deep in pan. Sauté crabs over medium heat for about 3 minutes per side or until crisp and golden brown. Remove and drain on paper towels. To serve arrange slaw on plate and arrange crabs on top.

Asian slaw
Mix all ingredients for slaw. Chill in covered container.

Softshell Crab Melt

PHILIP LADD

EXECUTIVE CHEF

Holiday Inn Executive Center, Chesterfield

Chef's Notes

• *To clean crabs, remove eyes, spongy gills, yellow-green digestive system, and apron or tail. Rinse under cool water. Body, legs, claws, and soft shell are edible.*

During late spring, summer, and early fall, the blue crab sheds its hard shell making it quite easy to devour. The timing for this open-faced sandwich is perfect for matching with meaty, red, ripe homegrown tomatoes. This quick and tasty item makes a special luncheon dish.

Complexity ✪   Yield: 6 servings

1 **bunch chopped basil**
1 **small (3 ounces) onion, finely diced**
½ **cup (4 ounces) olive oil**
¼ **cup (2 ounces) white vinegar**
2 **large tomatoes (10 ounces), cut into 6 slices each**
6 **jumbo (1½ pounds) softshell crabs, cleaned**
½ **cup (2 ounces) all-purpose flour, for coating crabs**
    freshly ground black pepper to taste
¼ **cup (2 ounces) clarified butter**
6 **slices freshly baked rye bread**
12 **thin slices (6 ounces) Emmentaler or Gruyère cheese**
    whole chives for garnish

Blend together basil, onion, oil, and vinegar. Spread out tomato slices and ladle with dressing. Marinate 2 hours, refrigerated. Dredge crabs in mixture of flour and pepper. In a large pan, sauté crabs in clarified butter over medium heat for about 2 minutes on each side or until firm. Toast bread, topping each with 2 tomato slices, a crab, and 2 cheese slices. Place under broiler until cheese is melted. Garnish with whole chives.

A Virginian's Maryland-Style Crab Cake

DAVID BRUCE CLARKE

CHEF-INSTRUCTOR

J. Sargeant Reynolds Community College, Richmond

Competition over who makes the best crab cakes is fierce among inhabitants of these two states. But all agree, there is nothing quite like fresh Chesapeake Bay crab when made into scrumptious crab cakes.

Complexity ✪　　　　　**Yield: 4 servings**

- 1 *pound lump or backfin crabmeat, picked over*
- ¼ *cup finely chopped parsley*
- 2 *pieces white bread, crust removed, made into crumbs*
- ¼ *teaspoon baking powder*
- ¼ *teaspoon Old Bay seasoning*
  pinch salt
  pinch white pepper
- 1 *teaspoon dry mustard*
- 2 *tablespoons (1 ounce) dry white wine*
  juice of 1 lemon
- 1 *tablespoon Worcestershire sauce*
- 1 *cup mayonnaise*
- 2 *whole eggs, beaten lightly*

In a medium stainless mixing bowl, place crab, parsley, and bread-crumbs. Mix lightly with fingers. Dust top with baking powder and refrigerate. Mix dry spices, wine, lemon juice, and Worcestershire. Blend well with mayonnaise and eggs. Combine the mixtures. Gently pat into 8 cakes. Pan-fry until golden brown.

Chef's Notes
- *Handle crabmeat delicately so as not to break up pieces when removing any stray bits of cartilage.*
- *These can also be served as sandwiches, but only make 4 cakes.*
- *Serve with tartar sauce and lemon wedges.*

Rue's Wharf Crab Cakes

JOHN LONG
ROUNDS CHEF, C.C.

The Williamsburg Inn, Colonial Williamsburg, Williamsburg

Chef's Notes

• *Using a small pan on a larger baking sheet will prevent cakes from burning. Crab is quite delicate.*

On the banks on the York River, crabbers haul in fresh crabs to Rue's Wharf. Unfortunately, the crab harvest in Virginia cannot keep pace with the demand. This version of crab cakes has no breading, just three ingredients to hold it together while baking.

Complexity ✪   **Yield: 6**

1 pound backfin crabmeat, picked over
¼ cup mayonnaise
2 tablespoons grainy mustard (Pommery)
1 egg, beaten

Remove any cartilage gently, trying to keep the crab in large chunks. Lightly mix all ingredients. Form into 6 cakes. Place on a small pan placed on a baking sheet. Bake at 400° for 15 to 20 minutes or until the cakes just start to brown.

Seared Salmon and Sea Scallops with Vegetable Julienne Cucumber Ginger Sauce

HANS SCHADLER
EXECUTIVE CHEF, C.E.C., A.A.C.

The Williamsburg Inn, Colonial Williamsburg, Williamsburg

The sauce of scallops, cucumber, and fresh ginger is prepared while swirling in cubes of chilled butter to the reduced cooking vegetable liquid of fish stock, shallots, and white wine. This flavor-building continues layer by layer with each new ingredient perfectly harmonized to the total finished array of delicately sauced vegetables—the perfect balance for seared fresh salmon fillets.

Complexity ✪✪✪ **Yield: 4 servings**

Chef's Notes
• *Flounder, sea bass, or brook trout are delicious alternatives to salmon fillets.*

SALMON

4 salmon fillets, 4 ounces each
½ cup (2 ounces) all-purpose flour
1 teaspoon paprika
   pinch salt
2 tablespoons (1 ounce) olive oil

VEGETABLES AND SAUCE

¼ cup (2 ounces) butter, cubed and chilled, mixed use
1 large shallot, peeled and chopped, mixed use
1 cup (8 ounces) dry white wine, mixed use
1 cup (8 ounces) fish or vegetable stock, mixed use
1 medium (4 ounces) carrot, julienned
1 medium (5 ounces) zucchini, julienned
1 medium (5 ounces) yellow squash, jullienned
4 large (2 ounces) shiitake mushrooms, sliced into fine strips
1 tablespoon chopped thyme
1 tablespoon chopped chervil
1 English cucumber (8 ounces), peeled, ¼-inch dice
4 large (2 ounces) sea scallops, ¼-inch dice

1   *teaspoon peeled and finely chopped ginger*
    salt to taste
    fresh cracked black pepper to taste
    juice of 1 lemon
1   *teaspoon Dijon mustard*

GARNISH

¼   *cup chopped chives, garnish*

salmon
Dredge salmon in mixture of flour, paprika, and salt. Lightly shake off all excess. Heat olive oil in a nonstick skillet. Sear salmon on each side for about 2 minutes or until lightly browned on each side. Set aside; keep warm. Wipe skillet clean.

vegetables and sauce
Return skillet to heat, add 1 teaspoon each butter and shallots with ¼ cup white wine and ¼ cup fish stock. Bring to a quick boil. Add julienned vegetables, mushrooms, and herbs. Cook for 5 to 8 minutes or until the vegetables are beginning to soften. With slotted spoon, remove vegetables and keep warm. Add remaining liquids and reduce by half. Add remaining shallots, cucumber, scallops, and ginger. While swiftly turning ingredients, swirl in cold butter cubes. Adjust seasoning with salt, pepper, and lemon juice. Finish with Dijon mustard.

presentation
Arrange vegetables in center of plate. Top with salmon fillet. Spoon cucumber scallop sauce over salmon. Garnish with chopped chives.

Scallops and Mushrooms in Pear and Brandy Sauce with Pecans on Pasta

MANFRED E. ROEHR
C.E.C., A.A.C.
**Chowning's and Christiana Campbell's Taverns,
Colonial Williamsburg, Williamsburg**

Chef Roehr's culinary surprise is teaming Seckel pears and plump, fresh sea scallops—an exquisite and original match. In a half-and-half-based sauce with major components of mushrooms, shallots, apple brandy, and lemon juice, the sweetness of the pears brings out the delicate sea taste of the scallops. Finishing the dish with chopped pecans adds a delightful crunch and even more flavor. Chef Roehr says this dish is "incredibly rich." While rotini was the initial pasta in the chef's development, experiment with your favorite pastas cooked al dente.

Complexity ✪✪   **Yield: 4 servings**

> ¾ *pound large sea scallops*
> ¼ *cup (2 ounces) butter*
> 3 *tablespoons fresh lemon juice*
> 2 *cups (12 ounces) Seckel pears, unpeeled*
> 2 *cups (5 ounces) sliced mushrooms*
> 2 *tablespoons chopped fresh shallots*
> ⅓ *cup chopped fresh parsley*
> ¼ *cup (2 ounces) apple brandy*
> 3 *cups half and half*
> ½ *cup (2 ounces) chopped pecans*
>   *salt and white pepper to taste*
> ½ *pound pasta, cooked and drained*

Chef's Notes
- *Half and half is 10 to 12 percent butterfat and is made of equal portions of cream and milk.*
- *Milk alone can be used instead for a less rich and lighter sauce.*
- *If Seckel pears are unavailable, try any other fresh pears.*
- *Scallops are done when they start to turn opaque. Be careful not to overcook so they maintain their moist, sweet taste, reminiscent of the deep sea.*
- *Pasta can be cooked in advance, then refreshed by plunging into boiling water for 1 minute. Drain completely before saucing.*
- *For an exotic twist try the black squid ink pasta available in specialty markets.*
- *Also try this dish for a sublime starter for 8.*

In a large skillet sauté scallops in 2 tablespoons butter for 1 minute. Add lemon juice. Place scallops in bowl and keep warm. Wash, core, and cut pears into 6 wedges—do not peel. Sauté pear wedges, mushrooms, shallots, and parsley in remaining butter for approximately 5 minutes or until mushrooms are cooked. Drain liquid. Add brandy, half and half, and half the liquid from scallops. Simmer until liquid is reduced by half. Add drained scallops, pecans, salt, and pepper and simmer for 2 to 4 minutes or until scallops are done. Place pasta in individual large bowls. Cover with scallops and sauce.

Steamed Mussels and Button Clams with Peppers in Basil Garlic Vinaigrette

HANS SCHADLER
EXECUTIVE CHEF, C.E.C., A.A.C.
The Williamsburg Inn, Colonial Williamsburg, Williamsburg

Chef's Notes
- *Button clams are smaller than cherrystones.*
- *Discard any raw shellfish that do not close when touched.*
- *Discard any cooked shellfish that do not open.*
- *Use a small food processor, pouring oil through top opening, to easily make an emulsion.*
- *Steamed shellfish may be served at room temperature or served chilled.*
- *Sprinkle finely chopped spring onion on vinaigrette.*

Shellfish steamed, then sauced with a lively basil garlic vinaigrette transforms a casual dinner into a lively event. Enjoying it is a hands-on experience with lots of dipping and savoring. Serve with a plethora of toasted garlic bread, a good bottle of crisp, chilled Sauvignon Blanc, and generous cloth napkins.

Complexity ✪✪   **Yield: 4 servings**

SHELLFISH

1 pound mussels (approximately 12 in shells)
1 pound button clams (approximately 16 in shells)
½ cup (4 ounces) white wine
1 sprig thyme
1 clove garlic
1 bay leaf

VEGETABLES AND VINAIGRETTE

1 small (4 ounces) green bell pepper, julienned
1 small (4 ounces) yellow bell pepper, julienned
1 small (4 ounces) red bell pepper, julienned
2 ripe tomatoes (10 ounces), peeled, seeded, and diced
half a (3 ounces) red onion, finely minced
1 clove garlic, finely minced
½ cup (4 ounces) olive oil, divided use
¼ cup (2 ounces) balsamic vinegar
4 basil leaves, chopped
  fresh cracked pepper
  salt to taste

shellfish

Soak shellfish in cold water. Scrub shells. Agitate and change water several times. In a large pot add shellfish, wine, thyme, garlic, and bay leaf. Cover with a tight lid. Steam for about 10 minutes or until shellfish opens. Remove one half of each shell. Chill seafood or keep at room temperature for a short period until vegetables are prepared.

vegetables and vinaigrette

Sauté peppers, tomatoes, onion, and garlic in 2 tablespoons olive oil until transparent. In a stainless steel bowl slowly whisk remaining oil into balsamic vinegar to form an emulsion. Add sautéed vegetables, basil, and season to taste.

presentation

Place shellfish on half-shells in a large bowl. Spoon vegetables and vinaigrette over top.

Flounder Paupiettes

ANTHONY CONTE
PASTRY CHEF, C.C.
Country Club of Virginia, Richmond

Chef's Notes

• *For presentation serve with baby carrots, haricots verts, fanned saffron potatoes, and beurre blanc as shown in the diagram.*

• *Purchase medium to small fresh flounder fillets. Remove any skin and trim off any small bones. Cut fillets lengthwise down center.*

• *Use an ovenproof dish just large enough to hold the paupiettes in place. They will bake into the circular shape and be beautifully held together with the farce.*

• *If only larger fillets are available, cut them into manageable lengths.*

• *Wash scallops carefully to remove any sand or grit. Bay scallops in equal weight may be used.*

• *Fresh backfin crabmeat is recommended. Be sure to remove all pieces of cartilage.*

• *Keep farce mixture well-chilled to maintain fresh flavors.*

• *Farce may be spooned into the centers of the flounder rolls if desired.*

• *The baking liquid is also a delicious sauce for the fish and quite tasty on baked golden potatoes.*

Flounder, a mild white fish abundantly fresh in Virginia waters, becomes an elegant entrée when rolled and stuffed with a mouthwatering crabmeat and scallop farce. Gentle baking in a bath of cream and wine creates a lovely sauce.

Complexity ✪✪✪   Yield: 4 servings

4 fillets (2 pounds) flounder, cut lengthwise

FARCE

4 jumbo (2 ounces) sea scallops
¼ pound backfin crabmeat, picked over
1 egg white
2 tablespoons (1 ounce) cream
1 teaspoon orange zest
1 teaspoon capers, fine
1 teaspoon fresh dill, chopped fine
½ teaspoon salt
¼ teaspoon ground white pepper

BAKING LIQUID

⅓ cup (2½ ounces) cream
⅓ cup (2½ ounces) white wine
⅓ cup water
2 teaspoons chopped shallots
1 bay leaf

Starting with the thickest part of the fish, roll individual fillet halves around the thumb. Pull off thumb and stand each roll on end in an ovenproof shallow 9-inch circular casserole dish. Purée scallops and crab in food processor until smooth. Add egg white and pulse until incorporated. Remove from processor to a bowl that is resting in a second bowl full of ice. Keep mixture chilled at all times. Fold in cream until completely incorporated. Fold in all remaining farce ingredients. Fit pastry bag with large tip. Fill with farce and pipe into middle of each flounder roll. With a spatula smooth off tops. Mix cream, wine, water, shallots, and bay leaf. Pour into casserole dish. Cover dish. Bake at 300° for approximately 30 minutes or until the centers are firm.

Steamed Whole Flounder

GRACE LIU
CHEF-OWNER
The Dynasty, Williamsburg

The Cantonese province produces some of the freshest, brightest Chinese foods. Chef Liu and her husband have carefully researched Chinese cooking styles to ensure authenticity for their customers. The microwave oven, while not the traditional technique, steams fish as expertly as any bamboo steamer.

Chef's Notes
- *Fresh fish is key to the success of this dish. Make sure fish eyes are still bright and skin shiny and taut.*
- *Remember one always "eats" first with one's eyes.*

Complexity ✪✪✪   **Yield: 4 servings**

- 1 *medium (1½ pounds) flounder, dressed*
- 3 *thin slices fresh ginger*
- ½ *cup (4 ounces) chicken stock*
- 1 *teaspoon dry white wine (or dry sherry)*
- ¼ *teaspoon salt*
  sprinkle white pepper
- 1 *teaspoon soy sauce*
- 1 *scallion, shredded*
- 1 *tablespoon (½ ounce) peanut oil*
  fresh cilantro, garnish

Make 3 angled cross-cuts to the bone of fish on the black side. Insert ginger slice in each slot.

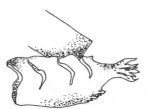

Lay fish on an oval plate with a rim. Add ½ cup stock and cooking wine. Sprinkle with salt and pepper. Top with soy sauce. Cover loosely with microwave-proof plastic wrap over plate. Seal at edges. Cook in microwave oven on high setting for 6 to 8 minutes until fish flakes easily. Remove from oven. Remove wrap carefully to avoid steam burns. Distribute shredded scallion over fish. Pour 1 tablespoon hot oil over the scallions and garnish with fresh cilantro.

Sautéed Salmon with Orange Mint Sauce

JEFF BLAND

EXECUTIVE CHEF

Buckhead Steak House, Richmond

CHEF-INSTRUCTOR

J. Sargeant Reynolds Community College

Chef's Notes

- *Before placing fish in pan, drain off excess egg wash.*
- *For cholesterol-sensitive diners, use egg substitutes or simply egg whites.*
- *While preparing the sauce, keep salmon warm in a slow oven. The sauté stage should leave the fish very pink inside. The carry-over heat will finish the process while the fish stands. Overcooking will dry out the fish.*
- *The butter may be completely eliminated from the sauce. Use the juice of 3 oranges. Reduce sauce by half and permit to naturally thicken. Use this natural reduction to spoon over salmon.*

"Chef Jeff," as he has become professionally known, dips fresh salmon in flour and egg wash just before a quick sauté. Its sauce is quickly made by deglazing the sauté pan with fresh orange juice and white wine. Then butter is swirled in with mint finishing the dish. The chef also recommends another approach of a natural reduction of the juice and wine using no butter. Try both.

Complexity ✪✪   Yield: 4 servings

1 **pound salmon fillets, divide into 4 portions**
½ **cup (2 ounces) all-purpose flour**
1 **egg**
1 **teaspoon water**
1 **tablespoon (½ ounce) vegetable oil**
2 **shallots (2 ounces), minced**
juice of 1 orange (3 ounces)
1 **tablespoon (½ ounce) white wine**
2 **tablespoons (1 ounce) butter**
4 **small mint leaves, julienned**
salt and pepper, to taste

Dust salmon with flour. Dip into wash of beaten egg and water. Place into a very hot sauté pan with oil. Cook for 2 minutes on each side. Remove salmon. Sauté shallots for 2 minutes. Add juice and white wine to deglaze pan. Reduce liquid by one-fourth. Stir in butter. Salt and pepper to taste. Remove from heat. Stir in mint just before serving. Spoon over salmon.

Grilled Marinated Salmon with Chorizo and Mussels, Smoked Tomato, and Chili Beurre Blanc

EDWARD DAGGERS
Executive Chef, C.E.C.
Country Club, Memphis, Tennessee

Complexity ✪✪✪	Yield: 4 servings

SEAFOOD, SAUSAGE, AND VEGETABLES

- 4 portions (5 ounces each) salmon fillet
- 3 cloves garlic, minced
- ¼ cup (2 ounces) olive oil
- 2 tablespoons (1 ounce) lemon juice
- 3 tablespoons (1½ ounces) teriyaki sauce
- 12 ounces chorizo sausage
- 20 mussels (1½ pounds), cleaned
- 2 yellow tomatoes, smoked and halved
- 2 plum tomatoes, smoked and halved
- 8 (2 ounces) asparagus tips, lightly steamed
- ⅓ cup (2 ounces) black beans, heated
  young chives, stems left whole

CHILI BEURRE BLANC

- 2 (2 ounces) shallots, minced
- ¼ teaspoon minced garlic
- ¼ teaspoon minced jalapeño pepper
- ½ cup (4 ounces) white wine
- ¼ cup (2 ounces) sherry wine
- 2 tablespoons lemon juice
- ¾ cup (6 ounces) heavy cream
- 2 tablespoons chili powder
- ¾ cup (6 ounces) butter, room temperature

Place fillets with garlic, olive oil, lemon juice, and teriyaki in a large plastic bag. Refrigerate for 1 hour, turning bag over several times. Grill salmon over hot coals about 3 minutes per side or until still reddish in the center. Do not overcook. Grill chorizo until thoroughly

Chef's Notes
- *Substitute any good-quality spicy sausage if chorizo is not available. An excellent choice is also Virginia's famous Surry sausages.*
- *A lower-calorie version of the sauce can be made by omitting both the cream and butter. After the initial wine reduction remove from heat and stir in ½ cup reduced-calorie sour cream.*

cooked through. Place mussels on grill until they open. To serve, place 2 tablespoons chili beurre blanc on center of plate. Place salmon on top. Make small piles of the smoked tomatoes. Fan chorizo around one side of the salmon and mussels on the other. Garnish with asparagus tips, black beans, and whole chives.

chili beurre blanc
In a small saucepan sauté shallots, garlic, and jalapeño in a small amount of butter. Add wines and lemon juice. Over low heat reduce by half. Stir in cream. Reduce by half. Stir in chili powder. Remove from heat. Cool slightly and whip in butter.

Grilled Salmon with Fire-roasted Pepper Salsa

JIM MAKINSON
EXECUTIVE CHEF, C.E.C.
Kingsmill Resort, Williamsburg

The Omega-3 fatty acids in salmon have received praise from the scientific community for their possible role in the reduction of cholesterol. Teamed here with an easy-to-prepare, low-fat, and very colorful salsa, the result is a healthy meal.

Complexity ✪   Yield: 4 servings

4	6-ounce salmon fillets
	olive oil vegetable spray
1	red bell pepper (6 ounces)
1	yellow bell pepper (6 ounces)
1	green bell pepper (6 ounces)
2	tablespoons (¾ ounce) chopped red onion
1	tablespoon chopped opal basil
1	teaspoon extra-virgin olive oil (or V-8 juice)
1	shallot, chopped (1 ounce)
	juice of 1 lime
	salt and cracked black pepper to taste

Grill salmon over hot coals using nonstick olive oil vegetable spray on grill. Roast peppers until black on all sides. Cover with plastic wrap for 5 minutes. Rinse off charred skin and remove seeds. Dice. Mix with remaining ingredients and season salsa to taste.

Chef's Notes
- *Salmon should be removed from the grill when the middle is still reddish. It will continue to cook somewhat and will remain moist.*
- *Do not spray grill grate over fire with vegetable spray as the can might ignite. Remove grate and spray.*

James River Rockfish Stew

EDWARD DAGGERS

EXECUTIVE CHEF, C.E.C.

Country Club, Memphis, Tennessee

Chef's Notes
- *Fish stock made from bones yields a superior tasting product.*
- *Substitute any firm fish for rockfish.*
- *For a less rich version substitute milk for cream.*
- *Serve in a rimmed cream soup bowl with fresh thyme garnish.*
- *When cleaning mushrooms it is fine to submerge them in water as they absorb very little water. A delightful scientific treatment of this is found in Harold McGee's* The Curious Cook *(San Francisco: North Point Press, 1990).*
- *For those desiring a bit of an alcoholic bite to their soup, skip the flaming step.*

The Kingsmill Resort—once the site of the Burwell family's plantation—sits majestically on the banks of the mighty James River. From the dining room, one can watch the steady progress as barges haul their cargo from Hampton Roads to Richmond.

Complexity ⊙⊙   Yield: 8 servings (8-ounce portions)

½ *pound smoked bacon, diced*
3 *medium (12 ounces) onions, diced*
1½ *cups (6 ounces) diced celery*
6 *tablespoons (3 ounces) butter*
1¼ *cups (5 ounces) all-purpose flour*
8 *large cloves (1 ounce) fresh garlic, minced*
2 *large (2 ounces) shallots, minced*
4 *cups fish stock*
2 *large (12 ounces) potatoes, diced*
2 *pounds rockfish fillets, chopped*
½ *pound mushrooms, cleaned and quartered*
1 *bunch fresh parsley, washed and minced*
1 *teaspoon fresh thyme, minced*
1 *teaspoon salt*
½ *teaspoon pepper*
½ *cup (4 ounces) sherry*
½ *cup (4 ounces) brandy*
1½ *cups (12 ounces) heavy cream*
   thyme sprigs, garnish

In a heavy soup pot, sauté smoked bacon with onions and celery. Add butter and flour to make a roux. Cook 5 minutes. Add garlic and shallots and cook for 3 minutes. Add fish stock, stirring constantly. Add potatoes. Simmer on low for 30 minutes. Add fish, mushrooms, and seasonings. In a separate sauté pan warm sherry and brandy. Flame to cook off alcohol. Add to soup. Simmer another 10 minutes and finish with cream.

Marble of Gingered Mahimahi in Savoy Cabbage with Thai Curry Butter Sauce

ROBERT D. CORLISS
SOUS CHEF

The Williamsburg Inn, Colonial Williamsburg, Williamsburg

Pale cabbage leaves wrap firm, white fish stuffed with fresh lobster mixed with toasted macadamia nuts. A rich butter sauce with delicate but haunting Thai curry elevates this creation to one of ecstasy. Present with Braised Lentils and Brunoise of Vegetables (see pages 141 and 156).

Complexity ❶❶❶　　　　**Yield: 2 servings**

2　whole leaves savoy cabbage
½　pound mahimahi fillets

MARINADE

2　tablespoons fresh ginger, finely chopped
　　zest of 1 lemon, finely chopped
　　zest of 1 orange, finely chopped
2　tablespoons finely chopped parsley
2　tablespoons finely chopped thyme
1　tablespoon (1 ounce) virgin olive oil
　　pinch white pepper

FARCE

2　ounces lobster meat, uncooked
¼　cup (2 ounces) heavy cream
1　egg white
1　orange (5 ounces), peeled and diced
6　leaves spinach (1 ounce), chopped and steamed (excess water removed)
1　tablespoon macadamia nuts, toasted and chopped
¼　teaspoon salt
　　pinch cayenne pepper

Chef's Notes
- *Monkfish (the poor man's lobster), flounder, or any white fish may be substituted. Either of these or scallops can be used in place of the lobster in the farce.*
- *The ice water shock for cabbage leaves prevents further cooking while retaining color and nutrients.*
- *Use your own creative ideas for the farce—try crabmeat, fruit compote, or spiced compound butters.*
- *Thai curry paste is available in Asian markets. Those that contain red Thai peppers, galangal, keffir limes, lemongrass, and garlic are preferred. Avoid any with peppers in a soybean paste.*
- *Save 1 tablespoon of marinade zest and herbs to sprinkle on plate for a colorful garnish.*
- *A lower-calorie Thai sauce can be made by eliminating both the butter and cream. Follow the above directions. After adding the Thai curry paste thicken with 1 tablespoon cornstarch mixed in ¼ cup cold water. Bring to a boil stirring constantly for about 2 minutes or until the sauce turns clear.*

THAI CURRY BUTTER

1 *cup (8 ounces) dry white wine*
½ *cup (4 ounces) fish stock*
1 *shallot (1 ounce), peeled, finely chopped*
1 *clove garlic, peeled, finely chopped*
   bay leaf
   sprig fresh thyme
   stem fresh parsley
1 *lemon, peeled and sliced*
2 *tablespoons (1 ounce) heavy cream*
4 *ounces unsalted butter, cut into tablespoon-size pieces*
2 *tablespoons Thai curry paste (available in Asian markets)*

Steam cabbage leaves for 6 to 8 minutes or until they easily bend. Plunge into ice water. Drain well and reserve. Cut fish into 2 pieces, then split the piece nearly in half horizontally. Open out fillets like butterfly wings. Place in glass dish. Combine marinade ingredients. Pour over fillets. Marinate, refrigerated, a minimum of 1 hour. Pulse lobster, cream, and egg white in food processor until smooth. By hand stir in orange, spinach, nuts, salt, and pepper.

To assemble, place two 12x8-inch pieces of plastic film on counter. Place a cabbage leaf in the center of each. Top each with fish fillet. Spread half the lobster farce on each fillet. Fold cabbage over to enclose the filling. Pull up all four corners of film and twist in center to form a marble-shaped ball. Tie with kitchen string. Poach in simmering water until fish is firm to the touch or for 12 to 15 minutes (interior temperature should be 135° to 140°). Remove from water. Let cool for 4 minutes before assembly.

For Thai sauce simmer wine, fish stock, shallot, garlic, herbs, and lemon in a heavy-bottomed saucepan. Reduce over medium heat, about 15 minutes, to 3 tablespoons. Whisk in heavy cream. Reduce for 3 minutes or until thickened. Whisk in butter, one tablespoon at a time, to form a creamy sauce. Whisk in curry paste until evenly blended. Strain through a fine strainer and reserve.

Arrange braised lentils and brunoise of vegetables (see recipes on pages 141 and 156) in circle in middle of plate. Lentils constitute half-circle with vegetables constituting the other half. Slice each fish marble into 4 or 5 slices. Arrange neatly on top of circle. Ladle 4 tablespoons of sauce around the plate. Serve hot.

Pan-Grilled Allegheny Mountain Trout with Baby Greens, Pine Nuts, and Chili Lime Aioli

HANS SCHADLER
EXECUTIVE CHEF, C.E.C., A.A.C.
The Williamsburg Inn, Colonial Williamsburg, Williamsburg

Chef's Notes
- *Soak 10-inch wooden skewers for about 10 minutes in water before threading. These are readily available in Asian markets.*
- *Haricots verts, the petite French green beans, can be immersed in ice water to stop cooking immediately and to maintain their delicate crispness. Handle fennel in a similar fashion.*
- *Poblano chilies are a 4-inch green, medium-hot pepper. After drying, the reddish-brown pepper is called an ancho. Use care in roasting chilies as the color change is quite subtle. The dried ancho can be used in the recipe by reconstituting in water, removing seeds and stem, and mixing with the roasted garlic and other aioli ingredients.*
- *Many markets stock dried peppers in the produce section. Pasillas could be used as a substitute.*
- *The puréed chilies and garlic should be thick, but a bit more water can be added if needed.*
- *Leftover aioli sauce can be stored in the refrigerator for up to one week in a tightly sealed glass jar.*

The southwestern flavors of chili peppers, lime, and cilantro give the French garlic-infused mayonnaise, aioli, an entirely new taste. Matched with prosciutto-wrapped morsels of trout accented with basil, it is presented as an entrée salad garnished with elegant haricots verts and julienned fennel. Farm-raised trout is a paean to aquaculture—the trout are readily available to consumers in most supermarkets. Have the fish monger fillet and skin the fish. Ask for the fillets to be wrapped in plastic, then set in a bag of crushed ice to preserve freshness. This can be stored for several hours in the refrigerator until preparation time. Be sure that fish never actually touches the ice.

Complexity ✪✪✪   **Yield: 4 servings**

FISH

- **4 6-ounce trout fillets, skinned**
- **4 basil leaves**
- **4 thin slices (2 ounces) prosciutto ham**
- **4 wooden skewers**

SALAD AND VEGETABLES

- **4 ounces haricots verts**
- **4 ounces fennel**
- **4 cups (8 ounces) mixed baby greens or curly leaf lettuce**
- **6 tablespoons (3 ounces) olive oil**
- **3 tablespoons (1½ ounces) red wine vinegar**
- **1 Belgian endive (3 ounces)**
- **½ cup (2 ounces) lightly toasted pine nuts**

AIOLI

2 poblano chilies, stem and seeds removed, but left as whole as
   possible
1 clove garlic, unpeeled
1 egg yolk
½ cup water
2½ tablespoons (1 ounce) olive oil
2 tablespoons lime juice
1 teaspoon chopped cilantro
1 teaspoon salt

fish
Cut trout into 1-inch pieces. Place a piece of basil leaf on each section. Wrap with ham and thread onto skewers. Chill for several
hours. Grill skewers carefully and set aside.

salad and vegetables
Blanch haricots verts until al dente. Cool quickly. Blanch fennel in
boiling water until al dente. Julienne and cool quickly. In a stainless
steel bowl toss salad greens with mixed oil and vinegar.

aioli
Wash chilies under running water. Drain and place in a small roasting
pan along with the garlic clove. Roast at 325° for 10 minutes or until
the chilies darken and the garlic is golden and soft. Remove from
oven and cool. Place chilies, garlic, egg yolk, and water in blender.
Purée well. Add oil slowly while blender is running. Add lime juice,
cilantro, and salt.

presentation
Place dressed salad greens on each plate. Remove trout pieces from
skewer and place on greens. Top each trout morsel with aioli. Attrac-
tively arrange fennel, haricots verts, and endive leaves. Sprinkle with
pine nuts.

- *Toast pine nuts for about 2 minutes in a sauté pan to give them
a "nuttier" flavor and crisper
texture. Be careful not to burn.*

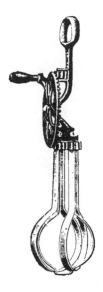

Pan-Smoked Bluefish

JOHN T. MAXWELL
EXECUTIVE CHEF-OWNER, C.E.C.

Chef Maxwell's Catering Company, Richmond

Chef's Notes
- *The fresher the fish, the better the results.*
- *Try this with other varieties of fish and seafood.*
- *Serve with ½ cup light cream sauce garnished with lemon rind.*
- *Because this smoking technique tends to fill a kitchen with great aromas (which may be a bit too much for some), move outside and use the side burner on a grill or a portable electric burner.*

Smoking fish over fresh herbs imparts a marvelous flavor to Virginia's favorite—bluefish. As bluefish season is limited, this indoor pan-smoking technique can also be used with any firm fish fillets. Use a large skillet with a tight-fitting cover and a rack.

Complexity ●● 　　　　　　　　　　 Yield: 6 servings

1　**bunch fresh thyme**
1　**bunch fresh rosemary**
¼　**cup whole black peppercorns**
6　**6-ounce bluefish fillets, skinned**
¼　**cup (1 ounce) all-purpose flour**
1　**tablespoon dried thyme**
½　**teaspoon salt**
⅛　**teaspoon pepper**
　　peanut oil

Soak fresh herbs and peppercorns in water for 15 minutes. Drain and set aside. Blend flour, dried thyme, salt, and pepper. Dredge fillets in flour mixture. Sauté in large skillet in oil for 3 minutes. Remove fillets. Wipe skillet with paper towel. Turn up heat under skillet until it is almost smoking. Sprinkle fresh herbs and peppercorns in skillet. Place fish on rack over herbs. Cover and smoke for 15 minutes or until fish are done. Serve with cream sauce with lemon rind garnish.

Sautéed Black Sea Bass, Shiitake Mushrooms, Caramelized Vidalia Onions with Summer Vegetables in Cilantro Butter Sauce

HANS SCHADLER
EXECUTIVE CHEF, C.E.C., A.A.C.
The Williamsburg Inn, Colonial Williamsburg, Williamsburg

Black sea bass is a hearty fish assertive enough to be matched with woodsy shiitake mushrooms and caramelized sweet Vidalia onions. Beautiful sea bass is imported from the chilly waters off Chile. In a medley of green and white accented by bright orange, the vegetables reiterate the celebration of fresh ingredients. The better the quality of the ingredients, the better the results.

Complexity ✪✪✪   Yield: 4 servings

FISH

---

4 6-ounce black sea bass fillets
¼ cup (1 ounce) all-purpose flour
    pinch salt
2 tablespoons (1 ounce) oil

ONION

---

1 tablespoon (½ ounce) butter
1 tablespoon (½ ounce) oil
1 teaspoon sugar
1 Vidalia onion (6 ounces), peeled, cut in half, sliced thin
1 cup shiitake mushrooms (2½ ounces), sliced
2 tablespoons (1 ounce) balsamic vinegar

Chef's Notes
- *Flounder is a delicious alternative to sea bass fillets.*
- *Celeriac, a popular European vegetable, is a cultivar of celery grown for its large knobby roots. The brown exterior skin should be removed. It may be eaten raw, but should be treated with lemon juice to prevent discoloration. Often these are available in speciality markets.*
- *Substitute parsnips if celeriac is unavailable.*
- *Use any sweet onion, such as Maui, Texas 10–15, Granex, or Walla Walla.*

VEGETABLES

2 tablespoons (1 ounce) butter
1 ounce carrot, julienned
1 ounce leek, julienned
1 ounce celeriac, julienned
1 ounce zucchini, julienned
1 ounce spinach, julienned
1 ounce sugar snap peas
¼ cup (2 ounces) dry white wine
¼ cup (2 ounces) fish stock
2 tablespoons (1 ounce) cream
2 tablespoons chopped cilantro
   salt and pepper to taste
   chives for garnish

fish

Trim bass into well-shaped pieces. Dust with flour mixed with salt on the skin side only. Heat a nonstick skillet and sear fish with skin side down. Allow to cook for 3 minutes or until bass is well-browned. Set aside.

onions and mushrooms

In same skillet heat mixture of oil and butter. Add sugar. Caramelize sugar until golden brown. Be careful not to burn. Add shiitake mushrooms and onions. Cook, stirring constantly until caramelization starts. Deglaze with vinegar. Reduce until almost all liquid evaporates and mixture becomes compote-like. Set mixture aside.

vegetables

Heat butter in skillet. Over low heat cook vegetables for approximately 5 minutes to soften slightly without browning. Add wine. Reduce by half. Add fish stock. Reduce again by half. Add cream and simmer for 2 minutes. Add chopped cilantro. Season to taste.

presentation

Spoon vegetables on plates. Place fillets on top. Garnish each with caramelized onions and mushrooms. Drizzle cilantro butter sauce from vegetables around plate. Garnish with fresh chives.

Vegetarian Penne Pasta

HANS SCHADLER
EXECUTIVE CHEF, C.E.C., A.A.C.
The Williamsburg Inn, Colonial Williamsburg, Williamsburg

Matched with pasta, the products and flavors from the sun-baked shores of the Mediterranean combine in a vegetarian triumph. Depending on the degree of vegetarianism, the chef suggests using heavy cream instead of stock for a richer texture. For a meat-free meal for nonvegetarian use, use a good quality chicken stock.

Chef's Notes
- *Serve with French, garlic, or focaccia bread.*
- *For a richer texture substitute ½ cup heavy cream for the vegetable stock.*
- *For a nonvegetarian version, substitute 1 cup of good quality chicken stock for the vegetable stock.*
- *If vegetarian instant bouillon is used, be careful not to add too much salt.*
- *If the dried version of sun-dried tomatoes is used, soak in water for 20 minutes before chopping.*

Complexity ✪✪   Yield: 4 servings

2 tablespoons (1 ounce) olive oil
2 tablespoons garlic cloves, crushed
2 shallots (2 ounces), minced
¾ cup (2 ounces) shiitake mushrooms, sliced
8 asparagus (8 ounces), peeled and cut into 2-inch pieces
1 medium zucchini (8 ounces)
½ cup (4 ounces) cooked, quartered artichoke hearts
1 medium red bell pepper (6 ounces), peeled, seeded, and julienned
1 medium green bell pepper (6 ounces), peeled, seeded, and julienned
¼ cup (1 ounce) pitted black olives
¼ cup (2 ounces) chopped sun-dried tomatoes (drained of olive oil)
1 cup (8 ounces) good quality vegetable stock
¼ cup (2 ounces) dry white wine
¼ cup fresh chopped herbs (thyme, basil, oregano)
    salt to taste
    freshly ground black pepper to taste
4 cups (8 ounces) cooked penne pasta
1 cup (3½ ounces) freshly grated Parmesan or Romano cheese
¼ cup (1 ounce) crumbled goat cheese

In a large nonstick pan, heat olive oil. Sauté garlic and shallots until transparent. Add mushrooms, asparagus, zucchini, artichoke, peppers, olives, and sun-dried tomatoes. Sauté for approximately 5 to 8 minutes over medium-high heat or until cooked but still crisp. Remove vegetables with a slotted spoon and keep warm. Add stock and wine, and reduce mixture by one-fourth. Add seasonings. Add pasta and vegetables mixing with a wooden spoon. Divide mixture into 4 soup or pasta bowls. Sprinkle with cheeses.

CHAPTER 4
Elegant Entrées
Poultry and Meats

Everything on the plate must be meaningful. It has to be edible, taste good, and make sense. If there is lemon, it must be large enough to squeeze—you cannot squeeze a slice. The center of the plate tells me the skill of the kitchen. It must be cooked properly.—*Chef Schadler*

There is a whole new flavor evolution. It is going away from the basic roux and using reduction. Start with chicken stock, shallot, and fresh herb reduction. Add a semi-sweet wine and reduce by one-third.—*Chef Schadler*

You can flavor with vinegar, with vegetable bases, with fruit bases.—*Chef Schadler*

Searing caramelizes the exterior of meat and is very important for appearance.—*Chef Corliss*

When serving, place starch on left at 9 or 10 o'clock, vegetable near 3 o'clock, and meat, the focal point, near the middle. Always serve bone away from guests and meat toward them.—*Chef Corliss*

Give guests something they cannot get at home.—*Chef Corliss*

Try for dimensionality on plates. Layer up into the air and have other items cascading down. Every plate should have a focal point and odd number—3, 5, 7.
—*Chef Corliss*

For a full range of tastes: salt taste first hits the tip of the tongue; white pepper hits toward the middle of the back of the mouth; red pepper hits down the throat.
—*Chef Corliss*

Currant jelly, rubbed over beef before baking, will render a taste reminiscent of a wood fire.—*Chef Fulton*

When roasting meat remember the cardinal rule—the lower the temperature the greater the yield, the higher the temperature the greater the shrinkage.—*Chef Fulton*

To vary the taste of a steak or chop, rub with a cut clove of garlic before cooking.—*Chef Fulton*

Because of its mild flavor, veal requires more seasoning and slower cooking than other meats.—*Chef Fulton*

One teaspoon of cornstarch can be substituted for each tablespoon of flour when making gravy.—*Chef Fulton*

A little baking powder added to chicken or turkey dressing will keep it from being soggy and make it light and fluffy. Always cook the stock before adding it to the bread.—*Chef Fulton*

For a stew that is out of this world, brown the meat on all sides in a little fat before adding any liquid. Add finely chopped onions during the browning process. Add other vegetables, according to type, so they will not be overcooked.—*Chef Fulton*

Beautify a stew with swirls from a pastry bag of mashed potatoes. Brown under the broiler.—*Chef Fulton*

Do not salt liver before frying, but afterwards. Salt causes liver in hot fat to toughen and shrivel.—*Chef Fulton*

Fresh lemon juice does amazing things to roast pork gravy.—*Chef Fulton*

Never wash meat in water. Clean by scraping with a sharp knife.—*Chef Fulton*

TIPS ON KNIVES

KNIVES are a fundamental kitchen tool. Often chefs can be seen carrying a toolbox or knife roll to work. Knives are rarely shared. Quality knives are worth every penny of their investment. If cared for properly, they will last for decades.

Expensive knives, like Henckels and Wüsthof, are hand-forged from high-quality steel, meaning they stay sharpened and respond better to a steel. The balance is highly noticeable. It takes very little effort to move a well sharpened and well balanced 10-inch chef knife through precise motions.

High-carbon stainless steel knives are made of an alloy that takes and keeps an edge, can be easily resharpened, and does not corrode or discolor foods. Look for one with the metal tang continuing inside the handle's full length, called a full tang knife.

Keep knives sharp at all times. A dull knife is much more dangerous than a sharp knife because you have to exert more pressure to cut. Use a steel for toning the blade. Hold blade at a 20° angle. Make a series of full-length strokes on each side of the blade, alternating sides. Occasionally sharpen with a stone. Commercial knife sharpeners are valuable for this job. Several mechanical sharpening machines provide excellent home sharpening. Select these very carefully, as many of these machines may remove too much metal or not be at the correct angle. Be particularly suspicious of those on an electric can opener.

French knives are the most versatile knife, coming in several sizes. Use for general cutting, chopping, slicing, and dicing. Hold with thumb and forefinger bent on the blade with the remaining three fingers wrapped around the handle.

Narrow knives with 6-inch to 8-inch blades, called utility knives, are suitable for lettuce, fruits, and in carving poultry.

With a 6-inch thin pointed blade, the boning knife is used for removing the bones from raw meats, poultry, and fish. Use one with a stiff blade for beef and a flexible one for fish filleting. Paring knives are small, pointed knives with a 2-inch blade perfect for paring vegetables and fruits and for trimming. Slicing knives with a long, slender, flexible blade in varying lengths, are for cooked meats. A similar knife, but with a serrated edge, is used for breads and cakes.

Prepare food so that a flat surface, if possible, is on the cutting board. For example start round items such as potatoes and onions by cutting in half. Put flat surface on board, then proceed. Hold items with fingers arched and curled under safely out of the blade's way.

For finely mincing foods such as the final stages of onions or fresh herbs, place both hands on the knife, one on the handle and one on the blade's end top, using a rocking motion. Fingers are completely out of the way.

Wash knives by hand immediately after using. One left in a sink is a booby trap for the unsuspecting victim. Store knives in a wooden holder or on a magnetic rack where the edges are protected. Never store unprotected in a drawer.

Some Cuts and Their Typical Dimensions

Matchsticks—
    Julienne, ⅛x⅛x2-inch,
    Batonnet or French fry ¼x¼x2-inch
Slice—uniform cross cuts
Paysanne—½-inch spheres or triangles
Parisienne—round shapes
Concassée—rough cut
Chop—irregular pieces

Cubes—
    brunoise ⅟₁₆ inch,
    macedone ⅛ inch,
    small dice or small baton ¼ inch,
    medium dice ½ inch, and
    large dice ¾ inch
Mince—fine chop

Breast of Chicken on a Roasted Red Pepper Sauce with Red Onion Marmalade and Spinach Fettuccine

WINSLOW GOODIER

EXECUTIVE CHEF, C.E.C.

Hermitage Country Club, Richmond

Chef's Notes

- *To make infused oil, place 2 crushed cloves of peeled garlic and 2 large sprigs of fresh rosemary into one pint virgin olive oil. Permit to sit for two weeks before using.*
- *Olive oils come in various levels of quality. Extra-virgin is the first pressing and is of the highest quality and flavor. Pure olive oil is from lower quality olives and usually the second pressing.*
- *Red peppers may be blackened over a gas flame or under the broiler. Turn constantly. When finished place in plastic bag. Close for 5 minutes. Peel off charred skin. Remove seeds. Rinsing is discouraged as some flavors are lost.*
- *Fresh shiitake mushrooms are widely available around the country. Dried ones are a poor substitute.*
- *Try this recipe with pheasant or turkey breasts.*

Here is positive proof that healthy gourmet food is not an oxymoron. Once tasted, this dish will be on the "please serve it again" list. Chef Winslow builds flavors in the red onion marmalade with brown sugar, red wine, and heady balsamic vinegar. In fact, this marmalade is so delicious that it might be wise to double the quantity, ensuring leftovers.

Complexity ✪✪   Yield: 2 servings

2 medium (12 ounces) red bell peppers, roasted, seeds and
    skin removed
    salt and pepper to taste
1 large (8 ounces) red onion, julienned
3 tablespoons (1½ ounces) firmly packed brown sugar
½ cup (4 ounces) dry red wine
3 tablespoons (1½ ounces) balsamic vinegar
2 medium (3½ ounces each) boneless chicken breasts
½ cup (1 ounce) fresh, sliced shiitake mushrooms
2 teaspoons garlic and rosemary infused olive oil
1 cup spinach fettuccine, cooked and drained

In a food processor purée peppers. Place in sauté pan. Cook until purée is reduced by half. Season to taste with salt and pepper. Reserve and keep warm. In a saucepan, combine onions and brown sugar. Cook over moderate heat until onions begin to caramelize. Stir in wine and vinegar. Bring to a boil. Reduce heat and stir until liquid is evaporated. In a sauté pan, cook breasts and mushrooms in olive oil until no longer pink inside. Ladle pepper sauce on each serving plate. Place breast and mushrooms on top. Garnish with red onion marmalade and cooked fettuccine.

Sautéed Chicken Breasts with Crab and Virginia Ham Dressing

EDWARD SWAN
CHEF

Shields Tavern, Colonial Williamsburg, Williamsburg

The crab and Virginia ham dressing are regional classics. Rolled in a large chicken breast and then in breadcrumbs, it is baked to a golden brown. Serve immediately with the creamy wine sauce as the breast will dry out if held too long.

Complexity ✪✪✪   **Yield: 8 servings**

DRESSING

2 teaspoons butter
¼ cup (1 ounce) celery, small dice
¼ cup (1½ ounces) onion, small dice
1 ounce backfin crabmeat, picked over
1 ounce Virginia ham, medium dice
2 teaspoons chicken bouillon granules
3 cups (4½ ounces) breadcrumbs, finely ground
1 teaspoon dry mustard
2 dashes Worcestershire sauce
    dash hot sauce

CHICKEN BREASTS

8 chicken breasts (6 ounces each), lightly pounded to an even
    thickness
½ cup (2 ounces) all-purpose flour
1 egg
½ cup (4 ounces) milk
1 cup (1½ ounces) fresh breadcrumbs

SAUCE

1 tablespoon finely diced onions
1 cup (8 ounces) white wine
1 teaspoon chicken bouillon granules
1 cup (8 ounces) whipping cream
2 teaspoons cornstarch
2 teaspoons cold water

Chef's Notes

- *For a richer dressing replace 1 cup of breadcrumbs with 1 cup of crabmeat.*
- *This wine sauce is excellent on fresh pasta.*
- *For variation, stuff breasts with shrimp Florentine and pass a Stilton cheese sauce, substituting sherry for the wine and adding ¼ cup (2 ounces) Stilton cheese.*
- *If a lighter entrée is desired, omit the sauce and try a lively fruit condiment such as Dried Cherry and Cranberry Fruit Compote (page 196).*

dressing
In a large skillet, sauté celery and onion in butter until translucent. Stir in crabmeat, ham, and chicken bouillon. Sauté 1 minute. Add breadcrumbs, dry mustard, and seasonings. Mix gently with a fork. Cool for about 10 minutes.

chicken breasts
Place 2 tablespoons crabmeat stuffing on each breast. Roll breast around stuffing, tucking in meat at both ends.

Dust in flour. Dip in egg wash. Lightly roll through breadcrumbs. Bake at 350° on a greased baking sheet for 15 to 20 minutes or until golden brown.

sauce
In medium saucepan, cook onions, wine, and chicken bouillon over medium heat for 2 minutes. Add cream. Cook over medium heat, stirring occasionally, for 10 minutes. Add cornstarch thoroughly mixed in cold water. Bring to a boil. Cook for 2 minutes or until the mixture is again clear. Serve sauce on side.

Breast of Chicken with Fresh Apple and Pear Compote

BILLIE RAPER
CHEF PRODUCTION MANAGER, C.C.
ARAMARK, Bell Atlantic, Richmond

Fresh fruit and spices create a sauce for chicken breasts, making a nonfat entrée that has no gastronomic sacrifices. The chicken is guaranteed to be moist as long as it is fresh and not overcooked. After searing, the chicken is removed from the pan where the compote is ready in about 6 minutes. It is crucial when the chicken is added to the compote to keep the heat low. High temperatures or a boiling compote will toughen the meat.

Complexity ☉	Yield: 6 servings

12 boneless chicken breast halves (about 3 ounces each), skin removed
1 medium (1 ounce) shallot, peeled and minced
3 pears (1 pound), peeled, cored, medium dice
3 Granny Smith apples (1 pound), peeled, cored, medium dice
¼ cup (2 ounces) applejack
   pinch ground cinnamon
   pinch ground nutmeg
   pinch ground clove
   pinch sugar
1 large Red Delicious apple (5 ounces), poached, for garnish
   chopped fresh mint, for garnish

Sear chicken breasts with shallots in a large nonstick pan treated with vegetable spray. Cook over high heat for 2 minutes on each side. Remove chicken from pan. Add pears, Granny Smith apples, applejack, and seasonings. Cook over medium heat until fruit is al dente, about 6 minutes. Add chicken breasts and cook over low heat for about 3 minutes until firm. Arrange 2 breasts on each plate with compote. Garnish with apple slices and sprinkle with mint.

Chef's Notes
• *This is particularly good when served with rice. Brown rice contains more fiber, but takes longer to prepare. Enriched white rice still contains all the vitamins and minerals and can be ready in only 20 minutes. Try to avoid instant rice—its flavor and texture are lacking. More exotic rices, such as the Italian arborio, Indian or Texas basmati, and Oriental jasmine provide subtle and exciting nuances. Other excellent carbohydrate sources to match with this entrée are orzo (tiny pasta), couscous, or whole barley.*

Chicken Breast in Two Sauces

MANFRED E. ROEHR
C.E.C., A.A.C.
Chowning's and Christiana Campbell's Taverns, Colonial Williamsburg, Williamsburg

EDWARD SWAN
CHEF
Shields Tavern, Colonial Williamsburg, Williamsburg

Chef's Notes
- *When caramelizing sugar, do not leave the stove as sugar can burn quite quickly.*
- *Sprinkle chopped pecans and fresh parsley as a garnish.*
- *Serve with pasta.*
- *Each of these excellent sauces can stand alone with the chicken.*

Combining their talents, these two chefs created this recipe that took first place in a Virginia Chefs Association Grey Poupon contest. The corn chowder instructions are on page 49. With pears, raspberry sauce, and salty tangy mustard, these chicken breasts are, indeed, both a winner and a robust entrée.

Complexity ✪✪✪   Yield: 10 servings

CHICKEN

10 chicken breasts (about 6 ounces each), skinless
½ cup (4½ ounces) Grey Poupon country-style mustard
¼ cup (2 ounces) white wine
¼ cup (1 ounce) all-purpose flour
¼ cup (2 ounces) olive oil
5 cups (2 pounds) julienned pears
½ cup (4 ounces) corn chowder sauce

RED RASPBERRY SAUCE

½ cup (4 ounces) butter
½ cup (3½ ounces) sugar
1 cup chicken stock
½ cup (4 ounces) red wine
1 (1 ounce) shallot, minced
½ cup (2½ ounces) red currants
½ cup (6 ounces) raspberry jam
1 teaspoon (½ ounce) cracked peppercorns
  salt and pepper to taste
1 tablespoon butter, softened
1 tablespoon chopped parsley

Brush both sides of chicken with mixture of mustard and white wine. Dust lightly with flour on both sides. Sauté in skillet in hot olive oil until golden brown on each side. Remove chicken from skillet and place in roasting pan. Place pears on top. Cover with corn chowder. Bake in 350° oven for 7 to 8 minutes or until pears are beginning to soften and chicken is cooked.

red raspberry sauce
Melt ½ cup butter in a small saucepan. Add sugar and cook, stirring constantly, until caramelized. Add stock, wine, and shallots and bring to a boil. Add currants, jam, and peppercorns. Simmer 15 minutes over low heat. Add salt and pepper to taste. Finish with 1 tablespoon butter and parsley. Stir until smooth.

presentation
Plate chicken, pears, and chowder sauce. Drizzle with raspberry sauce.

Grilled Breast of Chicken with Garlic, Parsley, and Lime

JIM MAKINSON
EXECUTIVE CHEF, C.E.C.
Kingsmill Resort, Williamsburg

Chef's Notes

• *Serve with two Japanese eggplants cut in rounds, seasoned with salt, pepper, and garlic, and grilled with a tomato, also cut into rounds. Serve with baked potato topped with herbed fat-free sour cream or low-fat cream cheese.*

Steeping garlic in skim milk removes all bitterness from the garlic, yielding a smooth, pungent flavoring. To avoid fat this recipe can be prepared with skin on or off. With skin on, the chicken remains moister while cooking with no char marks on the meat. Remove skin before eating. Grilling without the skin is also delicious. Spray grate (removed from the fire) with non-stick vegetable spray to prevent sticking.

Complexity ✪   **Yield: 4 servings**

CHICKEN

2 chicken breasts (about 8 ounces each), boneless
12 cloves garlic, peeled
1 cup (8 ounces) skim milk
2 tablespoons Italian flat-leaf parsley, chopped
2 limes, juiced
   salt
   black pepper

Remove all visible fat from chicken. Blanch garlic in milk until al dente. Dispose of milk. Rinse and slice garlic paper-thin. Mix garlic and parsley with lime juice. Fill chicken with mix under skin. (Alternately use skinless chicken. Make slit in breast and fill with mix.) Spray grill with olive oil vegetable spray. Grill on each side. Salt and pepper to taste.

California Sonoma Valley Chicken

U.S. ARMY CULINARY OLYMPIC TEAM

Fort Lee

The secret to stuffing is cutting a pocket in the breast, which is then filled with pesto piped from a pastry bag, folding over the tender to seal in the goodness. The pesto is a subtle combination of two fresh herbs—basil and parsley—with fresh spinach, pine nuts, garlic and two cheeses—Parmesan and ricotta. It is smoother with less garlic and oil than other pestos. Adding fresh Roma tomatoes with sweet red peppers and fresh herbs to canned tomato purée creates an intriguing, lively sauce. Served on a bed of roasted spaghetti squash with Kalamata olives (page 152), flavors dance wonderfully on the palate while calories are pretty tame.

Complexity ✪✪✪   **Yield: 6 servings**

PESTO

⅛ cup (1½ ounces) pine nuts
2 cloves garlic
4 large basil leaves
2 tablespoons chopped parsley
3 large leaves (½ ounce) fresh spinach, blanched
3 tablespoons (2 ounces) ricotta cheese
¼ cup (¾ ounce) Parmesan cheese, finely grated
1 tablespoon (½ ounce) virgin olive oil
1 teaspoon salt
½ teaspoon black pepper
  basil sprigs, garnish

TOMATO SAUCE

1 teaspoon virgin olive oil
half an onion (2 ounces), finely chopped
1 garlic clove, crushed
1 red bell pepper (6 ounces), seeded, veins removed, and roughly chopped
3 plum tomatoes (6 ounces), chopped
2 basil leaves
4 sprigs fresh thyme
1 teaspoon sugar

Chefs Notes

- *Sauce may be made 1 day ahead and reheated.*
- *Chicken breast can be prepared and refrigerated several hours.*
- *No pastry bag, no problem—the pesto can be chilled and rolled into a three-inch long tube with diameter of about ⅛ inch and placed in the chicken pocket.*
- *Start cooking chicken breast with the top stuffed pocket on the pan's surface. This will also seal the pocket, preventing leakage of the pesto. Chefs always start with presentation side down as this provides the best color. The presentation side is the top side with the pocket of pesto.*
- *During the Culinary Olympics in Frankfurt, the team served this with polenta gateau (page 143)—two layers of polenta stuffed with ratatouille covered with melted Gruyère cheese—and zucchini fans.*

> ¼ *cup (2 ounces) dry white wine*
> ¼ *cup (2 ounces) tomato purée*
> ½ *cup water*

CHICKEN

> 6 *medium (about 5 ounces each) chicken breast halves*
> ¼ *cup (1 ounce) all-purpose flour*
> ¼ *teaspoon salt*
> 1 *tablespoon (½ ounce) olive oil*

pesto

In a food processor fitted with the metal blade, process pine nuts, garlic, basil, parsley, and spinach into a smooth paste. Mix in ricotta and Parmesan cheese and olive oil with a brief pulsing motion. Season. Chill until needed.

tomato sauce

In 2-quart saucepan heat olive oil. Add onions and garlic. Cook without cover for 5 minutes over medium heat. Add bell pepper, cook for 5 minutes. Add chopped tomatoes, herbs, and sugar. Cook until tomatoes are softened. Add wine and tomato purée. Reduce by half. Add water, simmer for 45 minutes, stirring occasionally. Pour into food processor and pulse several times until the sauce is just chunky.

chicken

Remove any fat and sinew from chicken breast. Gently pull out chicken tender from the underside of the breast and cut off. Turn breast over. With a sharp fillet knife cut a pocket the length of the breast. The pocket is horizontal to the top of the breast, about ¾ inch deep, and must not cut through the breast. Fill a pastry bag fitted with a No. 5 tube with pesto. Pipe pesto into chicken breast. Roll breast lightly in flour mixture. Shake off any excess. Plug the pocket with the tender. Slightly flatten the breast carefully so as not to disturb the filling. In a nonstick pan, cook chicken in olive oil over high heat for 3 minutes on each side or until golden brown. Reduce heat to low and finish cooking, for about 8 more minutes.

  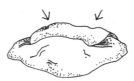

assembly

Make bed of spaghetti squash (see page 152). Place chicken breast on top and spoon on two spoonfuls of sauce. Garnish with fresh basil leaves.

Mexican Chicken

WINSLOW GOODIER
Executive Chef, C.E.C.
Hermitage Country Club, Richmond

Heart-smart diners not willing to sacrifice good taste will award this entrée a regular spot on their menus. Those with larger appetites may wish to double the serving of steamed rice, an excellent complex carbohydrate full of fiber without too many additional calories.

Complexity ✪✪   Yield: 2 servings

3 cloves garlic, minced
half a medium (3 ounces) green bell pepper, sliced
1 medium (4 ounces) onion, sliced
4 teaspoons (1 ounce) vegetable oil
2 medium (6 ounces) boneless chicken breasts, skin removed, cut into strips
2 Roma tomatoes (4 ounces), sliced
2 tablespoons fresh lime juice
2 teaspoons ground cumin
1 teaspoon taco seasoning
2 tablespoons chopped fresh cilantro
4 black olives, chopped
1 cup steamed rice

In a nonstick sauté pan sauté garlic, bell pepper, and onion in hot oil for 2 to 3 minutes. Add chicken and tomatoes. Continue cooking over medium heat for 3 minutes. Add lime juice, cumin, and taco seasoning. Sauté 2 more minutes. Add cilantro and black olives. Sauté 1 more minute. Cover two plates with rice and arrange chicken and vegetables on top.

Chef's Notes
- *The oil may be reduced if using nonstick vegetable spray.*
- *Substitute chili powder if taco seasoning is not available.*
- *For a fast fajita, roll the finished product sans rice in two heated flour tortillas.*

General Zuo's Chicken

GRACE LIU
CHEF-OWNER
The Dynasty, Williamsburg

Chef's Notes
- *Dissolve cornstarch in cold water and stir completely.*
- *The amount of oil can be decreased in the sauce.*

Chef Liu and I journeyed to a Taipei restaurant specializing in General Zuo's chicken. Liu, born in Hunan and a devotee of fine, spicy cuisine, deemed her version to be both more authentic and exotic. I feel confident she is absolutely correct. It is crucial, particularly in Chinese food preparation, to have all ingredients prepared before beginning the cooking process. A wok is suggested, but any large skillet will do.

Complexity ✪✪   Yield: 4 servings

CHICKEN

10	ounces boneless chicken meat (white or dark), cut into 10 pieces
1	tablespoon egg white
1	tablespoon (½ ounce) oil
	pinch salt
2	tablespoons cornstarch
	ginger slices

VEGETABLES

	half a sweet red bell pepper (3 ounces), cut into 1-inch squares
2	ounces snow peas
2	ounces bamboo shoots
1	cup (8 ounces) chicken stock

SAUCE MIXTURE

2	tablespoons (1 ounce) peanut oil
1	scallion, chopped
2	cloves garlic, sliced
1	tablespoon sugar
1	tablespoon (½ ounce) white vinegar
1	cup (8 ounces) stock, reserved from blanching vegetables
1	teaspoon hot sauce
1	teaspoon soy sauce
¼	teaspoon white pepper

ASSEMBLY

> 1 **teaspoon cornstarch in 2 teaspoons water**
>   **oil for deep frying**
> 2 **drops sesame oil**

chicken

Marinate chicken in ingredients for 30 minutes. Heat oil in wok. Deep fry chicken pieces one by one at a medium-high heat until golden brown. Drain chicken pieces.

vegetables

Blanch for 30 seconds in 1 cup stock. Remove vegetables, saving stock for sauce.

sauce mixture

Heat wok, then heat 2 tablespoons oil. Add scallion and garlic to season oil. Remove scallion and garlic. Add sauce mixture and stock reserved from blanching vegetables. Bring to a boil.

assembly

Add blanched vegetables to sauce mixture in wok. Cook for 15 seconds. Return chicken chunks to wok. Stir. Add cornstarch mixture for thickening. Mix well. Add sesame oil. Serve immediately.

Chicken Provençale with Saffron Linguine

WINSLOW GOODIER

EXECUTIVE CHEF, C.E.C.

Hermitage Country Club, Richmond

Chef's Notes
- *To make infused oil, place 1 teaspoon crushed peppercorns and 2 large sprigs of fresh thyme into 1 pint virgin olive oil. Permit to sit for two weeks before using.*
- *Try this recipe with chicken or turkey breasts.*

Using economical and flavorful chicken thighs is suitable impetus to splurge on fresh saffron linguine. For entertaining make the sauce up to a day in advance. For best pasta texture cook immediately before serving. With freshly made pasta, only cook 1 or 2 minutes or until al dente.

Complexity ✪   Yield: 2 servings

1 teaspoon olive oil infused with thyme and peppercorn
1 shallot, diced (1 ounce)
4 (7 ounces total) boneless, skinless chicken thighs
2 medium (10 ounces) tomatoes, diced
1 cup (2½ ounces) sliced mushrooms
2 cups (16 ounces) chicken consommé
½ cup (4 ounces) white wine
1 cup (2 ounces) fresh spinach, chopped
2 teaspoons tomato paste
½ teaspoon fresh thyme
½ teaspoon fresh tarragon
   salt and pepper to taste
1 cup saffron linguine, cooked and drained

Place oil in nonstick sauté pan. Bring to medium heat, add shallots, and cook until translucent. Add chicken and cook for 2 minutes on each side. Add tomatoes, mushrooms, consommé, and wine. Over low heat, reduce by half. Add spinach, tomato paste, herbs, and salt and pepper to taste. Serve over saffron linguine.

Chargrilled Quail with Crispy Potato Rounds and Garlic Vinaigrette

EDWARD DAGGERS

EXECUTIVE CHEF, C.E.C.

Country Club, Memphis, Tennessee

Farm-raised quail, available in many markets, tempt one to dispense with cumbersome cutlery. Reverting to the more natural fingers makes it possible to secure every last morsel. Fingers are fine even around the finest Virginia tables.

Chef's Notes
- *Frozen quail work well with grilling. Defrost in the refrigerator; never at room temperature.*
- *Rather than frying potatoes, spray directly with vegetable spray, place under broiler until crispy, turning once.*

Complexity ✪✪   **Yield: 4 servings**

QUAIL AND POTATOES

8 *5-ounce baby quail*
¼ *cup (2 ounces) peanut oil*
2 *tablespoons minced fresh thyme*
1 *teaspoon cracked pepper*
3 *potatoes (1 pound), peeled, sliced thin*
2 *cups (15 ounces) oil for deep frying*

VINAIGRETTE AND WATERCRESS

1 *tablespoon fresh garlic, minced*
2 *egg yolks*
1½ *cups (11 ounces) peanut oil*
¼ *cup (2 ounces) balsamic vinegar*
½ *teaspoon cracked pepper*
1 *teaspoon fresh minced chervil*
1 *bunch watercress*

Brush quail with oil. Sprinkle inside and out with thyme and pepper. Grill quail over hot coals for about 15 minutes. Remove and keep warm. In a heavy pan, fry potato slices in several cups oil until crisp and brown. Drain.

To make vinaigrette place egg yolks and garlic in mixing bowl of an electric beater. Slowly pour in oil while mixing until thick. Stir in vinegar, pepper, and chervil.

Shingle crispy potatoes in a circular pattern on dinner plates. Place 2 quail on bed of watercress in center of each plate. Drizzle with vinaigrette.

Roasted Cornish Hens with Virginia Chardonnay Garnished with Bread Mousse and Cranberries

DOMINADOR VALEROS
SUPERVISOR LEAD CHEF, C.C.

Shields Tavern, Colonial Williamsburg, Williamsburg

Delicate Cornish hens are roasted until golden brown. Individual bread mousses bake at the same time. The sauce can be started during baking and finished with drippings from the hens. Tangy berries add excellent color and texture to the final presentation.

Complexity ✪✪✪   **Yield: 4 servings**

4 Cornish game hens

SAUCE

2 teaspoons oil
2 shallots (2 ounces), chopped
¼ cup (1 ounce) chopped celery
5 mushrooms, sliced
1 juniper berry, crushed
1 sprig thyme
1½ cups (12 ounces) Virginia chardonnay
    defatted drippings from hens
1 teaspoon red currant jelly
    squeeze of fresh lemon
    salt and freshly ground pepper to taste

MOUSSE

1¼ cups (10 ounces) milk
 1 slice bread, crusts removed
 1 small onion (3 ounces), finely chopped
    pinch ground cloves
    pinch ground nutmeg
    pinch salt
    pinch white pepper
 1 egg, beaten
 2 egg whites, beaten to stiff peaks
    squeeze of fresh lemon

Chef's Notes
- *Mousse will be slightly convex when ready.*
- *Fill any unused muffin tin with water.*
- *One large roasting chicken may be used in place of hens.*
- *Try the Williamsburg Winery Chardonnay, whose grapes are grown on the banks of College Creek leading to the James River. We recommend their Act 12 Chardonnay in this recipe. The Williamsburg Winery, 2638 Lake Powell Road, welcomes visitors from 10:00 A.M. to 5:00 P.M. Tuesday through Sunday. Williamsburg Winery is producing outstanding wines with whites somewhere between French and California in taste and complexity. They are fruitier than the French. Rob Bickford of the winery says, "Treat them like a white Burgundy. The French taste them and say they taste American—thank goodness they are not Californian. The Californians taste and say they taste closer to the French—but thank goodness they are not."*

CRANBERRIES

2 tablespoons fresh cranberries, washed
2 teaspoons sugar
1 tablespoon water

Cornish hens
Preheat oven to 450°. Place cleaned hens on rack in roasting pan
breast side up. Reduce heat to 350°. Cook 30 minutes or until tender.

sauce
In a medium skillet, sauté in oil the shallots, celery, mushrooms,
juniper berry, and thyme for 5 minutes. Add chardonnay, drippings,
and jelly. Add lemon juice. Season. Reduce by two-thirds. Strain. Keep
warm.

mousse
In a medium saucepan, bring milk to a boil. Remove from heat. Add
bread, onion, and spices. Cool. Stir in egg. Fold in egg whites. Line
muffin tins with parchment paper. Fill with mousse. Place tin in
roasting pan filled two-thirds with hot water. Bake at 350° for 20 minutes or until done. Keep warm.

cranberries
Simmer all ingredients for 3 minutes.

assembly
Turn out bread mousse onto center of plates next to hens. Spoon
sauce around. Scatter cranberries. Serve hot.

Roast Duckling
à la Manfred

MANFRED E. ROEHR
C.E.C., A.A.C.

**Chowning's and Christiana Campbell's Taverns,
Colonial Williamsburg, Williamsburg**

Chef Roehr is one of the world-renown experts in international techniques of roasting ducks. This recipe is inspired by the Asian style of using vinegar to draw fat from the duckling. While he recommends fresh ducks with fat breasts, frozen ones are more than acceptable—and 90 percent of ducks are marketed in the frozen form. The farm-raised ducks, an excellent source, are leaner.

Complexity ❁❁   **Yield: 2 servings**

4- to 5-pound duckling
   salt and pepper to taste
1 cup (8 ounces) cider vinegar
1 cup (12 ounces) honey
2 oranges (12 ounces)
½ cup (4 ounces) chicken broth
½ cup (4 ounces) dry white wine or orange juice
1 teaspoon cornstarch

roasting

Preheat oven to 325°. Clean duck. Sprinkle with salt and pepper. Rub into both skin and cavity. Place on rack in a shallow roasting pan. Mix vinegar and honey. Brush on duck. Peel oranges. Cut into quarters. Scrape white pulp from peel. Cut peel into small thin strips to make 1 tablespoon. Place peel and chicken broth in bottom of pan. Roast on a rack uncovered, basting frequently with honey and vinegar, for 3 hours or until the thermometer reaches 155°. Place duck on platter.

saucing

In a small saucepan combine ½ cup of pan drippings with wine or orange juice. Blend cornstarch with 1 tablespoon cold water. Stir cornstarch mixture into sauce. Cook until sauce thickens, stirring occasionally. Pour sauce over duckling. Garnish with orange slices.

Chef's Notes
- *To clean duckling, remove giblets and neck. Rinse with water inside and out. Drain. The meat is done at 160°. Removing at 155° permits carry-over heat to complete the cooking process. Duckling will look pink when properly cooked.*
- *When roasting game always use a rack on bottom of the roasting pan to keep meat out of the greasy drippings.*
- *Frozen ducklings require 24 hours in original package to thaw in the refrigerator.*
- *Serve with wild rice.*
- *The German home-style method is to brown on both sides in a hot skillet, then finish in the oven.*

Roasted Breast of Turkey with Prosciutto Ham

ROBERT D. CORLISS
SOUS CHEF

The Williamsburg Inn, Colonial Williamsburg, Williamsburg

Chef's Notes
- *Prosciutto ham is a seasoned, salt-cured ham that is dried by air, not smoking. The ham is very dense due to its pressing. Parma ham is the original prosciutto, but others are available.*
- *Cut horizontally leaving the back seam intact.*
- *Rest to distribute the juices. During cooking, juices go outside. Resting, juices come back to the center.*

Stuffed with salty prosciutto and layered with herbed crumbs, this rolled triple-butterflied turkey breast is a flavorful twist to the traditional holiday turkey. Guests will imagine, though incorrectly, that this took significant effort, particularly when viewing its artistic pinwheel slices.

Complexity ✪✪   Yield: 12 servings

1	turkey breast (3 to 4 pounds), bone removed
9	paper-thin slices prosciutto ham (4 ounces)
½	cup breadcrumbs
2	teaspoons fresh ginger, minced
2	teaspoons finely chopped parsley
1	teaspoon finely chopped fresh thyme
2	teaspoons finely chopped lemon zest
¼	teaspoon cayenne pepper

Butterfly turkey breast 3 times still holding together in the back. Gently pound each section to a uniform thickness of ¼ inch. On each turkey piece place 3 slices ham, sprinkling herbed crumbs between the slices. Using butcher's twine tie each of the three pieces. Roast in a 375° oven for 1 hour or until a meat thermometer reaches 130° to 135°. Remove from oven. Let rest for 10 minutes. Remove twine, slice, and serve.

Brunswick Stews

DAVID BRUCE CLARKE

CHEF-INSTRUCTOR

J. Sargeant Reynolds Community College, Richmond

Chef Clarke's research on the beginnings of Brunswick stews offers delightful historical perspectives. Four different recipes from an old Virginia cookbook reveal marked diversity. Each recipe is identified only by initials as *proper* ladies still did not use their names in publishing such household information. The chef's heart-healthy rendition contains no squirrels, but a lean roasted pork loin and chicken with the fat removed.

Chef's Notes
- *Serve with fresh beaten biscuits and fruit salad or "Health Slaw" see recipe page 169.*
- *Chicken drippings can be used if the fat is first skimmed off.*
- *If fresh corn is not available use a 10- or 12-ounce package of frozen corn. Substitute a 10-ounce package of lima beans for fresh ones.*

Complexity ✪✪✪   Yield: 12 servings

---

1 *4-pound broiler chicken, cooked with skin and bones removed, cut into 3/4-inch dice*
3- *to 4-pound pork loin, boneless, roasted, cut into 1-inch dice*
3 *ears corn, scraped off cob (about 1½ cups or 9 ounces)*
2 *cups (1 pound) fresh lima beans*
   water to cover (or chicken drippings, see note)
4 *fresh tomatoes (1 pound), peeled, seeded, diced*
   salt and pepper to taste
1 *cup (8 ounces) white wine*

Combine all ingredients. Bring to a boil. Reduce heat to a simmer for 1½ hours or until broth is thickened and meats are tender. Adjust seasonings.

The following four Brunswick stew recipes from *Housekeeping in Old Virginia,* a nineteenth-century cookbook, provided the inspiration for Chef Clarke's recipe.

Brunswick Stew I, Mrs. R.P.
  A **twenty-five cent shank of beef**
  A **five-cent loaf of bread, a square loaf as it has more crumb and the
    crust is not used**
  1 **quart of potatoes, cooked and mashed**
  1 **quart of butter-beans**
  1 **quart of raw corn**
1½ **quarts raw tomatoes, peeled and chopped**

If served at two o'clock, put on the shank as for soup at the earliest possible hour; then about twelve o'clock take the shank out of the soup and shred and cut all of the meat as fine as you can, carefully taking out bone and gristle, and then return it to the soup-pot and add all of the vegetables; the bread and two slices of middling [scraps of salt pork left over from making bacon] are an improvement to it. Season with salt and pepper to taste; and when ready to serve, drop into the tureen two or three tablespoons butter. This makes a tureen and about a vegetable-dish full.

Brunswick Stew II: Mrs. M.M.D.
About 4 hours before dinner, put on two or three slices of bacon, two squirrels or chickens, one onion sliced, in one gallon of water. Stew some time, then add one quart peeled tomatoes, two ears of grated corn, three Irish potatoes sliced, and one handful of butter-beans and part pod of red pepper.
    Stew altogether about 1 hour, till you can take out the bones. When done, put in one spoonful breadcrumbs and one large spoonful butter.

Brunswick Stew III: Mrs. I.H.
Take one chicken or two squirrels, cut them up and put one-half gallon water to them. Let it stew until the bones can be removed. Add one-half dozen large tomatoes, one-half pint butter-beans and corn cut from a half dozen ears of corn, salt, pepper, and butter as seasoning.

Brunswick Stew IV: Mrs. R.
Take two chickens or three or four squirrels, let them boil in water. Cook one pint butter beans, and one quart of tomatoes; cook with the meat. When done, add one dozen ears of corn, one dozen large tomatoes, and one pound butter.
    Take out the chicken, cut it into small pieces and put back; cook until it is well done and thick enough to be eaten with a fork.
    Season with pepper and salt.

Pork Medallions Dijon

MICHAEL VOSBURG
EXECUTIVE CHEF
The Salisbury Country Club, Midlothian

Lean pork's popularity is partially due to its repositioned status as "white meat." Since its nutritional profile is similar to poultry, pork should appear often on home menus. These medallions have the illusion of "I spent hours preparing dinner," while requiring minimal preparation and cooking time.

Complexity ✪   Yield: 6 servings

2 pounds pork medallions, divided into 6 portions
⅓ cup (about 3 ounces) Dijon mustard
5 slices soft white bread, crusts removed, crumbed
¼ cup (2 ounces) peanut oil

Pat medallions dry. Spread with mustard. Roll in crumbs. In a 12-inch nonstick pan brown meat in peanut oil over moderate heat. Remove while interior is still pink.

Chef's Notes
• *Purchase the entire boneless pork tenderloin available in packaging in supermarkets. Trim fat and prepare medallions. Employ small pieces for another entrée, such as a stir-fry dish.*

• *To keep pork tender, do not overcook. It is done at 160° or when still slightly pink.*

• *To reduce fat content, spray pan with vegetable spray and eliminate peanut oil. Reduce cooking heat slightly.*

• *Fresh breadcrumbs are used as dry ones become too hard when used as a coating.*

• *For variety include 1 tablespoon seeds (sesame, poppy, or crushed fennel) to the crumb coating. Match herbs with different breads such as rosemary with French bread or jolt the taste buds with bits of pickled jalapeños in corn breadcrumbs.*

Roasted Stuffed Pork Loin

WILLIAM H. SWAN
EXECUTIVE SOUS CHEF
**Williamsburg Lodge, Colonial Williamsburg,
Williamsburg**

Chef's Notes
- *Sally Lunn bread is a rich egg-and-butter bread popular in the eighteenth century that is served by Colonial Williamsburg to adoring fans.*
- *When using an instant meat thermometer, remove meat when it is 5° less than its finished temperature to allow for carry-over cooking heat.*

Dried fruits provide sweetness and texture to this toothsome stuffing made with the rich eighteenth-century Sally Lunn bread. It can be made ahead, then oven-roasted to create incredible aromas to tantalize your guests.

Complexity ✪✪   **Yield: 8 to 12 servings**

1 pork loin (2 to 3 pounds), boneless

STUFFING

3 slices Sally Lunn bread or white bread, small cubes
2 tablespoons (1 ounce) dried cranberries
2 tablespoons (1 ounce) diced prunes
2 tablespoons (1 ounce) diced dried figs
1 teaspoon vegetable oil
2 tablespoons (¾ ounce) diced onions
2 tablespoons (½ ounce) diced celery
3 eggs
2 cups (8 ounces) chicken stock
   salt and pepper
¼ teaspoon ground sage
¼ teaspoon poultry seasoning, optional

Trim pork of excess fat. Make a lengthwise cut 4 inches deep. In a large bowl, mix bread cubes and dried fruits. In a small sauté pan, sauté onions and celery in vegetable oil until limp. Add to bread mix. Beat eggs. Add eggs, chicken stock, and seasonings to bread mix and mix well. Stuff mixture into pork cavity. Roast at 325° for 30 to 35 minutes per pound. Permit to sit at room temperature for 15 minutes before slicing.

Italian Sausage with Peppers and Onions

MATT PARTRIDGE
EXECUTIVE CHEF, C.W.C.
Willow Oaks Country Club, Richmond

This popular Italian sausage dish gets its unique taste from beer. Make the sausage the traditional way by stuffing into a casing or a shortcut way by wrapping in plastic wrap and poaching as detailed in the Chef's Notes. Top it with a rich tomato sauce and serve over fresh pasta. Fill Italian sub rolls with sausage and top with vegetables for a substantial grinder.

Complexity ✪✪✪   **Yield: 8 servings**

ITALIAN SAUSAGE

2½ pounds coarsely ground pork
2½ teaspoons salt
2½ teaspoons fennel seeds
 ¾ teaspoon black pepper
 ¾ teaspoon crushed red pepper flakes
 1 cup beer
 1 tube sausage casing

VEGETABLES

 3 large green bell peppers (1½ pounds), seeded and cut into
      ¼-inch strips
 2 large onions (12 ounces), sliced
 ¼ cup (2 ounces) butter

Italian sausage
Mix pork and spices for 1 minute using paddle attachment or with quick pulses in a food processor. Mix in beer. Put in grinder with a sausage attachment, fill casings and tie off ends with string. Bake for 20 minutes at 350°.

vegetables
Sauté peppers and onions in butter. Cut cooked sausages into 6- to 8-inch pieces and top with vegetables.

Chef's Notes
- *To make sausage without a casing, place sausage mixture on pieces of plastic wrap in sizes that will fit into a Dutch oven. Form meat into a long tube. Roll up plastic and twist ends to seal. Fill Dutch oven with water. Bring to a boil. Add sausage and immediately reduce heat to a light simmer. If water is too hot the casing will pop because ingredients are expanding too fast. Cook sausage for about 15 minutes. Let cool several minutes, then remove plastic wrap.*

Surry Sausage and White Beans

JOHN LONG
ROUNDS CHEF, C.C.

The Williamsburg Inn, Colonial Williamsburg, Williamsburg

Chef's Notes
- *Great northern beans or the larger Italian cannelli beans are also excellent white beans. For larger beans, cooking time may increase up to 1½ hours.*
- *To mail order smoked Surry sausage links and other cured Virginia ham products contact: E. Wallace Edwards & Sons, P.O. Box 25, Surry, VA 23883, (800) 222-4267.*

European bistro foods are adapted to Virginia with these smoked sausage links from Surry County (just a ferry ride from Williamsburg across the James River). This hearty meal can be prepared well in advance and will improve with a bit of aging.

Complexity ✪   Yield: 4 servings

1	**pound dried white beans, pea or navy**
6	**cups chicken stock**
2	**cloves fresh garlic, minced**
	sea salt
	freshly ground black pepper
12	**2-ounce links smoked Surry sausage, sliced**

For beans, soak overnight in cold water. Drain. Place in a large pot. Cover with stock. Simmer for 30 to 40 minutes or until tender. Drain off extra liquid. Reserve liquid. Add garlic and sausage. Add salt and pepper. Simmer for 15 minutes, adding reserved liquid if desired.

Roast Fresh Ham, Civil War Style

M. SCOTT KIZER

The Dining Room, Ford's Colony, Williamsburg

The South will rise again when the open fires are lit to cook this nineteenth-century cuisine. In living history Virginia Civil War encampments, Pvt. Scott Kizer, Fifty-third Infantry Volunteer (for Company B, Barhamsville Grays, and Company K, Charles City Southern Guards) completes the experience with a taste of the past.

The pits and coals have to be developed in early morning as it will be 8 to 12 hours before dinner is ready. The sides of the pit are lined with flat rocks while more rocks or logs are arranged around the pit as a wind breaker. Due to its fast burn, pine is not recommended.

Complexity ●●　　　　　　　**Yield: 25 to 40 servings**

1　12- to 14-pound ham
2　medium onions (8 ounces), minced
3　red chilies, minced
2　tablespoons (1 ounce) firmly packed brown sugar
1　tablespoon celery seed
1　tablespoon ground mustard
1　teaspoon turmeric
1　teaspoon ground pepper
1　teaspoon salt
　　cider vinegar to top off quart bottle

Score skin and fat of ham in crisscross fashion. Pierce meat with single or double spit. In a 1-quart jar add onions, chilies, sugar, and spices. Fill jar to top with vinegar. Shake. Place meat over developed wood coals for 8 to 12 hours or until meat reaches an internal temperature of 155°. Baste often with barbecue sauce. Keep on pit and slice. Serve with sprinkle of sauce.

Chef's Notes
- *A pair of camp irons, ½-inch forged iron bars, 3-inch long are sufficient for a single or double spit. To suspend ham above fire, use logs or another pair of irons.*

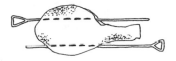

- *The barbecue sauce is styled after a North Carolina version found in M. C. Tyree's Housekeeping in Old Virginia.*

Pasta Primavera

DAVID BRUCE CLARKE

CHEF-INSTRUCTOR

J. Sargeant Reynolds Community College, Richmond

A celebration of spring, primavera, is deserved after the long, cold winter. Just when the first asparagus arrive is time to make this pasta dish. The sauce uses all the juices from the vegetables. The butter and cream make it just thick enough to hold on to the al dente strands of pasta.

Complexity ✪✪　　　　　　　　Yield: 4 to 6 servings

½ cup (4 ounces) unsalted butter
1 medium onion (4 ounces), minced
1 clove garlic, minced
1 pound thin asparagus, tough ends trimmed, cut diagonally into
　 ¼-inch slices, tips left intact
½ pound mushrooms, thinly sliced
6 ounces cauliflower, broken into small florets
1 medium zucchini (5 ounces), cut into ¼-inch rounds
1 small carrot (5 ounces), halved lengthwise, cut diagonally into
　 ⅛-inch slices
1 cup (8 ounces) whipping cream
½ cup (4 ounces) chicken stock
2 tablespoons fresh basil
1 cup (5 ounces) frozen tiny peas, thawed
2 ounces prosciutto or cooked ham, chopped
5 green onions (2 ounces), chopped
　 salt and pepper to taste
1 pound fettuccine or linguine, cooked al dente, thoroughly drained
1 cup (3 ounces) freshly grated Parmesan cheese

Chef's Notes

- After stir-frying vegetables, remove several pieces of asparagus tips, mushrooms, and zucchini and reserve for garnish.
- A large wok can be used in the place of a deep skillet.
- Frozen tiny peas tend to be sweeter than fresh peas from the market. If using fresh peas, shell just before adding and cook with the asparagus.
- Try to find imported Parmesan cheese; the flavor is unexcelled.
- Add 1 pound cooked shelled shrimp at the same time as the ham for variation.
- Enjoy a chilled bottle of Pinot Grigio and a crisp green salad with this pasta.

Heat a large, deep skillet over medium-high heat. Add butter. Sauté onion and garlic for 2 minutes or until softened. Add asparagus, mushrooms, cauliflower, zucchini, and carrot. Stir-fry for 2 minutes. Increase heat to high. Add cream, stock, and basil. Boil for 3 minutes or until the liquid is slightly reduced. Stir in peas, ham, and green onions. Cook 1 minute. Season with salt and pepper to taste. Add pasta and cheese, tossing until thoroughly combined and pasta is heated through. Turn onto a large serving platter. Garnish with vegetables. Serve immediately.

Applewood Smoked Angus Tenderloin Rémoulade

DAVID BRUCE CLARKE
CHEF-INSTRUCTOR
J. Sargeant Reynolds Community College, Richmond

Beef tenderloin, delicately marinated in Chef Clarke's special ingredients, cooking on the outdoor grill over applewood chunks tantalizes the entire neighborhood. Sliced and served with rémoulade sauce, it is an extravagant buffet centerpiece.

Complexity ❂❂❂   Yield: 10 to 12 servings

1 4- to 5-pound Angus beef tenderloin, trimmed, with all silver skin
   and fat removed
2 pounds seasoned applewood chips, 2- to 3-inch chunks
4 pounds charcoal

MARINADE

2 cups (16 ounces) cool water
1½ (12 ounces) cups cider vinegar
½ cup (4 ounces) balsamic vinegar
⅔ cups (6 ounces) grainy mustard
1 teaspoon salt
1 tablespoon freshly ground black pepper
¼ cup fresh tarragon leaves, chopped
½ cup (4 ounces) firmly packed brown sugar
½ cup (3 ounces) garlic purée

RÉMOULADE SAUCE

2 cups (16 ounces) mayonnaise
½ cup (4½ ounces) grainy mustard
½ cup finely chopped gherkins
3 tablespoons nonpareil capers
¼ cup chopped parsley
½ cup (3 ounces) finely chopped Vidalia onion, optional

beef
Fold small end of tenderloin underneath roast and tie with butcher's twine. Place meat in glass or porcelain dish. Mix all marinade ingredients. Pour over meat and cover with plastic wrap. Refrigerate overnight or for at least 8 hours. Rotate 2 or 3 times.

Chef's Notes
- *Remove all silver skin with a very sharp knife.*
- *The smoking chips impart a special flavor to this very tender cut of beef.*
- *Fill a new spray bottle with water and a few tablespoons of wine or vinegar to stop flare up on the smoking wood and coals. It also imparts a little flavor in the vapors.*
- *Juices will not be lost from hole made by an instant-read thermometer as it seals quickly. Cook to 140° for rare, 160° for medium, and 170° for well done.*
- *If optional Vidalia onions are not available, substitute any sweet onion such as Granax, Texas 10–15, or Maui. Do not use yellow onions as they are too bitter.*
- *The nonpareil capers are the petite variety from southern France. Brine-cured, it is best to rinse before using.*

Soak applewood chips in water for 4 to 5 hours. Prepare fire with charcoal. Remove tenderloin from marinade, reserving marinade for basting. Pat dry. When coals have turned white and all flame is gone, spread to both sides of grill. Drain applewood chips and place on both piles of hot embers. Place grate over wood. Place tenderloin on center of grill. Cover immediately with all vents, except one, closed. Every 10 minutes rotate tenderloin a quarter turn and baste with reserved marinade. Total cooking time will vary with the intensity of the fire. Use an instant thermometer for exact indication of doneness. Let meat cool for at least 30 minutes before slicing so the juices will be evenly distributed.

rémoulade sauce
Combine all ingredients. Chill before serving.

Sliced Beef with Shanghai Cabbage

GRACE LIU

CHEF-OWNER

The Dynasty, Williamsburg

Shanghai cabbages are blissfully tender heads of Chinese cabbage typically available fresh at Asian markets. Have all ingredients prepared before starting cooking, as it goes very fast.

Complexity ✪✪✪   **Yield: 4 servings**

MARINADE AND MEAT

6 ounces flank steak, 1½x2½-inch thin slices
1 tablespoon water
½ tablespoon dry sherry
½ tablespoon cornstarch
5 slices ginger
¼ teaspoon white pepper
¼ teaspoon sugar
  pinch salt

CABBAGE STIR-FRY

2½ cups Shanghai cabbage, 1x3-inch long strips
1 tablespoon (½ ounce) peanut oil (no substitutions)
1 tablespoon garlic slices, peeled
  pinch salt
¼ cup (2 ounces) chicken stock
½ teaspoon cornstarch mixed in ½ teaspoon water

MEAT STIR-FRY

1½ (¾ ounce) tablespoons peanut oil
1 teaspoon garlic slices
5 thin slices peeled ginger
⅓ cup (2½ ounces) chicken stock
1 teaspoon soy sauce
1 teaspoon oyster sauce
2 teaspoons cornstarch mixed in 2 teaspoons water
2 drops dark sesame oil

Chef's Notes
- *Blanch cabbage in heated chicken stock for better flavor.*
- *If Shanghai cabbage is unavailable, use an equivalent amount of fresh, tender spinach.*
- *Uniform-size cuts are important in Chinese cooking so that the cooking is even.*

marinade and meat
Marinate meat for 30 minutes in mixture of all ingredients.

cabbage stir-fry

Blanch cabbage for 30 seconds. Strain. Heat wok. Add oil. When hot add garlic and pinch of salt. Stir-fry cabbage for several seconds. Add stock. Heat until stock boils. Thicken with cornstarch mixture. Remove to serving plate.

meat stir-fry

Heat clean wok with oil. Add garlic, ginger slices, and beef. Stir-fry beef for 10 seconds. Add mixture of chicken stock, oyster sauce, and soy sauce. When sauce comes to a boil, add cornstarch mixture. Reduce heat, stirring for 1 minute or until sauce is thickened. Remove from heat. Add sesame oil.

assembly

Place meat and sauce on top of cabbage. Serve immediately.

Textbook Chili

DAVID J. BARRISH
PROGRAM DIRECTOR, C.H.A.

J. Sargeant Reynolds Community College, Richmond

No one will ever accuse Virginians of having "sissy" palates after tasting this chili, developed as a class project by the hospitality management students at J. Sargeant Reynolds Community College. "The Scholars of Spice" entered the Fifth Annual Richmond Chili Cook-off (a competition sanctioned by the International Chili Federation) and placed eleventh in a field of seventy-five. The subtle mixing of pepper flavors enhanced by Virginia dry-cured bacon results in a winning dish for a crowd. Any extra can be frozen.

Complexity ⭕⭕   Yield: 20 servings

20 slices (about 1¼ pounds) Virginia dry-cured bacon, sliced
3½ pounds ground beef round
 2 cups (12 ounces) coarsely chopped Spanish onions
 8 cloves garlic, finely minced
 6 tablespoons masa harina
 6 tablespoons ground chipotle chili powder
 1 tablespoon ground cumin
 1 teaspoon whole oregano
 1 teaspoon ground black pepper
 5 cups (40 ounces) tomato sauce, unsalted
 6 cups ripe plum tomatoes (4 pounds), peeled and coarsely chopped
 4 cups ripe plum tomatoes (2½ pounds), peeled and puréed
 2 cups (12 ounces) coarsely chopped red and yellow sweet bell peppers
 1 teaspoon finely minced red and green serrano peppers
 1 teaspoon finely minced green jalapeño peppers
 ½ cup (3 ounces) finely minced green Anaheim peppers
3½ cups warm water
 1 tablespoon ground cumin
 1 tablespoon mild chili powder

In a large skillet cook bacon until fat is browned. Drain on paper towels. Crumble and reserve. In a 3-gallon nonaluminum stock pot cook beef until no longer pink. Drain well. Add onion and garlic to beef. Cook over medium heat until onions are translucent. Add masa, chipotle chili powder, 1 tablespoon cumin, oregano, black pepper, and bacon to beef-onion mixture. Stir over low heat until thoroughly mixed. Add tomato sauce, tomatoes, peppers, and water. Simmer over low heat for 1 hour, stirring occasionally. Add remaining cumin and mild chili powder. Simmer over low heat for 25 minutes, stirring occasionally.

Chef's Notes
- *The Scholars of Spice promise that their chili is not too spicy. Adding the cumin and chili powders at various stages in the cooking process creates multidimensional layers of spice flavors. Serve in white stoneware bowls accompanied by great squares of corn bread and ice cold beer.*
- *Masa harina is a special corn flour found in Latino markets.*
- *The recipe can be halved or doubled easily.*
- *Foods of All Nations, 2121 Ivy Road, Charlottesville, VA 22903, (804) 296-6131, will mail chipotle chili powder to any continental U.S. postal address.*

Sicilian Meat Roll

JOHN T. MARLOWE
C.P.C.

European Specialties, Ukrop's Supermarket, Richmond

Chef's Notes

- *To achieve a light meat texture have it well chilled before beginning and handle as little as possible.*
- *The flat-leafed Italian has more flavor than the curly parsley and is easy to grow in most kitchen gardens.*
- *Cholesterol watchers may want to substitute ground turkey for the beef. Add 1 tablespoon white Worcestershire to the meat mixture. Also experiment with ground chicken seasoned with lemon thyme, filled with sharp Cheddar, and city ham. (City ham is the not-so-salty pink ham.)*
- *Serve with a side of polenta or fresh pasta with a light sauce.*
- *If you are fortunate enough to have leftovers, serve on toasted slices of Italian bread with red, ripe tomato slices.*

Local branches of the Sicilian families, having acquired a taste for fine Virginia cured hams, insist on this variation from the old country recipe. Filled and rolled in jelly roll fashion, the slices are fit for a godfather quietly dwelling on his James River plantation.

Complexity ✪✪   **Yield: 8 servings**

2 eggs, beaten
¾ cup (1 ounce) fresh breadcrumbs (from 1 slice fresh bread)
½ cup (4 ounces) tomato juice
2 tablespoons fresh snipped Italian parsley
½ teaspoon dried oregano, crushed
¼ teaspoon salt
¼ teaspoon pepper
1 clove garlic, minced
2 pounds lean ground beef
8 thin ham slices (4 ounces) (Virginia country recommended)
1½ cups (6 ounces) mozzarella cheese, shredded
4 square slices mozzarella cheese (4 ounces), halved diagonally

Mix eggs, crumbs, tomato juice, herbs, salt, pepper, and garlic. Add beef. Mix well. Pat out on waxed paper into a 10x12-inch rectangle. Fan the ham down the length of rectangle leaving a margin around all four sides. Sprinkle shredded cheese on top of ham. Start at short end of rectangle and roll up in jelly roll fashion using the waxed paper to aid in handling. Place seam side down on drip rack in roasting pan. Seal ends of roll. Bake at 350° for 75 minutes or until done. Top with cheese diagonals. Return to oven until melted. Slice.

Mongolian Lamb with Leeks

GRACE LIU
CHEF-OWNER
The Dynasty, Williamsburg

The secrets of the Orient are here revealed with this medium-spicy Peking lamb recipe. Serve family style on a large platter. Be authentic and use chopsticks. To serve, use opposite ends of sticks. Add more hot pepper sauce if desired.

Chef's Notes
- *To angle cut, place knife at a 45° angle to cutting board. Place trimmed meat in the freezer for about 30 minutes for easy slicing.*
- *A large fry pan can be used in the place of a wok.*
- *Add more hot pepper sauce if desired.*

Complexity ✪✪✪   Yield: 4 servings as part of a family-style Chinese dinner

LAMB AND MARINADE

5 ounces lamb, trimmed of all fat, sliced into thin slices
1 teaspoon soy sauce
½ teaspoon sugar
½ teaspoon dry sherry
1 teaspoon oil
¼ teaspoon ground white pepper
1½ teaspoons cornstarch
2 thin slices ginger

STIR-FRY

1½ (¾ ounce) tablespoons peanut oil
1 tablespoon garlic slices
5 ginger slices, thin
2 cups (1 large) leeks, angle cut into ¾-inch strips
¼ teaspoon salt
1 tablespoon stock (or water)
1 teaspoon sesame seeds
½ teaspoon hot pepper sauce (optional)

lamb and marinade
Cut lamb into thin slices approximately 1½x2½ inches. Mix marinade ingredients and pour over lamb for 30 minutes.

stir-fry
Heat wok over high heat. Add peanut oil. Stir in garlic and ginger slices. Stir-fry lamb for 10 seconds. Add leeks. Stir. Add salt and stock. Cook, stirring, for about 3 minutes or until leeks are soft. Place on warmed serving platter. Sprinkle with sesame seeds. Add optional hot pepper sauce. Serve immediately with steamed rice.

The New American Lamb Burger

U.S. ARMY CULINARY OLYMPIC TEAM

Fort Lee

Chef's Notes

- *For a quick version try using ground lamb with 2 tablespoons prepared curry powder and yogurt.*
- *Use ground turkey or chicken in the place of lamb for a lighter variation.*

This is a version of the winning sandwich that captured the highest gold medal in the world's Culinary Olympics in Frankfurt. The chefs' contest, held every four years, has teams competing from at least three dozen countries. Have the butcher remove the fat from a leg of lamb, then mince the meat. Alternatively, purchase ground lamb and briefly pulse in a food processor with the spices. Overprocessing results in a mushy burger. Grill over hot coals for an award-winning and unusual barbecue.

Complexity ✪✪   Yield: 6 servings

1½ pounds lamb, minced
 1 tablespoon finely ground fresh ginger
 2 teaspoons ground cumin
 2 teaspoons ground coriander
   pinch ground cloves
   pinch ground cinnamon
   pinch ground nutmeg
 ½ teaspoon black pepper
   cayenne pepper to taste
 1 teaspoon salt
 3 tablespoons (1½ ounces) plain yogurt

Mix all ingredients together. Shape into 6 oval lamb burgers. Chill until ready to grill. Grill over hot coals until medium-pink inside. Serve on a toasted sourdough bun with accompaniments—spicy tomato and cilantro relish; cucumber, yogurt, and mint; and dal.

CHAPTER 5
Stunning Side Dishes

RICHMOND NATIVE Bruce Baker, who has spent his life around vegetables, confesses that his favorite is still good old greens cooked in the Southern style. He suggests starting with several pounds of turnip greens. In Virginia grocery stores, very large plastic bags are placed next to the greens because their leafy abundance requires lots of room. Baker removes the stem and core keeping the leaf portion whole. In a large pot place cleaned greens with about 3 cups of water, several beef bouillon cubes, and some olive oil. Concern with cholesterol led him to switch from the traditional pork fat. He adds about ¼ cup olive oil or more, if his wife is not looking.

Over a slow fire simmer until the liquid is reduced by about half. Now you can start eating the greens, but they are better the next day. Heat, cook some more. Baker suggests adding new potatoes to the liquid. During the simmering phase they take on a magnificent golden color.

When asked what he likes to eat greens with, Baker laughed and clearly stated, "Pork chops."

🍍 *To clean greens* (turnip, kale, spinach, or mustard), fill sink with cool water. Whirl greens around the water with some force. With hand place greens in colander to drain. The sand particles and debris will sink to the bottom. Repeat process with fresh water if needed.

🍍 *Try sautéed cucumber* for a good side dish to baked bluefish or pompano. Peel the cucumber. Split in half. Scoop out seeds with a teaspoon. Slice flesh and sauté with freshly chopped dill, salt, and pepper.
—*Chef Bland*

🍍 *Mix dough for homemade pasta* in a food processor. Add flour and flavoring agent first, then egg and oil or water until a ball forms.—*Chef Bland*

🍍 *A high starch potato* such as red new potatoes make great fluffy mashed potatoes. Do not overmix or they will become very sticky.—*Chef Bland*

❧ *Keep sliced or peeled potatoes* in cold water to prevent oxidation. Strain before use. Let potatoes for fries or chips soak in ice water overnight.—*Chef Bland*

❧ *Cold water* will keep cut carrots crisp.
—*Chef Bland*

❧ *This may sound silly,* but it works. If you cry when chopping onions, open the freezer door and stick your head inside for a few seconds.—*Chef Bland*

❧ *Microwave cut potatoes* for 2 minutes then fry for crispy, less greasy French fries.
—*Chef Ozerdem*

❧ *Recipes using sour cream* can often use low-fat yogurt as a substitute. Add at the last minute as yogurt will separate if subjected to high heat.—*Chef Conte*

❧ *Finely chopped shallots* are excellent in vegetables. Heat in a little butter, add salt and pepper, emulsify with chicken or turkey stock. Vegetables look and taste much creamier.—*Chef Corliss*

❧ *Soak fresh unhusked corn* in salt water. Place under broiler, turning until husks turn black. Peel. Hold stem on top. Using serrated knife, cut straight down cob. Keep turning as you go to remove all the roasted kernels.—*Chef Corliss*

❧ *Make vegetable purees* without too much water or they will loose both color and texture. With rutabagas and turnips add some peeled red apple or celery to reduce bitterness. For broccoli use the tough ends, but do not cook too long.—*Chef Corliss*

❧ *Use 2- or 2½-ounce small dishes,* glass ramekins, soup cups or rice rings to mold rice. Make sure rice is al dente. If using a metal container, first place in chilled water. Pack with hot product. Flip right-side up. It will come right out. Make hollow in middle and fill with stir-fried vegetables. Top with a lobster or crab claw.—*Chef Corliss*

❧ *Oil outside of potatoes* to produce a crisper product, which heats up the skin faster, making a flakier skin. Fill sheet pan with rock salt to keep potatoes mounted.
—*Chef Corliss*

❧ *For wonderful flavor,* add roasted and minced garlic to mashed potatoes. Coat raw garlic with olive oil, sprinkle with salt, and bake in a 350° oven until golden brown. Make sure that garlic is completely roasted to avoid bitterness.—*Chef Corliss*

❧ *To keep okra* from sticking, add lemon juice or tamarind sauce.—*Chef Corliss*

❧ *For superior kernel texture* in grits cakes, use stone-ground corn. In humid climates store grits in freezer to protect flavor.
—*Chef Corliss*

❧ *In general, vegetables* should be cooked only in a small amount of water. Save liquids to add flavor, vitamins and minerals to soups, sauces and gravies.—*Chef Fulton*

❧ *A touch of curry powder* to baked beans adds a delightful new twist. Try a dip from mashed baked beans.—*Chef Fulton*

❧ *Celery is an automatic* convenience food—every part of this year-round vegetable can be eaten. Celery will not lose its flavor through cooking although it does undergo a change in texture.—*Chef Fulton*

❧ *To reduce potato baking time,* let stand in hot water a few minutes or parboil or give them a minute in the microwave.
—*Chef Fulton*

🍍 *Try some of these additions* to mashed potatoes. Hot milk makes them beat up much lighter while egg white adds flavor and improves appearance.—*Chef Fulton*

🍍 *Salt turnips after cooking* to retain their sweetness. Add a little sugar just prior to cooking to improve flavor and retard the strong cooking odor.—*Chef Fulton*

The Produce Marketing Association top 10 fruits in terms of pounds sold are: (1) banana, (2) apple, (3) watermelon, (4) orange, (5) cantaloupe, (6) grape, (7) grapefruit, (8) strawberry, (9) peach, and (10) pear. The Produce Marketing Association top 10 on its vegetable list based on pounds sold are: (1) potato, (2) iceberg lettuce, (3) tomato, (4) onion, (5) carrot, (6) celery, (7) corn, (8) broccoli, (9) green cabbage, and (10) cucumber. Sorry, Popeye, spinach ranked 21st.

Nutty Couscous

MARK KIMMEL
EXECUTIVE CHEF, C.E.C., A.A.C.
The Tobacco Company Restaurant, Richmond

Chef's Notes

- *Since the couscous has been pre-cooked, it only takes 3 minutes. Overcooking makes a sticky product—not the dry, fluffy side dish loved by many.*
- *Chicken base is a concentrated form of chicken stock and is available in warehouse outlets such as Price Club and Sam's around the country. Try to find one with no MSG and not too much sodium. Two bouillon cubes could be substituted, but the flavor is not as delightful. A better substitute is to eliminate the water and use 2 cups chicken stock.*
- *Whole-wheat couscous has much more flavor and may be found in health food stores and grocery stores with more extensive gourmet lines.*

Add a touch of exotic Morocco to dinner with couscous—the light, fluffy semolina wheat pasta, full of healthy complex carbohydrates. By the time you sing "As Times Goes By" and visualize the romance portrayed by Ingrid Bergman and Humphrey Bogart, this is done. "A kiss is just a kiss . . ."

Complexity ✪   **Yield: 6 servings**

¼ cup (2 ounces) butter
¼ cup fresh chopped chives
⅓ cup (1 ounce) chopped celery
2 tablespoons chopped fresh cilantro
1 bunch (3 ounces) scallions, chopped
½ cup (2 ounces) chopped pecans, toasted
½ cup (2 ounces) sliced almonds, toasted
1 teaspoon chicken base
2 cups water
2 cups (12 ounces) couscous

In large pan, melt butter. Sauté chives, celery, cilantro, and scallions for 3 minutes. Add pecans, almonds, and chicken base stirred into water. Bring to a boil. Add couscous and simmer for 3 minutes only. Fluff with a fork and serve.

Basic Fresh Pasta

RENNY PARZIALE

CHEF-OWNER

Virginia Culinary Company, Williamsburg

CHEF-INSTRUCTOR

P. D. Pruden Vo-Tech, Suffolk

A basic pasta machine eliminates using a rolling pin for this recipe. Machines are available at most kitchen shops for around $30. An electric one is not needed nor are the host of attachments for the dozens of pasta varieties.

Complexity ❂❂❂   Yield: about 1½ pounds or 8 to 10 servings

- 3 cups (12 ounces) all-purpose flour
- 4 whole eggs
- ¼ cup (2 ounces) olive oil
- 1 teaspoon salt

Place flour in mixing bowl and make a well. Crack eggs into well and add oil and salt. Pull flour with fingers into eggs, mixing slowly to avoid flour lumps. After all ingredients are mixed, remove from bowl and knead on a lightly floured board. Cover and refrigerate for 1 hour or more to relax dough. Remove and cut into four workable pieces. Pound flat and knead by rolling on the thickest setting on a pasta machine. Fold dough from machine into thirds, like folding a letter before placing into an envelope. Roll through machine again. Repeat this step until the dough is smooth and shiny. Change setting on machine by increments of one. Continue to roll dough through until reaching the desired thickness. Roll or cut with a large chef's knife or machine attachment as desired for noodles or sheets.

Cook pasta using a ratio of 1 gallon of boiling water with 2 tablespoons of salt to 1 pound of pasta to prevent pieces from sticking together. Fresh pasta, depending on its size, only takes minutes to cook. Do not overcook. The optimal texture is al dente or with a bit of a bite left in it.

Chef's Notes

- *Flour machine if pasta sticks.*
- *Different flavors and colors of pasta are obtained by adding finely chopped or finely ground vegetables to the flour well before mixing. If vegetables with a lot of moisture are added, try to squeeze out as much liquid as possible. Additional flour may be needed. Suggested additions are spinach, beets, garlic, herbs, and saffron.*
- *Working without the pasta machine requires kneading by hand. Roll, repeating the folding in thirds several times, until the dough is smooth and shiny.*
- *If making dough for ravioli, roll out thinner sheets as two layers will be used.*
- *Adding olive oil to the dough shortens the gluten strands, creating a softer pasta leavened by the eggs.*
- *Divide recipe in half for a smaller yield.*

Apple Walnut Stuffing

TED KRISTENSEN
CHEF-OWNER, C.E.C., A.A.C.
The Willows Bed and Breakfast, Gloucester

Chef's Notes

- *Given the difficulty of cooking stuffing inside a turkey—reaching the proper temperatures to kill possible bacteria—prepare in a separate pan. If it appears too dry, add up to 2 cups of stock before baking.*
- *Croutons can be made by cutting any high-quality bread into ¼-inch cubes and drying on a sheet pan in a 300° oven for about 30 minutes.*
- *Take advantage of the pulse option on a food processor to reduce the chopping effort.*
- *Do not wait for Thanksgiving to try this. Why not serve as a side dish for a roast loin of pork?*

The early English settlers brought over apple seeds, which successfully grew in the rich Virginia soil. At the site of Berkeley Plantation, along the James River, this would have been an excellent addition to the first Thanksgiving celebrated with the Indians in 1610—long before the celebration at Plymouth Rock by the Pilgrims from the Mayflower.

Complexity ✪   Yield: stuffing to accompany a
                              20-pound turkey

- 2 large onions (12 ounces), chopped
- 1 clove garlic, minced
- 3 stalks celery (7 ounces), diced
- 3 tablespoons (1½ ounces) vegetable oil
- 12 large Red Delicious apples (4 pounds), peeled, cored, and finely diced
- 2 cups (9 ounces) chopped English walnuts
- 5 eggs, beaten
- 1 teaspoon salt
- ⅛ teaspoon ground ginger
- ⅛ teaspoon ground sage
- ⅛ teaspoon ground white pepper
- 1 pound unseasoned croutons

In a large sauté pan, sauté onions, garlic, and celery in oil until tender. Remove from heat. Mix in apples, walnuts, eggs, and seasonings. In a very large mixing bowl, place croutons. Add onion-apple mixture to croutons. Toss well. Bake in a large greased baking pan at 375° for about 25 minutes or until browning begins on top.

Brandied Fruit Stuffing Roulade

ROBERT D. CORLISS

SOUS CHEF

The Williamsburg Inn, Colonial Williamsburg, Williamsburg

Chef Corliss's roulade revolutionizes stuffing presentation with tiny bits of brandied fruit and colorful vegetables. The aromatic vegetables and fruits are blended with dried bread croutons and formed into a long roulade that is formed and baked in plastic wrap (yes, plastic wrap, and it is perfectly safe) covered with foil. The roulade is sliced for serving.

Complexity ✪✪✪   Yield: 6 servings

1 cup (6 ounces) minced dried fruits
½ cup (4 ounces) brandy
1 stalk celery (2 ounces), diced
1 carrot (2 ounces), diced
1 small onion (3 ounces), diced
1 16-ounce loaf of white bread, diced, dry
2 tablespoons (1 ounce) butter
2 eggs, beaten
1 tablespoon chopped fresh parsley
1 teaspoon chopped fresh thyme
  salt and white pepper to taste
  pinch nutmeg
½ to ¾ cup (4 to 6 ounces) milk, warm

Marinate dry fruit overnight in brandy. In a large nonstick pan sauté celery, carrot, and onion over high heat until tender. Add fruit with brandy. Cook for 1 minute. Place dried bread in large mixing bowl. Stir in vegetable-fruit mixture and eggs. Add seasonings. Drizzle with warm milk and continue stirring to form a soft ball. Place stuffing on

Chef's Notes
- *Also try with whole-wheat bread and variations of herbs and nuts.*
- *Slicing on a diagonal bias and fanning slices makes an excellent presentation.*
- *The stuffing can be made ahead of time and stored wrapped in plastic and foil in the refrigerator. Just before service time, slice, place on a buking sheet. Cover with a damp towel and heat at 350° for about 8 minutes.*
- *Leaves can easily be removed from fresh thyme by holding top with one hand and running fingers of the other hand down the stem. Save stem for aromatic use in soup.*

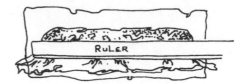

a piece of plastic wrap on top of foil the size of a baking sheet. Beginning with the plastic, pull top sheet over bottom sheet. Hold bottom plastic sheet in one hand. With a large ruler or knife pressing on the roll pull the bottom sheet toward you.

This will form the roulade. Repeat procedure with foil. Make a tight roll. Twist ends in opposing directions to seal foil. Bake at 375° for 40 to 45 minutes. Cool for 8 minutes. Unwrap, slice, and serve hot.

Cranberry Crème Salad

ROBERT D. CORLISS
SOUS CHEF
The Williamsburg Inn, Colonial Williamsburg, Williamsburg

At first this may appear to be a 1950s retro-food, but it has been upscaled with cranberry sauce, walnuts, and sour cream. Chef Corliss credits Linda Corliss, his ever-inspiring mother, for this creation. Serve as a side dish or as a pleasant salad over tender greens on a hot summer day, such as July 4th.

Complexity ✪   Yield: 6 servings

1 3-ounce box cherry-flavored gelatin
1 cup water, boiling
3 tablespoons sugar
1 8-ounce can whole-cranberry sauce
⅓ cup (1½ ounces) diced celery
⅓ cup (1½ ounces) chopped walnuts
1 cup (8 ounces) sour cream

In a small mixing bowl dissolve gelatin and sugar in boiling water. Stir in cranberry sauce. Pour into a 6-cup mold. Chill until thickened but not firm. Stir in remaining ingredients and chill for 1 hour. Serve chilled or at room temperature.

Chef's Notes
- A low-calorie version can be made by substituting sugar-free gelatin and low-fat sour cream or yogurt.
- Individually molded servings can be made using coffee cups, soufflé, or custard dishes.
- Try with a venison terrine for outstanding reviews.

Black Bean Cakes

MARK KIMMEL

EXECUTIVE CHEF, C.E.C., A.A.C.

The Tobacco Company Restaurant, Richmond

Chef's Notes

- *Liquid should be cooked down so that the top half of the beans are dry. Beans should be very soft.*
- *A #16 scoop is recommended for forming cakes. Scoop numbers refer to the number of scoops required to make a quart. The #16 is ¼ cup or 16 measures for 1 quart and the #12 is ⅓ cup.*

Black beans are inexpensive and a superb source of complex carbohydrates and protein. Eliminating the bouillon, this is a fabulous vegetarian dish. Team with Chef Kimmel's Fresh Salsa (page 202).

Complexity ✪✪   Yield: 8 servings

8 ounces dried black beans
1 tablespoon (½ ounce) olive oil
1 small (3 ounces) onion, chopped
2 cloves garlic, minced
1 slice bacon, diced
2 teaspoons beef bouillon
3 cups water
½ teaspoon salt
1 jalapeño, sliced
1 tablespoon dark chili powder
1½ teaspoons ground cumin
1 tablespoon (½ ounce) oil

Soak cleaned beans overnight in water. Drain. In a large kettle with 1 tablespoon of olive oil, sauté onion, garlic, and bacon for 3 minutes. Add bouillon, water, and salt. Add beans. Cook uncovered for approximately 2 hours or until the beans are tender. Place mixture in large bowl of electric mixer. Beat. Add jalapeño, chili, and cumin. In food processor run for about 2 minutes or until smooth. Chill mixture. Form into cakes with a #16 scoop or ¼ cup measure onto parchment or sheets lined with plastic wrap. Slightly flatten. In a large nonstick skillet or griddle sauté briefly in hot oil.

Braised Lentils

ROBERT D. CORLISS
SOUS CHEF

The Williamsburg Inn, Colonial Williamsburg, Williamsburg

Lentils are a versatile staple highly deserving of valuable pantry space. These little, inexpensive dried legumes cook faster than most dried beans, needing no presoaking. Chock full of complex carbohydrates, lentils respond beautifully to additions of stocks, herbs, and flavorings. Try these with the Marble of Gingered Mahimahi (page 83). They can stand alone as a meatless entrée or sit quietly, but deliciously, as a side dish.

Complexity ✪   Yield: 8 servings

2 strips lean bacon (2 ounces), julienned
1 onion (4 ounces), finely diced
2 tablespoons tomato paste
1 tablespoon (½ ounce) sherry wine vinegar
1 pound French green lentils
4 cups fresh fish stock
   salt to taste

In 3-quart pan sauté bacon over high heat. When halfway crisp, add onion. Cook until translucent. Add tomato paste. Cook for 1 minute. Add vinegar. Stir in lentils. Cover with stock. Bring to a boil. Reduce to a simmer. Cover pan. Cook for about 45 minutes or until lentils are tender. Adjust seasoning.

Chef's Notes
- *There is a richness of lentil types—brown, red, and green. Red are the fastest cooking as the skins have been removed. Look for these in bulk bins.*
- *For leaner cooking, substitute turkey ham, finely julienned, for the bacon.*
- *Any quality stock can be substituted in this recipe. If possible, try to match stock with any meat or fish being served. In a pinch, bouillon cubes can be used. Exercise caution as many varieties are monumentally high in sodium. A better substitute is a commercial chicken, beef, or fish-base concentrate available in gourmet markets and large, membership warehouse stores. These concentrates last for months under refrigeration. But again, be wary of high sodium contents.*
- *Any leftovers can be tossed into soups.*

Indian Corn Pudding

EDWARD DAGGERS

EXECUTIVE CHEF, C.E.C.

Country Club, Memphis, Tennessee

Chef's Notes
- *Fresh corn just scraped from a steamed ear is elegant. Out of season, use the canned version.*
- *Increase the sugar up to ½ cup and serve as a dessert, as do the Amish.*
- *The drained 17-ounce can of niblets yields approximately 1¾ cups.*

Of course this is not the style of dish enjoyed by native Indians, Powhatans, in the early years of colonization. But the Indians can certainly be credited with teaching the colonists how to raise, dry, and store corn. This is a twentieth-century upscale version that melts just like a soufflé.

Complexity ✪✪   Yield: 8 servings

1	teaspoon soft butter
1	tablespoon sugar
1¾	cups (12 ounces) corn kernels
1½	cups (13 ounces) heavy cream
½	teaspoon ground cinnamon
¼	teaspoon ground nutmeg
½	teaspoon salt
5	egg yolks, mixed
5	egg whites, whipped to stiff peaks

Butter a medium-size heavy-bottomed casserole dish. Sprinkle with sugar. In a large bowl, combine corn, cream, spices, and egg yolks. Fold in egg whites. Pour into prepared casserole dish. Bake at 350° for 40 to 50 minutes or until set up with a golden brown top.

Polenta Gateau with Ratatouille

U.S. ARMY CULINARY OLYMPIC TEAM

Fort Lee

Polenta is an Italian-style cornmeal that is slightly coarse. Stuffed with ratatouille between layers of creamy polenta and topped with nutty Gruyère cheese, this is a show stopper. The ratatouille is particularly outstanding, as each ingredient is sautéed separately so that each vegetable cooks to perfection.

Complexity ✪✪✪   **Yield: 6 servings**

POLENTA

3 cups chicken stock or water
1 cup (4½ ounces) yellow cornmeal
1 teaspoon salt
6 slices Gruyère cheese or mozzarella (6 ounces)

RATATOUILLE

1 medium eggplant (1 pound)
1 zucchini (8 ounces)
½ red bell pepper (3 ounces)
½ yellow bell pepper (3 ounces)
½ green bell pepper (3 ounces)
2 tablespoons (½ ounce) chopped onions
1 clove garlic, crushed
1 sprig fresh thyme
1 bay leaf
½ cup (4 ounces) tomato sauce
½ teaspoon salt
¼ teaspoon pepper
    olive oil to sauté (total of about 4 teaspoons)

polenta
Boil stock or water in a 3-quart saucepan. Whisk in cornmeal, getting rid of all lumps. Cook over low heat for 30 minutes, stirring occasionally. Season. Pour into a jelly roll pan. Spread out. Cool. Cut into 12 squares.

Chef's Notes
- *During the Culinary Olympics in Frankfurt, our team won a gold medal serving this as a side dish to the California Sonoma Valley Chicken breast stuffed with pesto (see page 103).*
- *The best cornmeal to use is a coarse-ground yellow.*
- *Cook all ratatouille ingredients together for a quicker, albeit not quite as good, product.*
- *Ratatouille chopping can be done with controlled pulses in a food processor.*
- *Make the polenta with water, double the recipe, and serve 6 as a vegetarian entrée.*
- *Polenta squares can be made up to one day in advance if carefully wrapped and refrigerated.*
- *If using the standard 14½-ounce canned chicken stock, use 2 cans stock plus ⅛ cup water.*

ratatouille

Cut all vegetables brunoise or into ¼-inch cubes. Sauté eggplant in 1 teaspoon olive oil in a nonstick skillet. Remove. Sauté zucchini in 1 teaspoon olive oil. Remove. Sauté peppers in 1 teaspoon olive oil. Remove. Sauté onions and garlic in remaining oil. Return all vegetables to skillet. Add herbs and tomato sauce and reduce several minutes until mixture thickens. Season. Remove from heat.

assembly

Lay 6 polenta squares on a greased baking sheet. Top each with one-sixth of the ratatouille. Top with another polenta square and finally with cheese. Bake 5 to 10 minutes at 375° or until completely heated through and the cheese melted.

Pan-Fried Grits with Virginia Country Ham

MARK KIMMEL
EXECUTIVE CHEF, C.E.C., A.A.C.

The Tobacco Company Restaurant, Richmond

The South is known for its love of grits. This corn is a naturally wonderful starchy side dish for other meals. Chef Kimmel added the intricate flavors of country ham and Cheddar cheese with just a hint of garlic and chives. Shaped in muffin tins, they are finished by pan frying. Fusion cuisine fans will love these teamed with Chef Kimmel's Fresh Salsa (page 202).

Complexity ✪✪   **Yield: 9 servings**

1 quart water
1¼ cups (½ pound) grits
2 teaspoons white pepper
1 teaspoon garlic powder
2 teaspoons salt
1 tablespoon dried chives
¼ cup finely chopped Virginia country ham (1½ ounces)
1 cup (4 ounces) grated Cheddar cheese
2 tablespoons (1 ounce) vegetable oil

In a large saucepan bring water to a boil. Stir in all ingredients except cheese and oil. Stir until smooth. Cook over medium heat whipping occasionally for 15 minutes or until thick. Remove from heat. Mix in cheese. Grease muffin tins with nonstick spray. Fill each to the top with mixture. Let cool. Remove from pans. Split lengthwise. Pan-fry on skillet in hot oil until golden on each side.

Chef's Notes
- *Stir grits thoroughly to avoid lumps.*
- *Try deep-frying these for a crunchy exterior. Or for less fat they can be run under the broiler for browning.*
- *Grits can be heated on a non-stick griddle treated with non-stick spray.*
- *Use 1 clove of fresh garlic and 3 tablespoons of fresh chives if available.*
- *Make ahead, refrigerate, and pan-fry for about 8 minutes just before serving.*
- *Use mini-muffin tins for petite starter-sizes.*
- *Edwards Hams sells ground Surry and Virginia ham in its shop on Richmond Road in Williamsburg. This is quite convenient for these grits and for other recipes needing just a little taste of flavorful ham.*

Pommes de Terre Dauphinois

RICHARD IVEY

EXECUTIVE CHEF

ARAMARK, Campus Dining Services, Randolph Macon College, Ashland

Chef's Notes
- *Check softness of potatoes with a toothpick or with a paring knife and lift. If the potato slides off it is done.*
- *There should be a double layer of potatoes to achieve the desired effect.*
- *If Jarlsberg is not available, try any variety of Swiss cheese.*
- *The 15-minute resting period after baking permits the dish to become firm. The slicing and serving are then quite easy and the potatoes are still warm.*

The lowly potato casts off its earthy status and ascends to royalty when dressed with heavy cream, eggs, and Jarlsberg cheese. The eggs make it more similar to a quiche than are most scalloped potatoes. Perhaps this might be just the dish to serve with a proper joint—a fine roast beef or rack of lamb.

Complexity ❸❸❸   Yield: 6 to 8 servings

4 *(about 2 pounds) baking-size Idaho potatoes*
1 *egg yolk*
1 *egg*
1 *cup (8 ounces) heavy cream*
1 *tablespoon chopped fresh garlic*
½ *teaspoon salt*
¼ *teaspoon pepper*
½ *cup (2 ounces) grated Jarlsberg cheese*
   parsley sprigs, garnish

Peel potatoes, removing eyes. Boil for about 20 to 30 minutes or until soft to the center. Drain water. Let potatoes cool to room temperature. In a 2-quart stainless bowl whisk eggs, cream, garlic, salt, and pepper. Evenly slice potatoes about ¼-inch thick. Shingle around a greased round 8-inch quiche pan or casserole dish. Pour cream and egg mixture over potatoes. Tops of potatoes should be slightly exposed. Top with grated Jarlsberg. Bake at 375° for about 30 minutes or until cheese is a light golden brown. After removing potatoes from oven, let them sit for 15 minutes before serving. Cut into wedges and garnish with parsley.

Potatoes Gruyère

JO OLSON

ACCOUNT EXECUTIVE

Atlantic Food Services, Inc., Richmond

Gruyère cheese, named after the Swiss canton where cows produce rich, sweet milk, gloriously crowns these otherwise lowly potatoes. While processed Gruyère, wedges wrapped in foil, is easy to find, it lacks the flavor of the original product.

Complexity ✪✪✪　　　　　　　**Yield: 6 servings**

　5　*medium potatoes (1½ pounds), peeled and sliced*
　1　*medium (4 ounces) onion, sliced*
　½　*cup (4 ounces) butter*
　¼　*cup (1 ounce) all-purpose flour*
　2　*cups milk*
　¾　*teaspoon salt*
　½　*teaspoon nutmeg*
　⅛　*teaspoon ground white pepper*
　½　*cup (2 ounces) Gruyère cheese, grated*
　3　*tablespoons freshly grated Parmesan cheese*
　　　dash cayenne pepper

Cook potatoes and onions in a 4-quart pan of boiling water. Drain for 10 minutes or until very dry. In medium saucepan melt butter. Stir in flour and cook for 3 minutes. Whisk in milk, salt, nutmeg, and white pepper. Simmer for 15 minutes, stirring occasionally. Butter a springform pan. Place a spoonful of sauce in bottom. Arrange potatoes and onions. Sprinkle with half the cheeses. Pour over remaining sauce. Sprinkle with remaining cheese. Shake on cayenne. In a 375° oven bake 15 minutes or until bubbly. Broil for 3 minutes or until top is golden brown. Remove rim of pan and cut into serving wedges.

Chef's Notes

• *After pouring off the water from the potatoes, the pan can be placed over a burner and heated to rid it of excess water. Watch this carefully so that the potatoes do not burn.*

• *After the milk-and-flour sauce has simmered, it can be strained if any lumps are obvious.*

Sliced Potatoes Lyonnaise

W. KEITH PEARCE
FOOD BROKER
Florida

Chef's Notes
- *Yukon gold potatoes magnificently color this dish and add a delicious taste variation. Use 4 medium golds.*

Chef Pearce has lightened up the classic treatment of potatoes using thickened chicken stock and flavor-enhanced it with caramelized onions, chives, and parsley in the place of butter and cream.

Complexity ●●   Yield: 4 servings

1 **large (6 ounces) onion**
¼ **cup chopped chives**
¼ **cup chopped parsley**
1 **cup (8 ounces) chicken stock**
1 **teaspoon cornstarch mixed in 1 tablespoon cold water**
1 **clove garlic, minced**
1 **teaspoon salt**
1 **teaspoon pepper**
2 **large baking potatoes (1 pound), peeled and sliced**

Slice onion in half, then slice into crescents. In a nonstick pan caramelize onions over low heat for approximately 8 minutes. Remove from heat. Mix in chives and parsley. In a small saucepan bring chicken stock to a boil. Stir in cornstarch mixture. Add garlic, salt, and pepper. Return to boil, stirring constantly for about 2 minutes or until stock thickens. In a shallow ovenproof dish, fan potatoes just overlapping each other and sprinkle with onion mixture. Pour stock mixture over top. Bake at 375° for 60 to 90 minutes or until potatoes are tender.

Sunday-Best Grated Potatoes au Gratin

DAVID BRUCE CLARKE

CHEF-INSTRUCTOR

J. Sargeant Reynolds Community College, Richmond

Adapted from a very old Virginia recipe lovingly written on a 2x3-inch yellowing scrap of paper, this "Sunday-Best" potato casserole always demands seconds and, yes, thirds.

Complexity ✪   **Yield: 6 to 8 servings**

1 clove garlic
1 tablespoon (½ ounce) butter
9 potatoes (3 pounds), grated
2 cups (½ pound) grated Cheddar cheese
2 eggs
2 cups milk
2 teaspoons salt
½ teaspoon pepper
¼ teaspoon grated nutmeg

Rub the inside of a large casserole dish with garlic clove. Butter dish. Fill with grated potatoes and mix with 1½ cups cheese. In a small mixing bowl combine eggs, milk, salt, pepper, and nutmeg. Pour over potatoes. Top with remaining cheese. Bake in a 350° oven for 1½ hours or until potatoes are fork-tender and the top is golden brown.

Chef's Notes
- *Grate potatoes and cheese in the food processor for speedy preparation.*
- *A small amount of crushed fresh rosemary provides a tasty variation with Cheddar or try a combination of mozzarella with Italian crushed herbs.*
- *The sharper the cheese, the more flavor. In fact we have reduced the amount of cheese to 1 cup in this recipe and still had stunning results.*

Potato and Onion Stew, Civil War Style

M. SCOTT KIZER

The Dining Room, Ford's Colony, Williamsburg

Chef's Notes
- *Flavor can be added by starting with rendered bacon or smoked hog jowls.*
- *Can be made one day in advance.*

Often this hearty and easy-to-prepare stew accompanies roasted meat during a Civil War reenactment. Only one pot is needed to cook these root vegetables in the nineteenth-century style. And given its ease of preparation, try indoors for a hearty meal.

Complexity ✪   Yield: 10 servings

9 *potatoes (3 pounds), medium dice*
6 *onions (2 pounds), small dice*
    water to cover
    salt and pepper to taste

Combine all ingredients in a deep cast-iron kettle over medium heat. Simmer until potatoes are past well done and the stew begins to thicken. Serve out of the kettle.

Sweet Potato Purée on Potato Leaves

BILLIE RAPER

CHEF PRODUCTION MANAGER, C.C.

ARAMARK, Bell Atlantic, Richmond

Now for a little art lesson with slow-roasted, golden sweet potatoes. Load up the pastry tube with purée, give it a generous squeeze, and decorate dinner plates guaranteed for raves from the audience. And it is so easy while artistically satisfying.

Complexity ✪✪   **Yield: 6 servings**

PURÉE

4 *medium sweet potatoes (2 pounds)*
⅓ *cup (2½ ounces) skim milk*
½ *teaspoon ground cinnamon*
2 *pinches ground nutmeg*
1 *tablespoon firmly packed brown sugar*

LEAVES

1 *medium sweet potato (8 ounces), peeled*
1 *teaspoon sugar*

purée
Roast potatoes for 45 minutes at 350°. Remove peels. Run through sieve or purée with hand mixer. Add skim milk and seasonings. Place purée in a large pastry bag fitted with a star tip.

leaves
Slice raw potato into ¼-inch slices. Cut each slice in half (these will look like half-circles). With a small, flexible knife sculpt leaf markings on each slice. Place on a baking sheet covered with parchment paper. Spray top of each leaf with nonstick vegetable spray and sprinkle with sugar. Bake at 350° for 12 to 15 minutes, until slices just begin to soften. Do not overcook.

assembly
Place 3 to 5 leaves on individual serving plates. Pipe purée on leaves. A branch may be formed by using a vertically sliced scallion top.

Chef's Notes
- *Potatoes may be cooked in the microwave for convenience, but they will lack the earthy sweetness that comes from slow roasting.*
- *The same carving technique can be used with cucumbers, zucchini, or other squash. Another attractive presentation is to place cooked potatoes in a glass bowl and garnish with the leaves.*
- *Decorating plates with other vegetables can be accomplished with tiny vegetable cutters that make hearts, flowers, moons, and circles.*

Spaghetti Squash with Kalamata Olives

U.S. ARMY CULINARY OLYMPIC TEAM

Fort Lee

Chef's Notes
- *The best tool we found for removing squash seeds is our fingers after running a small knife around the seed area.*
- *If the squash is overcooked, it will become mushy, ruining the spaghetti effect.*
- *During the Culinary Olympics in Frankfurt, our team won a gold medal serving this squash under the California Sonoma Valley Chicken breast stuffed with pesto (see page 103).*

Slowly roasting this squash yields perfectly formed spaghetti-like strands when scraped gently with a fork. Black-purple Greek Kalamata olives perk up the dish with their rich, bitter, aromatic taste. While Kalamatas can be purchased in jars, we like the ones from the old barrels in the ethnic markets where often an olive tasting, to discern subtleties, precedes any purchases.

Complexity ✪   Yield: 6 servings

1	(about 3 pounds) spaghetti squash
2	ounces Kalamata olives
¼	teaspoon black pepper

With a large chef's knife, cut squash horizontally. Scoop out seeds and strings. Place cut side down on an ungreased baking sheet. Bake for 30 to 40 minutes at 350°. Scrape out flesh. Chop olives. Fold into squash. Season with pepper.

ATLAS SPECIAL MASON

Squash Half Moons with Asparagus

BILLIE RAPER
CHEF PRODUCTION MANAGER, C.C.
ARAMARK, Bell Atlantic, Richmond

Contrasting colors provide gorgeous visual appeal for the diner. Be careful not to overcook the vegetables. This dish is quite flexible—an inspiration to the imagination. Try other winter squashes or pumpkin in the place of the acorn squash. Each has its own wonderful flavor. For the green vegetable, use what is fresh in the market—green beans, fresh spinach leaves, broccoli spears.

Complexity ✪   Yield: 6 servings

2 *acorn squash*
1 *pound fresh asparagus, tough ends removed*
2 *tablespoons (1 ounce) dry white wine*
1 *shallot (1 ounce), chopped*
  salt and pepper to taste

Cut squash in half lengthwise. Remove seeds and peel. Cut squash in ⅓-inch slices. Steam slices for 5 minutes or until al dente. On a baking sheet sprayed with vegetable oil, roast slices at 350° for 10 to 12 minutes or until soft. Blanch asparagus in boiling water for 2 minutes. Drop into cold water. Drain. Sauté asparagus in white wine and shallots until al dente. Adjust seasonings. On serving plate, place 2 squash half moons about 2 inches apart. Fill center with asparagus.

Chef's Notes
- *Roasting the squash creates flavors richer than only steaming. The skin can be left on the squash, but will create a slight discoloration on the squash.*
- *For a very healthy low-calorie meal, serve the above for two people. Create a circular pinwheel pattern with the squash half moons leaving space in the center for 2-inch asparagus pieces. Garnish with either a red onion confit or dried cherries poached in red wine.*

Ratatouille Terrine

W. KEITH PEARCE
FOOD BROKER
Florida

Chef's Notes
- *Use fresh, in-season vegetables to create other terrines.*

Made in individual ovenproof cups with fanned zucchini around the edges, the tender zucchini, eggplant, onions, peppers, and tomatoes are suspended in a light egg-white mixture.

Complexity ✪✪   Yield: 6 servings

1 zucchini (8 ounces), diced
1 small (8 ounces) eggplant, diced
2 onions (8 ounces), diced
1 small (4 ounces) green bell pepper, diced
1½ teaspoons chopped garlic
6 tablespoons (3 ounces) virgin olive oil
3 tomatoes (1 pound), peeled, seeded, chopped
½ cup (4 ounces) tomato purée
¼ cup chopped, fresh parsley
1 bay leaf
1½ teaspoons leaf oregano
¼ teaspoon leaf thyme
¾ teaspoon salt
½ teaspoon ground black pepper
¾ teaspoon sugar
1 egg white, beaten
2 zucchini (1 pound), thinly sliced

Sauté all vegetables except zucchini slices in olive oil for about 5 minutes or until just tender. Stir in tomato, tomato purée, herbs, and seasonings. Remove from heat and cool. Remove bay leaf and discard. Fold in egg white. Lightly grease 6-ounce ovenproof cups. Arrange zucchini slices around inside perimeter of cup. Fill with ratatouille mixture and bake 15 to 20 minutes. To serve, run sharp knife to loosen edges. Unmold directly onto serving plate.

Sichuan Eggplant in Garlic Sauce

GRACE LIU
CHEF-OWNER
The Dynasty, Williamsburg

Stir-frying only takes minutes from start to finish in this spicy eggplant dish. Have meat shredded, vegetables sliced, and sauce ingredients mixed. After cooking, the thickener is added, stirred briefly, and removed from the fire. In the restaurant kitchen, huge woks sit on fire-blasting hot gas units. At intensely high heats, the food cooks much faster than in a wok over a home unit. However, the results with this eggplant are excellent.

Chef's Notes
- *Make cornstarch mixture by stirring 1 teaspoon cornstarch in ¼ cup cold water. Stir well before using.*
- *A large skillet may be substituted for a wok. Since the liquid from the eggplant will not evaporate as quickly, try reducing the chicken stock to ⅔ cup.*

Complexity ✪✪   Yield: 4 servings

EGGPLANT

2 *medium (1 pound) Chinese eggplants (or 1 medium eggplant)*
2 *tablespoons (1 ounce) peanut oil*
1 *tablespoon garlic, cut into thin slices*
2 *scallions, cut into 3-inch sections*
2 *ounces shredded pork (or chicken)*

SAUCE

1 *cup (8 ounces) chicken stock*
1½ *teaspoons soy sauce*
1 *tablespoon (½ ounce) sugar*
1 *tablespoon (½ ounce) white vinegar*
1 *teaspoon hot sauce*

THICKENER

1 *teaspoon cornstarch mixture*

Cut eggplant into 3 horizontal sections. Cut each section into 4 to 6 strips. Heat oil in wok. Add garlic, scallion, and shredded pork. Stir-fry for 10 seconds. Stir-fry eggplant for 1 minute. Add sauce mixture and cook until the eggplant is soft. Thicken with cornstarch mixture. Place on serving dish.

Brunoise of Vegetables

ROBERT D. CORLISS

SOUS CHEF

The Williamsburg Inn, Colonial Williamsburg, Williamsburg

Chef's Notes
- *Salsify, often called the oyster plant, is a root vegetable usually available in Spanish, Italian, or Greek markets.*
- *For variety try other root vegetables such as celeriac, turnips, and rutabagas.*
- *For low-fat cooking, spray pan with vegetable spray and cook in ½ cup chicken stock.*

Brunoise is the French term for a mixture of vegetables finely diced. Often it is the building block vegetable mixture for soups and sauces.

Complexity ✪   Yield: 8 servings

2 tablespoons (1 ounce) butter
1 cucumber (6 ounces), peeled and finely diced
1 red onion (6 ounces), peeled and finely diced
1 stalk celery (3 ounces), chopped and finely diced
1 salsify (8 ounces), peeled and finely diced
1 carrot (4 ounces), peeled and finely diced

Heat butter in large sauté pan. Add vegetables. Cook over medium heat for about 15 minutes or until just tender and still firm and colorful.

CHAPTER 6
Snazzy Salads and Dressings

🍍 *When boiling eggs,* use cold water and cold eggs and 1 teaspoon salt. Bring to a boil. Reduce heat and simmer for a total cooking time of 15 minutes. (When overcooked the yolks will have a green ring. Properly cooked eggs have yellow yolks.) Drain. Cover with ice and cold water. Give the pan a jerk with one hand to break the shells. Allow to cool for 5 to 10 minutes. The ice and water cause the eggs to shrink inside the shells and make peeling fast and easy.—*Chef Clarke*

🍍 *Another test* to see if eggs are properly hard cooked is to grasp the egg between index finger and thumb the long way. Do this gingerly as egg will be quite hot. Spin like a top. If it turns up on the end while spinning it is perfectly done. If egg spins on the side, return it to the pot and cook at a simmer for 2 to 3 more minutes.—*Chef Clarke*

🍍 *To make perfect shrimp* for cocktails, make sure the poaching water contains no salt. The salt tends to draw moisture out of the shrimp. Put salt in ice water to chill shrimp after cooking. The salt will draw water into the shrimp and make it more plump, giving it a slightly salty taste that will be pleasing to the palate.—*Chef Goodier*

🍍 *For a quick dressing* for a fruit salad or a fresh fruit dessert try this Yogurt Dressing. Mix 1 cup low-fat plain yogurt, 2 tablespoons sugar or sugar substitute, and juice of 1 lemon. This makes about 1 cup. Each tablespoon has 14 calories.—*Chef Connell*

🍍 *For salads,* create unique concoctions. Avoid the hackneyed iceberg lettuce trap. Try red and green leaf, romaine, Boston, and oak leaf lettuces. Endive and radicchio add a nice bitter bite, but too much is overpowering. From the pantry candidates include whole tiny beets, hearts of palms, water chestnuts, kidney beans, chickpeas, and black beans. Drain well before using. In the freezer try peas, lima beans, and French-cut string beans. Rinse under warm water for several minutes, drain, and toss into the salad.

Things that go crunch add interest, such as sunflower seeds, sesame seeds, Virginia peanuts, chopped carrots, and croutons. Healthy croutons can be made by cutting cubes from any bread, sprinkling with herbs, and toasting in a slow 300° oven for approximately 20 minutes, stirring occasionally. No fat is needed.

Edible flowers, including rose, chive, geranium, pinks, nasturtium, day lily, lavender, viola, pansy, Johnny-jump-up, and violet, visually excite and add interesting tastes. Some poisonous flowers include iris, lantana, lily-of-the-valley, narcissus, daffodils, tansy, wisteria, sweet peas, rhododendron, amaryllis, anemone, and belladonna lily. Questionable, and therefore not to be eaten, are snapdragons, primrose, petunias, impatiens, and bachelor's button.—*M. H. Robinson*

Classic vinaigrettes are 3 parts oil to 1 part vinegar. Use a thickened stock to replace two-thirds of the oil. A 1-ounce portion of the classic has 175 calories and 20 grams of fat while the newer version has 50 calories and 5 grams of fat. The thickened stock version has an excellent coating ability and the texture can "fool" the mouth. Mixing with a regular or immersion blender not only adds to the body but also thoroughly distributes the oil. Also try as a marinade for vegetables, meats, poultry, and fish.—*Chef Corliss*

Fresh orange, ginger, and black pepper in homemade vinegar on romaine lettuce or iceberg with chicken or shrimp make a neat little taste.—*Chef Corliss*

For an impressive plate design, lay down a bed of lettuce or mixed greens. Next, cut a zucchini in half lengthwise. Using a potato peeler, take one even peel ⅟₁₆-inch thick down the center of the zucchini. Wrap strip around two fingers to create a cylinder. Stand on end and stuff with watercress or red oak leaf. This will add the dimensionality that most salads lack.—*Chef Conte*

Peel a carrot. Save outer peelings for your compost pile. Peel the rest of the carrot. Stack peels in piles, then cut into small strips. Fry in oil until crisp. Drain on paper towel. Lightly salt. Sprinkle over a salad for a unique garnish that adds a nice texture and bright flavor.—*Chef Conte*

Make a cone from waxed paper and cut off the point with a sharp knife or scissors. Fill with mayonnaise. Squeeze to make beautiful design on salads with no utensils to wash. Try coloring mayonnaise with food coloring for a new twist.
—*Chef Fulton*

Slice hard-cooked eggs with a knife dipped in warm water to prevent breakage. Drop leftover egg yolks in a pan of boiling and salted water. Use for salads.—*Chef Fulton*

Dress up chicken salad with chopped unpeeled apple, chopped black olives, and walnut meats. Serve in a hollowed-out loaf of French bread. Slice for portions.
—*Chef Fulton*

Wild Duck Salad with Granny Smith Apples

DOMINADOR VALEROS

SUPERVISOR LEAD CHEF, C.C.

Shields Tavern, Colonial Williamsburg, Williamsburg

Make friends with a duck hunter to ensure your supply of in-season wild ducks. Try calling a local Ducks Unlimited chapter to find duck enthusiasts. This organization works diligently for duck conservation and maintaining the balance of ducks in the wild. Their headquarters are at Kingsmill Resort in Williamsburg. The breast meat is used for the salad and the legs and thighs are reserved for another use. All remaining pieces are roasted and made into a wild sauce tempered with cognac to dress the salad greens and sautéed apples.

Complexity ❸❸❸   Yield: 4 servings

DUCK

2 wild ducks (4 pounds each)
1 teaspoon olive oil
¼ cup (2 ounces) white wine vinegar
¼ cup (2 ounces) cognac
2 cups cold water
   salt and white pepper to taste
   dash soy sauce

SALAD

1 Granny Smith apple (5 ounces), peeled and diced
2 stalks celery (5 ounces)
1 tablespoon (½ ounce) vegetable oil
4 ounces Boston lettuce, bite-size pieces
4 ounces romaine lettuce, bite-size pieces

duck
Cut off legs and thighs. Reserve with livers for another dish. Remove breasts and refrigerate until sauce is started. Chop all remaining pieces with skin. Sauté in a large skillet in hot oil for 3 to 4 minutes. Place in a roasting pan. Cook in a 450° oven for 20 minutes until well-colored. Remove from oven and spoon off fat. Use vinegar to deglaze pan. Add cognac and bring to a boil. Immediately add cold water. Transfer duck pieces with juices to a large saucepan. Bring to a

Chef's Notes

• Domestic duck can also be used. Turkey dark meat is also quite adaptable to this recipe.

• The vinegar to deglaze pan should be brought to a rolling boil in the roaster pan over a cook top. This step is vital to assimilate all the tasty bits that would otherwise adhere to the pan.

• For an elegant presentation garnish with deep-fried celery leaves and pan-fried wild mushrooms. Serve with a light Burgundy or Beaujolais wine.

• Roast legs and thighs while roasting the other duck pieces.

boil. Reduce heat. Simmer for 15 minutes. Strain juices and reduce until it is richly colored and thick. Adjust seasonings with salt, pepper, and soy sauce. Set aside. Roast duck breast brushed lightly with oil and seasoned with salt and pepper, breast side up, for 15 minutes at 400°. Remove from oven. Cover loosely with foil. Let rest 10 minutes. Remove skin and bone. Make thin diagonal slices. Hold in duck reduction sauce until time for salad assembly.

salad

In a large nonstick skillet sauté apples and celery in vegetable oil until wilted. Place mound of lettuce on center of 4 plates. Top with apple, celery, and juices. Place one-fourth breast slices with duck reduction on each plate.

Game Salad

MANFRED E. ROEHR
C.E.C., A.A.C.

**Chowning's and Christiana Campbell's Taverns,
Colonial Williamsburg, Williamsburg**

While it is highly unlikely that any duck will be leftover from Manfred's Roast Duckling (page 113) try it with "planned-over" turkey meat and sweet fresh pineapple, grapes, orange slices, and toasted pecans. Better yet, when preparing Roast Duckling make two—the additional effort is minimal relative to the gastronomic payoff.

Chef's Notes
- *This is a good hot summer dish and also quite healthy with the nonfat dressing and yogurt.*
- *As an entrée this is excellent for lunch or a light summer dinner.*
- *Team game salad with a crisp bottle of Riesling and a loaf of Chef Kogelman's Polish rye (page 181).*

Complexity ✪   Yield: 8 servings

 2 pounds cooked turkey, cubed light and dark meat
 1 pound roast duckling, cubed without skin
 1 cup (8 ounces) pineapple, cubed
 ½ cup (2 ounces) celery, finely chopped
 ¾ cup (6 ounces) plain nonfat yogurt
 ½ cup (4 ounces) fat-free French dressing
 2 tablespoons (1 ounce) fresh lemon juice
 ¼ teaspoon Tabasco sauce
    salt and pepper to taste
16 romaine lettuce leaves
 ¼ cup (1 ounce) chopped pecans, toasted
    seedless grapes, garnish
    orange slices, garnish
    spring onions, garnish

Combine turkey, duck, pineapple, and celery in a large bowl. Mix well. In a separate bowl mix yogurt, French dressing, and lemon juice. Add Tabasco, salt, and pepper. Mix well. Pour dressing over meat mixture and toss until just blended. Chill for 2 hours. Just before serving place bed of lettuce on each plate. Toss pecans with meat mixture and place one-eighth on each plate. Garnish with grapes, orange slices, and spring onions.

Roasted Corn Salad

DONALD E. BLEAU

The Butlery, Ltd., Richmond

Chef's Notes

- *Use either yellow or white corn, but make sure that it is fresh. In a matter of hours, the sugars change to starches—and refrigeration does not retard this change very effectively.*

- *The garlic press makes easy work of adding fresh ginger. Try to find a sturdy press (such as the Zygliss model) that comes with the handy plastic cleaning device.*

- *Hot chili oil, 3 to 4 drops, may be substituted for the fresh jalapeño.*

- *A soft brush is helpful for removing silk.*

What a pity that the original Indians never had access to these Asian condiments to enhance their roasted corn. Representing Virginia chefs in "A Taste of Elegance Cook-off," this East-West fusion dish was enthusiastically received. Try it as an accompaniment to grilled fish, chicken, or pork.

Complexity ✪✪   Yield: 4 servings

5 ears fresh corn (2 pounds), husks and silks removed
¼ cup (1½ ounces) chopped red bell pepper
1 fresh hot pepper (jalapeño), seeded, ribs removed, and finely minced
¼ cup minced fresh cilantro
2 tablespoons (1 ounce) peanut oil
4 teaspoons rice wine vinegar (Marokan)
1 walnut-size piece fresh ginger, peeled

In a large pot of lightly salted boiling water, cook corn, covered, for 7 minutes. Remove and plunge into cold water to immediately stop cooking. Roast on grid of gas or charcoal grill turning several times for 6 to 8 minutes or until some of the kernels brown. Let cool. Scrape kernels into a large mixing bowl. Add peppers and cilantro. In a small mixing bowl whisk oil and vinegar. Place ginger in a garlic press and squeeze into bowl. Drizzle dressing over salad and mix thoroughly. Allow flavors to develop for at least 1 hour.

Spaghetti Squash Salad

MICHAEL VOSBURG

EXECUTIVE CHEF

The Salisbury Country Club, Midlothian

Like the glorious golds, reds, and greens of fall foliage, this inventive salad mirrors autumn's hues. Spaghetti squashes are abundant, with other gourds and squashes, this time of year.

Complexity ✪✪   Yield: 6 servings

1 *medium spaghetti squash (3 pounds), cut lengthwise*
1 *large green bell pepper (6 ounces), cleaned, with ribs removed,*
    ¼-inch dice
1 *large red bell pepper (6 ounces), cleaned, with ribs removed,*
    ¼-inch dice
1 *small red onion (3 ounces), peeled and minced*
1 *ripe tomato (4 ounces), seeded and roughly chopped*
5 *fresh basil leaves, chopped*
¼ *cup (2 ounces) virgin olive oil*
1½ *tablespoons (¾ ounce) red wine vinegar*
    freshly ground black pepper and salt to taste
6 *romaine lettuce leaves, garnish*

Cook squash on an oiled cookie sheet, cut side down, in 350° oven for 20 to 30 minutes or until tender. Allow to cool enough to handle. With a large metal spoon remove seeds. Spoon out squash strands into a large mixing bowl. Refrigerate until cold. Add vegetables and basil. Mix oil and vinegar. Pour over ingredients. Toss well. Season with pepper and salt. Arrange on individual salad plates with lettuce garnish.

Chef's Notes
• *Scrape squash out with a fork to create spaghetti-like strands.*
• *Also try serving this as a hot salad or side dish. After stranding the spaghetti squash, lightly sauté all vegetables in the olive oil. Omit vinegar.*

Local Tomatoes and Cucumbers with Herb Vinaigrette

MARCEL DESAULNIERS

CHEF-OWNER, C.E.C., A.A.C.

The Trellis, Williamsburg

Chef's Notes

- *A mandoline is the best piece of equipment for cutting vegetables into long, spaghetti-like strands. Otherwise use a sharp French knife.*

- *After washing watercress, shake dry in a colander or, preferably, spin dry in a lettuce spinner. For crisper greens refrigerate 1 to 2 hours before serving.*

- *Although not recommended, when fresh herbs are simply not available, substitute 1 teaspoon of dried tarragon and ½ teaspoon dried basil.*

- *If tomatoes are not at their peak, prepare additional dressing and marinate the tomato slices in dressing for 1 hour.*

- *The better the quality of olive oil, the better the dressing. Try to find oil that still has a greenish olive tint.*

Fresh ingredients at their peak are essential to this garden-proud salad. Finding the perfect juicy tomato to pair with a young cucumber, not touched by any bitterness, to be accented by the heady fragrance of freshly picked herbs sometimes proves to be easier to write about than to actually locate!

Complexity ✪	Yield: 8 servings

1¼ cups (9 ounces) extra-virgin olive oil
6 tablespoons (3 ounces) red wine vinegar
1 tablespoon chopped fresh tarragon
1½ teaspoons chopped fresh basil
salt and pepper to season
1 large bunch (6 ounces) watercress, stems trimmed, washed, and dried
3 large (2¼ pounds) cucumbers, peeled, cut in half lengthwise, seeded, and cut into ⅛-inch wide full-length strips
8 medium (3½ pounds) vine-ripe local tomatoes, sliced ¼-inch thick (about 40 slices)

In a stainless steel bowl whisk oil, vinegar, tarragon, and basil. Adjust seasoning with salt and pepper. Combine thoroughly. Arrange spray of watercress in a 5-inch long border along edge of chilled 10-inch plates. On opposite side arrange the cucumber strips in a 2½x6-inch semicircle. Overlap 5 tomato slices in the center of each plate with tomatoes slightly covering both the cucumbers and the watercress. Pour dressing over.

Mixed Greens and Citrus Salad with Honey Dijon Vinaigrette

RICHARD IVEY
EXECUTIVE CHEF
**ARAMARK, Campus Dining Services,
Randolph Macon College, Ashland**

As the bees busily make their rounds on the fragrant citrus blossoms, chefs are already anticipating this year's crop of fruits. Combining the match made in warm climates of the honey bees and citrus with crispy winter greens touched with French mustard and other goodies, this salad may cause someone to sweetly call you "Honey."

Complexity ✪✪   **Yield: 6 servings**

MIXED GREENS

18 *outside leaves Belgian endive*
 1 *ounce curly endive*
 4 *ounces spinach*
 5 *ounces romaine or other green lettuce*
 3 *pink grapefruit (3 pounds)*
 3 *oranges (1 pound)*
 ½ *pint alfalfa sprouts*
 6 *chive blossoms, optional*

HONEY DIJON VINAIGRETTE

 ⅓ *cup (4 ounces) honey*
 ⅓ *cup (3 ounces) country-style Dijon mustard*
 ¼ *cup (2 ounces) apple cider vinegar*
 1 *shallot (1 ounce), chopped*
 1 *tablespoon fresh chopped garlic*
 ¼ *cup (2 ounces) walnut or peanut oil*
 1 *pinch coarsely ground pepper*

mixed greens
Clean endive leaves. Set in refrigerator. Chop coarsely curly endive, spinach, and romaine. Rinse under cold water, drain, and refrigerate. Using a sharp paring knife, remove peel and all skin from citrus fruits. To section, cut in-between skins of fruit and remove section.

Chef's Notes
- *To peel citrus fruit: Start with a very sharp knife and cut ends off so that the "meat" is showing. Stand on one end and slice down inside of rind and skins. Be careful to remove all white outside as it is bitter. Continue this process until entire fruit is clean of all skin and pith. Cut sections from peeled fruit in between so that sections are removed individually with no skin. Keep knife parallel to table to aid in even cutting of fruit.*

honey Dijon vinaigrette
Combine honey, mustard, vinegar, shallots, and garlic in stainless
bowl. Whisk together. Slowly whisk in the oil. Add pepper a little at a
time until the desired taste is achieved.

assembly
On a 7-inch glass salad plate place 3 Belgian endive leaves in a fan
position coming from center of plate with tips of leaves on top edge.
Place greens on base of endive near center of plate leaving tops of
endive exposed. Then place 3 alternating sections of grapefruit and 3
sections of oranges on the bottom of each plate in a fan position.
Place small pinches of sprouts in between Belgian endive on top of
plate. Dress greens with vinaigrette. A chive blossom makes a nice
garnish for the salad.

Spinach Salad with Orange Dill Dressing

GORDON ADAMS

ROUNDS CHEF

Stein Erickson Lodge, Park City, Utah

Salads with lots of "things" in them are guaranteed to create lots of interest. Try this as a light summer entrée to serve two. Use every bit of the oranges except for the bitter white pith—the zest gives sharp punctuation, the segments, bright bursts of flavor, and the juices make the dressing mellow. Peel and prepare segments over a bowl to collect juices and squeeze any juice from membrane pieces cut away from segments.

Complexity ✪   Yield: 4 servings

SALAD

    1 **pound fresh spinach**
    1 **14-ounce can hearts of palm, cut into ½-inch slices**
    6 **strips bacon (6 ounces), cooked and cut into 1-inch pieces**
    2 **hard-cooked eggs, sliced**
    1 **small (3 ounces) red onion, cut into thin rings**
 12 **medium mushrooms (6 ounces), sliced**
    2 **oranges (8 ounces) cut into segments, saving all juices for dressing**

DRESSING

 ⅓ **cup (2½ ounces) vegetable oil**
    2 **teaspoons grated orange peel**
    2 **teaspoons fresh dill (or ½ teaspoon dried)**
    1 **clove garlic, finely minced**
        orange juice reserved

Toss together all salad ingredients in a large salad bowl. Whisk together dressing ingredients in a small bowl. Let sit for 2 hours before using. Toss again with dressing. Compose salads on 4 separate plates. Drizzle dressing over salad.

Chef's Notes

- *To make perfect hard-cooked eggs: Place eggs in 2-quart pan. Cover with water. Bring to a boil. Cover. Turn off heat and let sit for 16 minutes. Pour off hot water and cover with cool water. Eggs that are overcooked will have greenish ring around yoke. Eggs that are several days old will peel more easily than freshly laid eggs.*
- *Hearts of palm are taken from the inside of tender shoots.*
- *Spinach may be thoroughly cleaned by filling a large sink with water. Add spinach. Swirl around. Lift leaves out and drain or swirl in a lettuce spinner. Grit and sand will fall to the bottom of sink.*
- *Try turkey bacon or reduced-fat pork bacon for a healthier salad.*

Cucumber Salad with Yogurt

MANFRED E. ROEHR
C.E.C., A.A.C.
Chowning's and Christiana Campbell's Taverns, Colonial Williamsburg, Williamsburg

Chef's Notes
- *Unwaxed cucumbers fresh from the garden do not need to be peeled.*
- *Snipping dill in a small glass with kitchen scissors makes fast work of processing.*
- *If fresh dill is unavailable, lamentingly use 2 teaspoons of dried dill.*
- *Try growing dill in your kitchen garden or in pots. It is prolific, returns every year, and so delicious when absolutely fresh.*
- *Use nonfat yogurt to make this a nice diet dish.*

Nothing could be as cool and refreshing as this salad. Made ahead, it is easy to team with grilled poultry or meats for a summer barbecue. Letting the cucumbers sit for 1 hour before mixing with other ingredients draws off any bitter tastes and a bit of moisture.

Complexity ✪	Yield: 6 to 8 servings

3 large cucumbers (1 pound), peeled and sliced paper thin
1 teaspoon salt
1 medium (4 ounces) onion
2 tablespoons (1 ounce) white vinegar
¼ cup chopped fresh chives
  salt and pepper to taste
1¾ cups (14 ounces) plain yogurt
¼ cup chopped fresh dill

Place cucumbers in a large glass bowl. Sprinkle with salt and toss. Let sit for 1 hour. Drain off all liquid. In a small bowl combine onion, vinegar, chives, salt and pepper, and yogurt. Add to cucumbers and toss. Chill for several hours. Sprinkle with dill before serving.

Health Slaw

DAVID BRUCE CLARKE
CHEF-INSTRUCTOR

J. Sargeant Reynolds Community College, Richmond

Fats are out, but the taste is still here. Corn syrup cleverly provides both body and a touch of sweetness to this slaw. And the vinegar features Virginia's prolific fruit, apples.

Complexity ✪   Yield: 15 servings (3½- to 4-ounce portions)

1 medium (about 2½ pounds) green cabbage
2 medium carrots (8 ounces), scrubbed, not peeled
1 small (3 ounces) onion, peeled
¼ cup (2½ ounces) light corn syrup
1 cup water
½ cup (4 ounces) apple cider vinegar
½ teaspoon salt
1 teaspoon white pepper
   parsley, garnish

Shred cabbage. Rinse in colander. Using a grater on large holes, grate carrots and onion. Combine remaining ingredients and toss with vegetables. Chill well. Garnish with parsley.

Chef's Notes
- *For an attractive presentation, make lettuce cups out of iceberg lettuce leaves to hold slaw while providing elevation.*
- *For color variation, substitute half red cabbage or radicchio.*
- *An optional ingredient is ½ tablespoon peanut oil.*
- *A food processor fitted with a small hole grater makes this a speedy salad. But shredding and grating by hand is a sure way to release tensions.*

Cabbage and Pepper Salad

WILLIAM F. FULTON

C.E.C.

Chester

Chef's Notes
- *Mix red and green cabbages for additional flavor, color, and interest.*
- *More ingredients can be added to this salad over time.*
- *This goes well with poultry, ham, barbecue, or roast beef.*
- *Glass jars make good storage containers.*

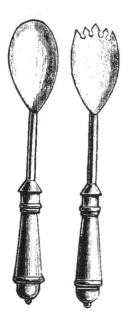

Chef Fulton's salad brings back an old-fashioned Virginia technique of the boiled salad dressing. It is rather clever since the cooking makes it easier to dissolve the sugar while reducing the acidity of the vinegar. And it has the added bonus of being fat-free. If that were not enough, Fulton claims the salad will last up to two weeks refrigerated, becoming crisper and more flavorful as time passes.

Complexity ✪   Yield: 8 servings

1 **pound cabbage, stalk removed and leaves shredded**
1 **red bell pepper (6 ounces), cored, seeded, and diced**
1 **green bell pepper (6 ounces), cored, seeded, and diced**
2 **small (6 ounces) onions, diced**
1 **cup (8 ounces) apple cider vinegar**
1 **cup (7 ounces) sugar**
1 **teaspoon salt**
1 **teaspoon mustard seed**
1 **teaspoon celery seed**
¼ **teaspoon turmeric**

Shred cabbage with hand grater or with food processor blade. Place cabbage, peppers, and onions in a large stainless steel or glass container. In a small saucepan bring all remaining ingredients to a boil. Pour over vegetable mixture. Cover and refrigerate for at least 4 hours before serving.

Through the Garden Potato Salad

MANFRED E. ROEHR
C.E.C., A.A.C.

**Chowning's and Christiana Campbell's Taverns,
Colonial Williamsburg, Williamsburg**

Try this unique—with tomatoes, apples, and pickles—and very healthy garden potato salad. Made with yogurt, it is a lovely change from a mayonnaise dressing.

Complexity ✪   **Yield: 6 to 8 servings**

9 potatoes (3 pounds)
3 tablespoons (1½ ounces) vinegar
5 tablespoons (2½ ounces) oil
1 small (4 ounces) cucumber, peeled, seeded, and finely chopped
2 firm tomatoes (8 ounces), finely chopped
1 medium (4 ounces) onion, diced
1 small (4 ounces) Granny Smith apple, chopped
½ cup (3 ounces) diced dill pickles
1¼ cups (10 ounces) plain yogurt
1 tablespoon (½ ounce) sugar
   salt and pepper to taste
¼ cup chopped fresh parsley, garnish
5 radishes, sliced, for garnish

Wash potatoes. Bring to a boil in a 3-quart pot. Simmer until tender, but not falling apart. Drain, peel, and slice while still warm. In a large mixing bowl combine potatoes, vinegar, and oil. Mix in vegetables, apple, pickles, yogurt, and sugar. Lightly season with salt and pepper. Garnish with fresh parsley and radishes. Chill for 2 hours before serving.

Chef's Notes
- *Instead of oil and vinegar, try ½ cup of a fat-free Italian dressing.*
- *Use a waxy white potato, not mealy baking potatoes. These will hold up with a crisper taste. Also try new red potatoes.*
- *It is not necessary to peel potatoes if they have been well-scrubbed.*
- *Granny Smith apples do brown just as red apples do.*

Seafood Salad Dressing

TED KRISTENSEN

CHEF-OWNER, C.E.C., A.A.C.

The Willows Bed and Breakfast, Gloucester

Chef's Notes
- *For easier preparation, let a food processor do all the chopping and blending.*
- *Mix with well-drained albacore tuna for the ultimate tuna salad.*

Lightly seasoned sour cream and buttermilk perfectly bind fresh seafood for the perfect salads. Try the reduced-calorie sour cream for a healthier dressing. Remember that buttermilk is a low-calorie product in comparison to mayonnaise.

Complexity ✪   **Yield: 4 to 6 servings**

1 *cup (8 ounces) sour cream (reduced-calorie recommended)*
1 *cup (8 ounces) buttermilk*
1 *tablespoon finely diced onions*
2 *cloves garlic, minced*
2 *anchovy fillets, finely chopped*
2 *teaspoons lemon juice*
1 *teaspoon celery salt*
1 *teaspoon Worcestershire sauce*

Place sour cream and buttermilk into a blender. Add onions, garlic, and anchovies. Blend at low speed for 2 minutes. Add remaining ingredients and blend for 2 more minutes.

Chive and Chardonnay Light Dressing

DENNIS CONNELL
EXECUTIVE CHEF
Pittsburgh, Pennsylvania

Dressings zip up salads, but fats in the classic vinaigrette ratio of 3 parts oil to 1 part vinegar are excessive. Chef Connell's healthy dressing, based on his Culinary Institute of America training at forward-looking St. Andrews Cafe, suggests portions of 25 percent acid (lemon juice, wine, vinegar), 25 percent oil (safflower or canola), and 50 percent stock or juice thickened with arrowroot or cornstarch.

Complexity ✪   Yield: 2 cups

1½ teaspoons arrowroot or cornstarch
1 cup (8 ounces) apple juice
¼ cup (2 ounces) wine vinegar
¼ cup (2 ounces) Chardonnay or other dry white wine
½ cup (4 ounces) safflower oil
¼ cup chopped fresh chives

Mix arrowroot with ¼ cup apple juice. Pour arrowroot mixture into ¾ cup apple juice and bring to a boil. Continue to cook, constantly stirring, until mixture thickens, approximately 1 minute. Cool. Mix with remaining ingredients.

Chef's Notes
- *Suggested serving size 1 to 2 tablespoons.*
- *Toss dressing with salad before plating. The flavors are better distributed.*

Raspberry Lime Salad Dressing

TED KRISTENSEN
CHEF-OWNER, C.E.C., A.A.C.
The Willows Bed and Breakfast, Gloucester

Chef's Notes
- *To make raspberry purée, place a scant ⅔ cup fresh (or defrosted and drained) raspberries in a food processor. Pulse until smooth. Force through a sieve. Discard seeds.*
- *For a sweeter dressing add 2 teaspoons sugar. Then try on a citrus and avocado salad.*
- *Lemon juice may be substituted for lime juice.*
- *Store in a glass container refrigerated for up to one week.*

On a bed of mixed salad greens, this light and tangy, refreshing dressing shows its pizzazz. Garnish with a few chopped toasted almond slivers and fresh raspberries.

Complexity ✪   **Yield: 4 2½-ounce servings**

¼ cup (2 ounces) red wine vinegar
½ cup (4 ounces) vegetable oil (canola recommended)
⅛ teaspoon ground oregano
⅛ teaspoon salt
⅛ teaspoon white pepper
⅛ teaspoon minced garlic
½ cup (4 ounces) raspberry purée
  juice of half a lime
⅛ teaspoon dill seed

Mix in order given. Shake. Chill. Pour over salad just before serving.

Citrus Yogurt Dressing

JIM MAKINSON
EXECUTIVE CHEF, C.E.C.
Kingsmill Resort, Williamsburg

Salad dressings do not need to contain fat to be delicious. Bursting with citrus grove flavors, nonfat yogurt forms the base of this light dressing. Its sweet notes match magnificently with bitter greens such as those found in mesclun mixes.

Complexity ✪   Yield: 8 servings

⅓ cup (2½ ounces) orange juice, freshly squeezed
3 tablespoons (1½ ounces) grapefruit juice, freshly squeezed
½ lime, juiced
1½ cups (11 ounces) nonfat yogurt
3 tablespoons prepared whole-grain mustard (pommery)
    orange juice to correct consistency
    salt and pepper to taste

In a small saucepan reduce juices for about 5 minutes, or to a sticky consistency. In another bowl, whisk together yogurt and mustard with reduced juices. Add more orange juice to correct consistency. Add salt and pepper to taste.

Chef's Notes
- *Also use on fruit salads or as a sauce for grilled fish.*
- *The dressing can be stored for several days in the refrigerator.*

Honey Mustard Dressing

ANTHONY CONTE
PASTRY CHEF, C.C.
Country Club of Virginia, Richmond

Using a mixer and slowly drizzling the oil into egg yolks makes a lovely emulsified dressing. Particularly during warmer weather it matches well with salads, especially those containing meats, poultry, or seafood. Serve as a dip for fresh vegetables, such as lightly steamed asparagus and raw strips of crisp red and yellow bell peppers.

- *Use a whip attachment if available. Beaters will also work fine.*
- *Let the emulsion form slowly. Drizzle in a teaspoon at a time, whip for 10 seconds, then add more.*
- *Try brushing 1 teaspoon of this dressing on a fresh fish fillet. Broil on one side. Flip. Brush with another teaspoon and finish cooking. The oil keeps in the moisture and forms a simple, flavorful glaze.*

Complexity ✪✪   Yield: 1½ cups (8 1½-ounce portions)

4   large egg yolks
3   tablespoons (1½ ounces) red wine vinegar
1   tablespoon (½ ounce) Dijon mustard
1   tablespoon (¾ ounce) honey
¾   cup (5½ ounces) salad oil (canola recommended)
    salt and white pepper to taste

In a medium mixer bowl whip egg yolks, vinegar, mustard, and honey. On medium speed slowly drizzle in oil as mixture becomes creamy. Add salt and pepper to taste. Store in the refrigerator in a glass container.

Potatoes Gruyère (page 147), Marinated Mushrooms (page 37), Swiss Ham Croissants (page 36), Baby Green Beans with Grilled Scallops (page 20) [BILL BOXER]

Sweet Potato Soup with Toasted Almonds and Currants (page 44),
She Crab Soup (page 60), Summer Gazpacho with Lump Crabmeat and Creme Fraîche (page 53) [BILL BOXER]

Shrimp with Angel Hair Pasta (page 65), Sautéed Black Sea Bass, Shiitake Mushrooms, Caramelized Vidalia Onions with Summer Vegetables in Cilantro Butter Sauce (page 89), A Virginian's Maryland-Style Crab Cake (page 69), Sautéed Salmon with Orange Mint Sauce (page 78), Grilled Scallops on a Rosemary Stem with Sautéed Shiitake Mushrooms (page 19), Flounder Paupiettes (page 76) [BILL BOXER]

Above: Roast Duckling à la Manfred (page 113), Spaghetti Squash Salad (page 163), Brandied Fruit Stuffing Roulade (page 137), Roasted Breast of Turkey with Prosciutto Ham (page 114) [BILL BOXER]

Right: Refrigerator Biscuits (page 186), Orange Blossom Muffins (page 189), Parmesan Cheese Straws (page 281), Sourdough Hot Cakes (page 286), Pan-Fried Grits with Virginia Country Ham (page 145), Spinach and Bacon Quiche (page 277) [BILL BOXER]

Above: Poached Pears with Stilton Filling on Shortbread with Raspberry Sauce (page 251), Soufflé Grand Marnier (page 265), Zimetsterne, Cinnamon Star Cookies (page 247) [BILL BOXER]

Right: Black and White Truffles (page 273), Grapefruit Champagne Granite (page 269), Truffles (page 272), Chocolate Pâté with Melba Swirled Whipped Cream (page 257) [BILL BOXER]

From Colonial Williamsburg to Historic Richmond

Top left: The reconstructed Governor's Palace at Colonial Williamsburg
[COLONIAL WILLIAMSBURG FOUNDATION]

Top right: Daily life during the American Revolution depicted at the
Yorktown Victory Center's Continental Army camp
[YORKTOWN VICTORY CENTER]

Bottom left: Evelynton Plantation, overlooking the James River, where
the Ruffin family has lived for five generations [EVELYNTON PLANTATION]

Bottom right: Monument Avenue in Richmond
[RICHARD T. NOWITZ, METROPOLITAN RICHMOND VISITORS AND CONVENTION BUREAU]

CHAPTER 7
Bountiful Breads

🍍 *Treat bread* like a baby. Give your yeast warmth (with water) and food (a little sugar). Make sure the water is not too warm or too cold. Give it love, warmth, and patience to grow.—*Chef Bland*

🍍 *Before shaping dough* for bread, cut it with a knife or scissors, never pull dough apart.—*Chef Bland*

🍍 *Melted butter or margarine* is absorbed by bread and is not advisable for spreading.
—*Chef Fulton*

🍍 *Offer a flavored butter* with hot breads. Suggestions are: honey for baking powder biscuits, orange for blueberry muffins, maple for pancakes or waffles, herbs for French bread, and spice for toast.
—*Chef Fulton*

🍍 *Bread flours have* the maximum amount of proteins. Progressively smaller amounts are found in whole wheats, all-purpose flours, then soft wheat flours. In Virginia, traditional biscuits and cakes are made with a low-protein, soft flour sometimes sold as "biscuit" flour.

🍍 *Yeast,* a living fungus, will grow when coming into contact with moisture,

warmth, or sugars. Its growth is actually the excretion of carbon dioxide and alcohol. Dry yeast, if stored in a cool, dry place, has a shelf life of one year.

🍍 *The new rapid-rise* yeasts, not first dissolved, are mixed directly with the dry ingredients. They work at warp speeds so change cooking directions according to the package guidelines.

🍍 *Yeast doughs benefit* from development of the gluten strands in flour—usually 10 to 15 minutes' worth of kneading. The use of a food processor diminishes this time considerably.

🍍 *Salt retards* the action of yeast. Measure carefully.

Shortening makes bread tender. These breads will keep longer than fat-free breads such as French baguettes.

If too much baking soda is used in a quick bread it will have a bitter taste. If too much baking powder is used, the grain is coarse while the color is yellowish. Measure exactly.

Quick breads, muffins, and biscuits will become tough if the gluten strands or the protein in the flour is developed. Keep mixing to a minimum after combining the wet and dry ingredients.

A muffin baked at too low a temperature has poor color and low volume while baking at too high a temperature results in a pronounced peak.

Bernard Clayton's **Complete Book of Breads** is absolutely essential for the library of any serious bread baker. And Carol Field's *The Italian Baker* is indispensable for specialty baked products of that country—particularly focaccia and amaretto cookies.

After baking breads, rolls, and other items, remove from baking pans to prevent continued cooking from carry-over heat.

Cool bread on a rack in a draft-free location. Refrigeration will retard molds while increasing the speed of staling. Store at room temperature well-wrapped. Freeze any excess quantities.

Hazelnut Raisin Bread

MARCEL DESAULNIERS
CHEF-OWNER, C.E.C., A.A.C.
The Trellis Restaurant, Williamsburg

Sunday brunch would be the perfect time for indulging in French toast made with hazelnut raisin bread. Imagine just-warmed strawberries and toasted hazelnuts as the crowning touch.

Complexity ❸❸❸   Yield: 1 loaf, 16 half-inch slices

½ *cup (2½ ounces) hazelnuts*
3 *cups (12 ounces) all-purpose flour*
½ *cup (3 ounces) raisins*
2 *tablespoons firmly packed light brown sugar*
2 *teaspoons salt*
½ *teaspoon ground cinnamon*
2 *teaspoons sugar*
½ *cup warm water (110°)*
2 *tablespoons (about 2 ¼-ounce packages) active dry yeast*
2 *large eggs*
5 *tablespoons (2½ ounces) unsalted butter, softened*
¼ *cup (1 ounce) all-purpose flour, for kneading*

Chef's Notes
- *The kneading process develops the glutens (proteins) by stretching the dough so it will be smooth and well-developed. Use the heel of the hand to knead dough.*
- *Be cautious not to add too much additional flour while kneading or the dough may toughen. The suggested amount of flour is sufficient.*

Toast the hazelnuts on a baking sheet in a preheated 325° oven for 20 to 25 minutes. Remove from the oven and immediately cover with a damp kitchen towel. Invert another baking sheet over the top. (This creates steam that will make the nuts easier to skin). After 5 minutes, remove the skins from the nuts by placing small quantities inside a folded dry kitchen towel and rubbing vigorously. Lightly crush the skinned nuts with the bottom of a sauté pan.

Combine the crushed hazelnuts, 3 cups flour, raisins, brown sugar, salt, and cinnamon. Cover with plastic wrap and keep at room temperature. In the bowl of an electric mixer, dissolve the sugar in warm water. Add yeast and stir gently to dissolve. Allow the mixture to stand and foam for 2 to 3 minutes. Add hazelnuts and flour mixture to the dissolved sugar and yeast. Combine on low speed of mixer fitted with a dough hook for 1 minute. Lightly whisk the eggs and combine with the ingredients in mixing bowl, then mix ingredients on medium speed until dough forms a ball, about 3 minutes.

Adjust speed to low. Add 4 tablespoons of softened butter, one at a time, and mix for 2 additional minutes. Transfer dough to a floured work surface. Knead by hand for 5 minutes until smooth. Use ¼ cup flour as necessary to prevent dough from becoming tacky.

Coat a stainless steel bowl with 1½ teaspoons of butter. Place kneaded dough in bowl, wiping the bowl with the dough. Turn dough over so that buttered portion of dough is facing up. Cover with a towel. Rise in warm location (70° to 80°) until dough has doubled in volume, about 2 hours. Punch down to original size. Form into a loaf. Place in loaf pan coated with 1½ teaspoons butter. Cover with towel. Allow to rise in a warm location until it reaches the top of the pan, about 30 minutes. Bake in 325° oven for 50 to 60 minutes. Cool in pan for 15 minutes. Remove from pan. Allow to cool to room temperature before slicing.

Polish Rye Bread

JOHN KOGELMAN
HEAD BAKER, C.M.B., C.E.P.C.
The Boca Raton Resort and Club, Florida

This is one of those marvelously flavorful, European-style breads that can stand up to even the grandest of fillings. Close your eyes while baking for an inexpensive sensory trip to the old country. Play a little polka music during the kneading phase.

Complexity ✪✪   Yield: 2 loaves

2½ teaspoons (1 ¼-ounce package) active dry yeast
1 cup warm water (100° to 115°)
1⅔ cups (6½ ounces) medium rye flour
½ teaspoon liquid malt or firmly packed brown sugar
3⅔ cups (18 ounces) bread flour
1 tablespoon (½ ounce) butter
1 tablespoon (¾ ounce) dark molasses
¼ medium (1 ounce) red onion, fine dice
2 tablespoons caraway seeds
1 cup cool water
½ teaspoon salt
coarse yellow cornmeal

Chef's Notes
- *Try the rapid-rise yeast and simply add with flour and water.*
- *To create steam place a pan with ¼-inch water on the oven floor 30 minutes into the last proof. Only open oven door once to put loaves in. An alternative is to throw in several handfuls of ice cubes when placing bread in oven.*
- *Enjoy with lots of butter.*
- *Even though this bread has no preservatives, it will keep at room temperature for several days if tightly wrapped.*

In a large bowl (about 3-quart) mix yeast in warm water and let stand for 5 minutes. Add rye flour and malt to yeast mixture and mix. Cover bowl and let rest for 50 minutes. Add bread flour, butter, molasses, onion, caraway seeds, and cool water until slightly damp. Knead until smooth for 5 to 7 minutes by machine or 10 to 12 minutes by hand. Add salt and mix for 2 more minutes. Divide dough in half and roll into two balls. Cover and let rest for 45 minutes. Punch down dough and reroll into balls. Let rest 20 minutes. Punch again and roll into balls, tightly. Place each ball on baking pan sprinkled with cornmeal on the bottom. Cover and proof until size increases by a third, about 1 to 1½ hours. Bake in a preheated 375° oven with some steam (see Chef's Notes) for 30 to 40 minutes or until a dark golden brown. Cool for 20 minutes.

French Bread

W. KEITH PEARCE
FOOD BROKER
Florida

Chef's Notes
- *Add ice cubes to the oven when first starting to bake to create a crisper crust.*
- *Spray large baking sheet with nonstick spray and roll and form loaf right on sheet.*
- *Bread is cooked at an internal temperature of 190° to 200°. Read with an instant thermometer.*
- *Substitute up to half the flour with stone-ground whole wheat for variety.*

Long thin loaves of no-fat-added breads add quality substance to any meal. The smell and taste are so reminiscent of France that you might be tempted to don a beret and ride a bicycle while carrying a freshly baked loaf. And while on the bicycle why not stop for a picnic if you've brought along a hearty chunk of cheese? Bon appétit.

Complexity ✪✪✪   Yield: 2 loaves

1 **tablespoon (1 ¼-ounce package) active dry yeast**
⅓ **cup warm water (110°)**
¼ **teaspoon sugar**
1 **tablespoon rye flour**
2 **teaspoons salt**
3½ **cups (17½ ounces) bread flour**
1 **cup water or less**

In a large mixing bowl sprinkle yeast on ⅓ cup warm water. Stir in sugar and rye flour. Allow to rest for 5 minutes. Whisk in salt, then bread flour. With dough hook blend ingredients on low speed. Add up to 1 cup water and beat until dough forms into a ball and becomes elastic. Put dough in lightly greased bowl. Lay damp towel over bowl. Allow to double in size in a warm place. Knock down dough and divide into two equal pieces. Roll into 14-inch long loaves. Make three long diagonal slashes on top. Permit to double in size. Bake at 400° for 20 minutes until golden brown.

Sourdough Bread

U.S. ARMY CULINARY OLYMPIC TEAM

Fort Lee

For the New American Lamb Burger (page 130), the gold-medal sandwich in the world's Culinary Olympics in Frankfurt, the chefs created this secret oval bun. Make the starter of flour, water, and sugar several days in advance to give it a chance to ferment and develop a personality of its own.

Complexity ✪✪✪   Yield: 1½ dozen buns

STARTER

1 cup (4 ounces) all-purpose flour
1 cup water
1 tablespoon sugar

BREAD

1 tablespoon (1 ¼-ounce package) active dry yeast
1½ cups warm water (110°)
1 cup starter
6 cups (24 ounces) all-purpose flour
1½ teaspoons salt
¾ teaspoon baking soda
½ cup (2 ounces) all-purpose flour

starter
Mix sourdough starter ingredients. Cover. Let stand in warm place for 2 to 3 days to ferment.

bread
In a large mixing bowl dissolve yeast in water. Stir in 1 cup starter, 6 cups of flour and salt. Stir for 3 minutes until well incorporated. Cover. Place in a warm location and proof for 2 hours. Mix soda with ½ cup flour. Turn dough onto large pastry board or work surface covered with soda/flour mix. Knead until flour is incorporated and dough is smooth. Make 18 oval buns. Place on baking trays. Let rise for 1 hour or until doubled in size. Brush with water. Using a sharp knife, slash top diagonally. Bake in a 400° oven for 30 to 40 minutes.

Chef's Notes
• *Try substituting up to half stone-ground whole-wheat flour for variety.*
• *Place a pan of hot water on the bottom shelf of oven to increase humidity and improve quality of the sourdough crust.*
• *Bread is finished cooking when its internal temperature reaches 190° to 200°.*

English Muffin Bread

GORDON ADAMS
ROUNDS CHEF
Stein Erickson Lodge, Park City, Utah

With only one rise of 45 minutes and absolutely no kneading, the airy bread takes little effort. Let fresh butter drip all over its nooks and crannies while warm. It will become a favorite.

Complexity ✪✪   Yield: 2 loaves

6 *cups (24 ounces) all-purpose flour*
2 *tablespoons (2 ¼-ounce packages) active dry yeast*
1 *tablespoon sugar*
2 *teaspoons salt*
¼ *teaspoon baking soda*
2 *cups (16 ounces) milk*
½ *cup water*
cornmeal

In a large mixing bowl combine 3 cups flour, yeast, sugar, salt, and soda. Heat milk and water until warm (about 115°). Stir liquid into dry ingredients. Beat well. Stir in remaining 3 cups of flour to make a stiff batter. Spoon into two 8½x4½-inch loaf pans that have been greased and sprinkled with cornmeal. Cover. Let rise in a warm place for 45 minutes. Bake at 400° for 25 minutes.

Chef's Notes
• *Use any leftovers for an unusual French bread.*
• *For an even faster loaf of bread use the new rapid-rise yeast. Mix the yeast in with dry ingredients, then add liquid ingredients. Follow package instructions for the abbreviated rise.*

Buttermilk Dinner Rolls

KAREN SHERWOOD
CHEF-OWNER
Sherwood Consulting, Richmond

Chef Sherwood's many loyal clients always request these delicious soft rolls. She recommends that the rolls not be frozen after baking. If desired, the rolls may be formed after the first rise, then frozen. The day of use, let dough complete the final rise, then bake and serve.

Complexity ✪✪   Yield: 4 dozen rolls

2 *cups (16 ounces) buttermilk, warm (110°)*
3 *tablespoons (1 ounce) active dry yeast*
1 *tablespoon sugar*
8 *cups (2½ pounds) bread flour*
½ *cup (3½ ounces) sugar*
1 *tablespoon salt*
2 *eggs*
½ *cup (4 ounces) butter, melted and cooled*
1 *tablespoon (½ ounce) vegetable oil*
1 *egg, beaten, plus 1 tablespoon water for glaze*
   poppy or sesame seeds, optional for topping

Place warmed buttermilk in 1-quart bowl. Whisk in yeast and sugar. Permit to sit for about 10 minutes while the yeast begins to activate. In a 5 quart mixing bowl mix bread flour, sugar, and salt. Stir in proofed yeast mixture. Stir in eggs and butter. Knead dough until smooth and elastic. Coat large bowl with oil. Place dough in bowl and let rise in a warm place for about 1½ hours or until double in volume.

On a lightly floured dough board form 1-ounce round rolls. Place on a greased baking sheet about 3 inches apart and permit to go through second rise, about 1 hour. Brush with egg glaze. Sprinkle with optional poppy or sesame seeds, if desired.

Bake at 350° for 25 minutes or until the tops are golden brown. Cool on a rack.

Chef's Notes
- *Kneading time is about 8 minutes using a dough hook or 12 minutes by hand. Extra water or flour may be added at this time if needed.*
- *An oven turned off with only the electric light bulb on is the perfect rising environment.*
- *The second rise is completed when a gentle press by the finger into the dough stays indented.*
- *The eggs and butter cut the gluten strands making the bread soft. For perfect results, weigh ingredients.*
- *After portioning 1-ounce dough pieces, roll into a 6- to 8-inch "sausage." Form a figure eight or a simple knot.*
- *Baking is easier if sheet pans are lined with parchment paper.*
- *For a richer, sweeter roll, substitute heavy cream for the buttermilk.*

Refrigerator Biscuits

WILLIAM F. FULTON
C.E.C.
Chester

Biscuits, a cornerstone of the Virginia tradition, make any meal "southern." Keep the dough tightly wrapped in the refrigerator for up to ten days for freshly baked biscuits. These are the perfect foil for the salty Virginia-cured hams from Surry and Smithfield.

Chef's Notes

- *Store dough in closed container or plastic bag in refrigerator. Do not let dough rise at any time.*
- *The dough is easier to work with if chilled before rolling and cutting. Brush tops with either milk or butter before baking for a richer color. For cheese sticks, roll thinly and sprinkle with Parmesan cheese. Cut in strips and twists.*
- *Do not even answer the telephone during the final minutes of baking at this high a temperature. When they are done, quickly get them out of the oven to prevent any burning.*
- *For smaller batches, halve the recipe.*

Complexity ✪   Yield: about 7 dozen 2-inch biscuits

2½ teaspoons (1 ¼-ounce package) active dry yeast
2 tablespoons lukewarm water
5 cups (20 ounces) all-purpose flour
1 tablespoon baking powder
¼ cup sugar
2 teaspoons salt
1 teaspoon baking soda
1 cup (7 ounces) butter-flavored solid shortening
2 cups (16 ounces) buttermilk, room temperature

Dissolve yeast in warm water. Sift all dry ingredients together. In a large mixing bowl cut shortening into half of dry ingredients. Pieces should be the size of large peas. Add remaining dry ingredients and mix. Pour yeast mixture into buttermilk. Add to bowl mixing well until a soft dough is formed. Roll dough on floured board to ½-inch thick. Cut with floured biscuit cutter. Place on a greased pan. Bake at 450° for about 10 minutes or until golden brown.

Sweet Potato Biscuits

JOHN LONG
ROUNDS CHEF, C.C.

The Williamsburg Inn, Colonial Williamsburg, Williamsburg

Southern biscuits made with creamy, golden sweet potatoes are superb with any meal. These also freeze well.

Complexity ✪   Yield: 2½ dozen 2¼-inch biscuits

2 *medium sweet potatoes (1 pound)*
¾ *cup (5 ounces) sugar*
¾ *teaspoon salt*
⅔ *cup (4½ ounces) solid shortening*
3 *cups (12 ounces) all-purpose flour*
2 *tablespoons baking powder*

Boil potatoes until tender. Peel. Mash. While potatoes are still hot mix in sugar, salt, and shortening with an electric mixer. Let cool. Mix flour and baking powder. Stir in part of the flour mixture. Move dough to a floured bread board. Knead in remaining flour until the mixture is no longer sticky. Roll to ¾-inch thickness. Cut into circles with a biscuit cutter. Bake at 375° for 18 to 20 minutes or until the edges start to brown.

Chef's Notes
- *If mixture is sticky, add up to ½ cup more flour.*
- *Peeling sweet potatoes while still hot is easiest.*
- *Low-protein flours with about 9 grams protein per cup (4 ounces) are the popular "soft" flours used for true "southern" biscuits.*

Muffins, Muffins, and More Muffins

HOSNI ZEID
EXECUTIVE CHEF
Indian Creek Yacht and Country Club, Kilmarnock

Chef's Notes

- *For fruit muffins, use 1 egg and ½ to 1 cup of fresh or frozen fruits such as raspberries, blueberries, or diced peaches, apples, plums, mangoes. One quarter cup of dried apricots, raisins, papaya, pineapple, cherries, blueberries are excellent. For crunch and flavor add 2 tablespoons almonds, cashews, walnuts, hazelnuts, peanuts (this is Virginia), or 1 tablespoon of seeds, such as poppy, chia, sunflower, or sesame.*
- *Up to half the flour may be replaced by other whole grains.*
- *Flavoring extracts to try in the place of vanilla are cherry, lemon, maple, almond, or rum.*
- *Use a ¼ cup measuring cup to scoop batter into tins. Muffins of the same size will bake in the same amount of time.*
- *If batter is insufficient to fill all holes in tin, fill empty ones with water to promote even baking.*
- *Have oven preheated before beginning.*
- *Bake muffins on a single shelf in the center of the oven.*
- *Place frozen fruit in colander, rinse for several minutes under warm water, and drain before adding to the combined dry and wet ingredients.*
- *Add nuts last to keep crisp. If tunnels appear in the final product, or a low volume, or toughness, the batter may have been overmixed.*

Warm muffins, fresh from the oven, are sure to envelop your family and friends with love and fond memories of special times. Preparation time is less than 5 minutes and no special equipment is needed. Chef Zeid shares his basic muffin with many variations. Be creative and develop your own signature muffins with combinations of fruits, nuts, seeds, and flavorings. The number of possible combinations are staggering.

Complexity ✪   Yield: 12 muffins

WET INGREDIENTS

2   eggs
⅔ cup (5 ounces) milk
⅓ cup (2½ ounces) melted butter or shortening
1   teaspoon vanilla extract

DRY INGREDIENTS

⅓ to ½ (2½ to 3½ ounces) cup sugar
2   cups (8 ounces) all-purpose flour
1   tablespoon baking powder
½ teaspoon salt

Mix wet ingredients in a small bowl. Sift all dry ingredients together in a large mixing bowl. Add wet ingredients to dry ones. Quickly mix. A few lumps may remain. Pour into greased muffin tins. Bake at 400° for 15 to 20 minutes or until browned on top. Let sit for 2 minutes for muffins to shrink from the sides of the pan. Run a knife around the edges, if necessary. Serve warm.

Orange Blossom Muffins

JO OLSON

ACCOUNT EXECUTIVE

Atlantic Food Services, Inc., Richmond

After baking these petite muffins redolent of an orange grove in blossom, cut them in half and serve with smoked turkey, smoked duck, country ham, or rare beef tenderloin. The sugar and butter content is much higher than in most muffins, yielding a fine, cakey crumb.

Chef's Notes
- *Use 2 lemons and their zest in the place of orange for lemon blossom muffins.*
- *This very sweet cakelike muffin is particularly delightful for tea.*

Complexity ✪   Yield: 3 dozen muffins

1 cup (7 ounces) sugar
½ cup (4 ounces) butter
2 eggs
1 teaspoon baking soda
1 cup (8 ounces) buttermilk
2 cups (8 ounces) all-purpose flour
½ teaspoon salt
   zest and juice of 1 large (6 ounces) orange

Butter small muffin tins. Using an electric mixer cream sugar and butter until fluffy. Add eggs and beat until fluffy. Add soda to buttermilk. Beat into butter mixture. Sift flour and salt together. Add to the sugar and butter mixture. Stir until blended. Add orange and zest to batter. Spoon into muffin tins. Bake at 400° for about 10 minutes or until golden brown. Let rest in pans 5 minutes, then remove.

Cranberry Lemon Almond Bread

GORDON ADAMS
ROUNDS CHEF
Stein Erickson Lodge, Park City, Utah

When cranberries are fresh, purchase an extra bag for the freezer so this can be enjoyed out of season. The delicate lemon undertones will make the kitchen smell like the blossoms in the springtime.

Chef's Notes
- *Have all ingredients and pans ready before starting. Overmixing will create a tough loaf.*
- *As most cranberries are sold in 12-ounce bags, triple this recipe, freeze one loaf, and give a fresh one to a deserving neighbor.*

Complexity ✪   Yield: 1 large loaf or 5 small loaves

- 2 cups (8 ounces) all-purpose flour
- 1 cup (7 ounces) sugar
- 1½ teaspoons baking powder
- 1 teaspoon salt
- ½ teaspoon baking soda
  juice of 1 lemon (1½ ounces)
  zest of 1 lemon, grated
- 1 teaspoon lemon extract
- ⅔ cup (5 ounces) milk
- 1 egg, well-beaten
- ¼ cup (2 ounces) vegetable oil
- 1 cup (4 ounces) frozen or fresh cranberries, coarsely chopped
- ½ cup (2 ounces) chopped almonds

In a large mixing bowl, mix flour, sugar, baking powder, salt, and soda. Add lemon juice, zest, extract, milk, egg, and vegetable oil to dry ingredients. Mix until well blended. Stir in cranberries and nuts. Pour into a 9x5-inch loaf pan greased only on the bottom. Bake at 350° for 55 to 60 minutes or until cake tester comes out clean. Cool thoroughly before serving.

Spiced Pumpkin Bread

GORDON ADAMS
ROUNDS CHEF
Stein Erickson Lodge, Park City, Utah

This fragrant loaf is spiced with cinnamon, nutmeg, and ginger. Have all ingredients and pan prepared before starting the mixing process. Since the bread is leavened with baking soda it is best to mix lightly and then immediately place into the oven.

Chef's Notes
- *One quart of fresh pumpkin, cooked, drained, and mashed can also be used.*
- *The recipe will make 8 small loaves. Cooking time is approximately 40 minutes.*
- *Pumpkin bread freezes beautifully.*
- *Keep ground spices tightly covered in a dark, cool cabinet. Remember to rotate spices every six months to maintain freshness.*

Complexity ✪   Yield: 3 large loaves or 8 small ones

- 5 cups (20 ounces) all-purpose flour
- 1 tablespoon baking soda
- 1 teaspoon salt
- 1 teaspoon ground cinnamon
- 1 teaspoon ground nutmeg
- 1 teaspoon ground ginger
- 3 cups (21 ounces) sugar
- 1 cup (7½ ounces) vegetable oil
- 1 large can (29 ounces) pumpkin
- 3 eggs

Sift all dry ingredients together in a large mixing bowl. Mix in oil, pumpkin, and eggs. Stir until just mixed. Bake in greased loaf pans at 325° for 50 to 60 minutes or until a toothpick inserted in the center comes out clean.

Savory Zucchini Cheddar Bread

EDWARD DAGGERS

EXECUTIVE CHEF, C.E.C.

Country Club, Memphis, Tennessee

Chef's Notes
- *Use a sharp Cheddar variety for a more pronounced taste.*
- *A small food processor will quickly purée the zucchini.*
- *For variety add 1 tablespoon chopped sun-dried tomatoes and vary the herbs.*

This unique loaf will use up any garden excess and is so easy, you will probably make it often. Toast slices and top with fresh, red tomatoes for an unbelievable sandwich. Make an unusual French-style toast for a savory treat.

Complexity ✪   Yield: 1 loaf

- 2 cups (8 ounces) all-purpose flour
- 2 teaspoons baking powder
- 1½ teaspoons baking soda
- ¾ teaspoon salt
- ⅛ teaspoon cayenne pepper
- ¼ teaspoon dried ground basil
- ½ teaspoon minced onion
- 1 tablespoon (½ ounce) sugar
- ¾ cup (6 ounces) shredded zucchini
- 2 eggs, lightly beaten
- ½ cup (4 ounces) puréed zucchini
- ¼ cup (2 ounces) vegetable oil
- ¼ cup water
- ¾ cup (3 ounces) shredded Cheddar cheese
- 1 tablespoon lemon juice

In a large mixing bowl combine flour, baking powder, baking soda, salt, cayenne, basil, onion, sugar, and shredded zucchini. In another mixing bowl mix eggs, puréed zucchini, oil, water, cheese, and lemon juice. Stir liquid into flour mixture. Continue to stir until just mixed. Pour into a greased loaf pan. Bake at 350° for 45 to 50 minutes. Cool for at least 10 minutes before slicing.

Old-fashioned Spoon Bread

WILLIAM F. FULTON
C.E.C.
Chester

Spoon bread is a Virginia specialty. Traditionalists insist on the more "refined" white cornmeal. But today's trend is toward the more robust yellow cornmeal. The taverns at Colonial Williamsburg serve this with the entrée, using a large spoon to roll a perfect golf ball-size serving. Skill is required to get the perfect mix of the crusty exterior and the creamy moist interior. The answer to "what does spoon bread go with?" is an unqualified "everything."

Complexity ✪   **Yield: 6 servings**

1 cup boiling water
2 cups (9 ounces) white or yellow cornmeal
1½ teaspoons salt
1½ tablespoons (¾ ounce) butter or margarine, melted
2 large eggs
2 teaspoons baking powder
1½ cups (12 ounces) whole milk

Pour boiling water over the cornmeal to make a thick mush consistency. Add the salt and melted butter. Cool. Stir in beaten eggs. Add baking powder and milk. Stir until smooth. Pour into a well-buttered 2-quart casserole dish. Bake at 350° approximately 40 minutes or until golden brown. The center will still be jiggly.

Chef's Notes
- *Adding more eggs and increasing the amount of butter results in a richer product and approaches the level of a soufflé.*
- *A pat of fresh butter melting just on top of the spoon bread is a test of the diner's patience. Will the diner start before the butter finishes melting? That dilemma can be avoided by serving with melted butter.*

Hush Puppies

RICHARD IVEY

EXECUTIVE CHEF

ARAMARK, Campus Dining Services, Randolph Macon College, Ashland

Chef's Notes

- *Slowly mixing in the eggs will help prevent lumps.*
- *Before refrigeration, the mix should be of medium consistency—not runny, not stiff. The 1-hour rest in the refrigerator thickens the mixture up slightly.*
- *Use 2 tablespoons to form 1 tablespoon of mixture. Use one spoon to guide dough off the other and drop into the hot oil. The oil must be maintained at 350° to create the golden crisp exterior and the fragrant moist interior so loved by hush puppy devotees.*
- *Electric woks are excellent for deep-fat frying as the temperature may be easily controlled.*

Chef Ivey, frustrated with frozen hush puppies, spent a day testing and retesting hush puppies until he "finally got it right." The result is a hush puppy that is tastier and lighter than most. At the university they are a hit with a Cajun meal of shrimp etoufée, blackened redfish, corn on the cob, and dirty rice.

Complexity ✪✪	Yield: 4 dozen

2 strips bacon (2 ounces), fine dice
half a medium (2 ounces) onion, fine dice
half a green bell pepper (3 ounces), fine dice
3 cups (14 ounces) stone-ground yellow cornmeal
1 cup (4 ounces) all-purpose flour
1 tablespoon baking powder
3 tablespoons sugar
1 teaspoon salt
3 eggs
1½ cups (12 ounces) milk
1 tablespoon finely chopped parsley
1 cup (6 ounces) cooked corn kernels
   vegetable oil for frying

Sauté bacon, onion, and green pepper in a skillet until limp. In a large mixing bowl combine cornmeal, flour, baking powder, sugar, and salt. Push mixture to outside of bowl to create a hole in the center. While mixing, add eggs slowly. Slowly stir in milk. Stir in bacon mixture, parsley, and corn kernels. Let stand in refrigerator 1 hour. Drop tablespoon-size quantities in 350° oil in a skillet or deep-fat fryer. When golden on one side, turn over with a slotted spoon. When other side is golden, remove with slotted spoon. Drain on paper towels. Serve immediately.

CHAPTER 8
Condiments, Chutneys, and Other Tempters

TASTES ARE as individual as the individual. Some folks love vinegars, others react with a sour pucker and a chagrined toss of the head. While some get excited with marinated and sauced meats, others complain "why can't you just leave it alone?"

Part of the wonderment of eating is trying new tastes and flavors. Often within the same family or group of diners there is a wide range of tastes and preferences. That is one reason why it is so much fun to go to a restaurant, order exactly what you want, and how you want it to be prepared. After all, the chefs are there to please you. If they do not, they will lose both your repeat business and your valuable word-of-mouth pronouncements.

At home condiments and chutneys offer a wide range of variety. Just like a painter selects colors to blend, contrast, and enhance so does the diner select flavors.

Condiments are such a blessing when cooking includes regular meals for children, who might still have a limited eating repertoire ("Ick, those are disgusting") or who fear being gagged by wild mushrooms. It is the food preparer's goal to please everyone. We respect those who always want the same old thing, day after day. For others that might just be boring—then condiments come to the rescue.

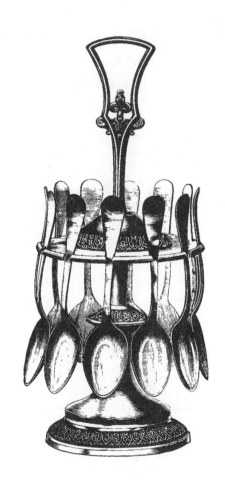

Dried Cherry and Cranberry Fruit Compote

STEPHEN PERKINS

CHEF GARDE MANGER

The Williamsburg Inn, Colonial Williamsburg, Williamsburg

Chef's Notes

- *To make sachet cut a 6-inch square of cheesecloth. Place ingredients inside. Tie with kitchen string.*
- *Increase cayenne pepper to ¾ teaspoon for a hotter result.*
- *Make special gifts by canning this compote.*
- *Unsulphured, preservative-free, dried berries may be obtain by mail order from L'Espirit De Campagne, P.O. Box 3130, Winchester, VA 22604, (703) 955-1014, fax (703) 955-1018.*

The regal deep magenta of this compote along with its dueling tart berries is bewitching. One minute it seems to be an exotic new fruit, then cherries, and next cranberries. Many simply shrug and describe it as luscious.

Complexity ✪   Yield: approximately 4 cups

8 ounces dried cherries
8 ounces dried cranberries
1½ cups (10 ounces) sugar
1 750 ml bottle Riesling
1 apple (3 ounces), peeled, cored, and diced
half an orange, zest and juice
half a lemon, zest and juice
sachet of cinnamon stick and clove
½ teaspoon cayenne pepper
1½ teaspoons arrowroot dissolved in ¼ cup cold water

Combine all ingredients except arrowroot in a 3-quart saucepan. Bring to a boil. Reduce heat and simmer for 45 minutes. Stir in dissolved arrowroot. Cook for 2 more minutes or until thickened. Remove sachet. Cool and store in glass jars, refrigerated, until ready for use.

Bing Cherry Chutney

RAOUL B. HEBERT

EXECUTIVE CHEF

Bull and Bear Club, Richmond

Never will poultry suffer from the stigma of ordinary when this glorious sweet-and-tart chutney is presented. Its spices are exotic with mysterious intrigue, which magnify when presented with grilled duck breast or chicken pâté.

Complexity ✪   **Yield: 6 to 8 servings**

2 16-ounce cans dark bing cherries, pitted
1½ cups (9 ounces) dark raisins
1 cup (8 ounces) firmly packed brown sugar
1 cup (8 ounces) white champagne vinegar
¼ teaspoon cayenne pepper
½ teaspoon ground ginger
½ teaspoon tandoori spice
1 teaspoon mustard powder or seeds
1 large (6 ounces) diced red onion
   zest and juice of 3 oranges (1 pound)

Drain cherries, set aside. Place cherry liquid and all other ingredients in 3-quart saucepan. Bring to a boil. Decrease heat to low. Reduce liquid, stirring occasionally, by two-thirds. Add cherries and remove from heat.

Chef's Notes
• *Vann's tandoori spice, available in specialty markets, is recommended. In an emergency, substitute curry powder.*
• *Chutney may be made up to 3 days in advance.*
• *Do not freeze.*

Strawberry Catsup

ANTHONY CONTE
PASTRY CHEF, C.C.
Country Club of Virginia, Richmond

Chef's Notes
- *Store refrigerated in a glass jar. Allowing flavors to marry for a day improves the catsup.*
- *For simple entertaining, serve cold over cream cheese and pass with crackers.*

When fresh strawberries are abundant make this easy glaze. Just toss the berries in the food processor, add the other ingredients, then reduce slightly on the stove. Serve warm on a roast chicken or a pork loin slice. The red color fires up the plate while the sweet-and-sour style sauce excites the palate.

Complexity ✪✪   Yield: 24 1-ounce servings

2 cups (10 ounces) fresh strawberries, washed and stemmed
¼ cup (2 ounces) water
½ cup (4 ounces) cider vinegar
¾ cup (6 ounces) firmly packed light brown sugar
1 teaspoon ground cinnamon
½ teaspoon salt
½ teaspoon ground ginger
½ teaspoon ground cloves
¼ teaspoon cayenne pepper

Combine all ingredients in food processor. Process until smooth. Place in a medium saucepan. Bring to a boil. Lower heat to a simmer. Reduce by one-third. Serve hot or cold.

Old Virginia Tomato Catsup

LIZ McCANN
C.C.
The Tobacco Warehouse, Richmond

In one of her great-grandmother's books, Chef McCann found a recipe for Old Virginia Catsup (reprinted below). Fascinated by the condiment, she experimented and created this intriguing version. Freshly made tomato catsup will surprise those who have lived only by the bottled versions. This is truly gourmet catsup.

Chef's Notes
- *The catsup requires approximately 1½ cups of vinegar.*
- *A very simplified "country" version can be made without peeling and seeding the tomatoes and processing the cooked ingredients until just still chunky. It will bring "wows" from gourmet catsup lovers.*

Complexity ✪✪   Yield: 2 cups

16 *tomatoes (4 pounds), peeled, seeded, and chopped*
 8 *medium (2 pounds) white onions, chopped*
   salt
 ½ *cup (4 ounces) firmly packed brown sugar*
 ¼ *cup (2 ounces) prepared mustard*
 2 *teaspoons allspice*
 2 *teaspoons whole cloves*
 1 *tablespoon mustard seed*
 2 *teaspoons black pepper*
 2 *teaspoons celery seed*
   white vinegar

Put tomatoes and onions in a large pan and sprinkle with salt. Let stand for 2 to 3 hours. Drain off liquid and discard. Place tomatoes and onions in sauce pot over medium heat. Stir in brown sugar and mustard. Tie spices in sachet bag. Drop in pot. Cover with vinegar. Boil slowly for 1 hour, occasionally stirring. When cooked remove sachet bag and discard. Purée in food processor or blender till smooth. Press through sieve or cheesecloth for extra smooth texture. Store in airtight jars in the refrigerator.

OLD VIRGINIA CATSUP

Take 1 peck of green tomatoes, ½ peck of white onions, 3 ounces of white mustard seed, 1 ounce each of allspice and cloves, half a pint of mixed mustard, an ounce each of black pepper and celery seed and 1 pound of brown sugar. Chop the tomatoes and onions, sprinkle with salt, and let stand 3 hours; drain the water off; put in a preserve kettle with the other ingredients. Cover with vinegar. Set on the fire to boil slowly for 1 hour. The vinegar should be pure and strong. A porcelain-lined kettle is best for cooking catsups. In making catsups, if whole spices tied up in cloth are used while boiling down, the article will be left a clear red. Tomato catsup is many percent improved if served hot.

Tomato and Cilantro Relish

U.S. ARMY CULINARY OLYMPIC TEAM

Fort Lee

Chef's Notes
- *The quality of this relish depends on the tomatoes' ripeness.*
- *To make fast work of this relish, put all ingredients into a mini food processor and give it a couple of pulses.*

This is the gold medal–winning relish accompanying the team's incredible showing in the world's Culinary Olympics in Frankfurt. While they served it with their lamb burger (page 130), try with virtually any sandwich or grilled fish or poultry.

Complexity ☉   **Yield: 6 servings**

1 *medium (5 ounces) tomato, peeled, seeded, 1/4-inch dice*
½ *medium onion (2 ounces), diced*
2 *tablespoons fresh chopped cilantro*
   salt, pepper, and cayenne pepper to taste
1 *tablespoon lemon juice*

Mix all ingredients together in a stainless bowl. Chill.

Corn and Tomato Relish

ANTHONY CONTE

PASTRY CHEF, C.C.

Country Club of Virginia, Richmond

Tomato concassée and corn relish are folded together to develop this garden-fresh medley. Serve with grilled fish on a bed of greens perhaps enhanced with a simple vinaigrette. Chef Conte obtained this recipe while working at the Eastern Standard Restaurant, a trendy little bistro in Charlottesville. The chef, Bob Ginader, a very adventurous young chef, had a knack for simple food with well-married flavors.

Complexity ✪✪   Yield: 8 servings

2 cups (12 ounces) whole kernel corn, canned and drained
1 green bell pepper (6 ounces), fine dice
½ cup (1½ ounces) red cabbage, diced
1 small (3 ounces) yellow onion, fine dice
¾ cup (5 ounces) sugar
2 tablespoons celery seeds
2 tablespoons mustard seed
2 cups (16 ounces) white vinegar
1 teaspoon salt
½ teaspoon ground white pepper
1 cup (8 ounces) tomato concassée (see note)

Combine all ingredients except tomato concassée in a 3-quart pot. Adjust vinegar so that it just covers ingredients. Place on moderate heat and let cook until vinegar is gone. Stir occasionally. Watch the corn relish carefully. Be sure not to scorch ingredients. Cool. Fold tomato concassée into corn relish.

Chef's Notes
- *For concassée, cut stems out of top of 2 large tomatoes. Make a small x on bottom of each tomato with a sharp knife. No need to cut any deeper than the tomato skin. Submerge tomatoes in scalding hot water until skin begins to peel away. Then submerge tomatoes in an ice bath. Once chilled remove from water with a slotted spoon. Remove skin. Split in half horizontally and squeeze seeds out. Dice to the desired size in a uniform fashion.*

Fresh Salsa

MARK KIMMEL
EXECUTIVE CHEF, C.E.C., A.A.C.
The Tobacco Company Restaurant, Richmond

Chef's Notes
- *Make only up to 1 day ahead of use. Freshness is imperative!*
- *A food processor can be used for chopping. Use a controlled pulse action so as not to overprocess ingredients.*
- *Cilantro lovers may wish to use more in the place of parsley.*
- *Heat seekers may double or (call the fire department) triple the jalapeños. Since the major factor in pepper heat is the inner ribs, use with discretion. To avoid a burning sensation in your hands, use gloves when working with peppers.*

The salsa in a jar is as close to the real thing as tomato ketchup is to a tomato. This salsa is fresh, fresh, fresh. What a difference it makes.

Complexity ✪   Yield: about 3 cups

1½ pounds red, ripe tomatoes, diced
 1 medium (4 ounces) red onion, diced
 1 cup green onions, thinly sliced
 2 jalapeño peppers, finely chopped
 2 tablespoons chopped cilantro
 ½ cup chopped parsley
1¼ cups (10 ounces) red wine vinegar
 1 tablespoon salt
 2 teaspoons coarse-ground black pepper

Mix all ingredients. Serve.

Black-eyed Pea Salsa

ANTHONY CONTE

PASTRY CHEF, C.C.

Country Club of Virginia, Richmond

As this soul-food-salsa-of-the-South sits and flavors meld together, it moves from just a pea to a grand culinary sauce. It is wonderful with a generous piece of piping hot corn bread.

Complexity ✪✪　　　　　**Yield: 16 2-ounce servings**

- 2 cups (1 pound) black-eyed peas, dried
- 1 medium (4 ounces) red onion, small dice
- 1 green bell pepper (6 ounces), small dice
- 1 red bell pepper (6 ounces), small dice
- 5 green spring onions, thinly sliced on the bias
- 4 stalks celery (10 ounces), small dice
- 2 teaspoons celery seed
- 1 tablespoon mustard seeds
- 2 tablespoons ground cumin
- 1 tablespoon salt
- ½ teaspoon Tabasco sauce
- 1 cup (7½ ounces) olive oil
- ½ cup (4 ounces) red wine vinegar
- ½ cup (4 ounces) tomato concassée

Chef's Notes
- Use 1 large tomato to prepare the tomato concassée according to the directions in Chef's Notes with Corn and Tomato Relish (page 201).
- Black-eyed peas require no soaking.
- Serve the salsa chilled with tortilla chips.
- Stuff warm salsa inside crisp taco shells and top with shredded lettuce and cheese.
- For a lower-fat version, olive oil can be eliminated.

Wash and pick over the dried peas carefully. Cook in several quarts of water for about 1 hour or until tender. Drain. Place all remaining ingredients except the tomato concassée in a mixing bowl. Fold in peas and tomato concassée (see tip on page 201).

Dal

U.S. ARMY CULINARY OLYMPIC TEAM

Fort Lee

Chef's Notes
- *Double or triple this recipe and freeze leftovers in ice cube trays. Defrost only as much as needed.*
- *Substitute red lentils—the casings have been removed. These will cook in about half the time.*

This is the gold medal–winning sauce accompanying the team's incredible showing in the world's Culinary Olympics in Frankfurt. While they served it as a side with their lamb burger, try it as a side to any lamb dish, Indian-inspired cuisine, or as an unusual sauce for rice or pasta.

Complexity ✪   **Yield: 6 servings**

1	tablespoon (½ ounce) vegetable oil
½	teaspoon whole cumin seeds
1	clove garlic, peeled and finely chopped
1	small (3 ounces) onion, peeled and chopped
½	cup (3½ ounces) dried lentils
1½	cups water
½	teaspoon salt
2	pinches cayenne pepper

Heat oil in 2-quart pan. Fry cumin seeds for 2 to 3 seconds. Add garlic and onion. Fry until brown. Add lentils, water, and salt. Bring to a boil. Simmer for about 1 hour or until lentils are soft. Season with cayenne.

Red Onion Confit

STEPHEN PERKINS

Chef Garde Manger

The Williamsburg Inn, Colonial Williamsburg, Williamsburg

This accompanied the Quail Galantine (page 31) at the 1992 Horizons 2000 benefit dinner. We find its slow-roasted, sweet-and-sour taste astonishingly agreeable with poultry and pork. For a gourmet sandwich slip several spoonfuls on pumpernickel bread with slices of turkey.

Chef's Notes
- *The trick to safely slicing onions is to cut the onion in half and place each half on the cutting board. With a secure surface and fingers tucked out of harm's way, thin slices are efficiently produced.*

Complexity ✪   **Yield: 12 servings**

 5 *medium red onions (20 ounces), peeled and thinly sliced*
 2 *tablespoons (1 ounce) vegetable oil*
2⅓ *cups (1 pound) sugar*
1¾ *cups (14 ounces) red wine*
 ¼ *cup (2 ounces) raspberry vinegar*
 2 *tablespoons (1 ounce) lemon juice*

In a large skillet over a low fire slowly sweat onions in oil until translucent. Add sugar and wine. Reduce until dry. Remove from fire. Stir in vinegar and lemon juice. Serve warm or chilled.

Red Pepper Compote

RAOUL B. HEBERT

EXECUTIVE CHEF

Bull and Bear Club, Richmond

Chef's Notes
- *Try to find the Holland red peppers.*
- *Make a sachet bag out of an 8-inch square of cheesecloth and tie with a 2-inch piece of kitchen string.*
- *Be careful not to reduce liquid too much or the honey will burn, creating a bitter taste.*
- *Make 3 or 4 days in advance. Do not freeze.*

This sweet sauce, as an accompaniment for grilled salmon fillets or freshly steamed asparagus, melts in your mouth. Food pyramid followers will love its fat-free composition.

Complexity ✪   Yield: 4 servings

3 medium (18 ounces) red bell peppers
¼ cup (2 ounces) cider vinegar
½ cup (6 ounces) honey
    sachet bag of 2 tablespoons black peppercorns and 1 bay leaf

Seed peppers, removing inner white membrane. Slice into strips. Combine with vinegar and honey. Place all ingredients in a 3-quart saucepan. Bring to a fast boil. Reduce heat to a simmer occasionally stirring. Cook for 20 minutes or until liquid caramelizes.

Sweet Red Pepper Coulis

JEFF BLAND

EXECUTIVE CHEF

Buckhead Steak House, Richmond

CHEF-INSTRUCTOR

J. Sargeant Reynolds Community College

The red peppers' hours of basking in the sun are tastily apparent in this salubrious sauce. Their natural sweetness, enhanced with a light touch of onion and garlic in chicken broth, is an excellent counterpoint for poached or grilled salmon, grilled prawns, or chicken breasts. Only 1 teaspoon of olive oil is used to create this sun-drenched sauce.

Complexity ✪   Yield: 4 servings

1 small (3 ounces) onion, *fine dice*
1 teaspoon (½ ounce) olive oil
2 large red bell peppers (12 ounces), *fine dice*
2 cloves garlic, crushed
½ cup (4 ounces) defatted chicken stock
salt and pepper to taste

In a medium nonstick skillet, sauté onions until translucent in olive oil. Add peppers. Sauté about 5 minutes or until soft. Add garlic. Sauté 1 more minute. Add chicken stock. Simmer over low heat for 5 minutes. Purée in blender until smooth. Strain if desired. Add salt and pepper to taste.

Chef's Notes
- *To prepare peppers cut off tops and bottoms. Remove core, seeds, and all the white membrane inside.*
- *After puréeing sauce, strain through a fine Chinoise (the strainer that looks like a pointed cap). This will catch any seeds that may have escaped as well as remove the skins of the pepper, which can sour the sauce.*
- *The longer the onions are sautéed, the sweeter the sauce will be due to the caramelization of the sugar.*

Pickled Pumpkin

MANFRED E. ROEHR
C.E.C., A.A.C.

**Chowning's and Christiana Campbell's Taverns,
Colonial Williamsburg, Williamsburg**

Chef's Notes
- *While any pumpkin can be pickled, the pie pumpkin varieties are suggested.*
- *Refrigerated, these pickles will keep for weeks.*

In Germany, the pickled pumpkin is frequently served as either an appetizer or dessert. The sweet and sour taste with pumpkin's unusual texture is delightful. Serve as an exciting new side dish with turkey.

Complexity ✪   Yield: 16 servings

4 *pounds pumpkin*
2 *cups (1 pound) firmly packed brown sugar*
1 *cup (8 ounces) cider vinegar*
½ *teaspoon ground allspice*
1 *teaspoon salt*
8 *whole cloves*
3 *cups water*

Remove skin and seeds from pumpkin and dice into medium-size cubes. In a 4-quart saucepan, combine all remaining ingredients. Bring to a boil and continue until all the sugar is dissolved. Add pumpkin. Simmer until pumpkin is tender. Place pumpkin with liquid in a glass container and refrigerate.

Jack Daniel's Butter

MATT PARTRIDGE
EXECUTIVE CHEF, C.W.C.
Willow Oaks Country Club, Richmond

Chef Partridge grills two pieces of beef tenderloin with a small piece of his herbed, spirited butter on top. As the steak melts the butter it turns into something of a sauce. It works on any steak: Delmonico, New York strip, and sirloin. The bourbon complements the steak's robust flavor. Start with a slightly softened stick of butter. Be extremely careful to cool ingredients before adding to the mixer so the butter does not melt.

Complexity ✪✪   Yield: 8 to 12 servings

one-quarter medium (1 ounce) onion, minced
1 clove garlic, minced
1 tablespoon (½ ounce) butter
½ cup (4 ounces) Jack Daniel's whiskey
½ cup (4 ounces) butter, unsalted
½ teaspoon salt
½ teaspoon pepper
5 sprigs fresh parsley, stems removed and leaves chopped
½ teaspoon sugar

In a medium skillet, sauté onions and garlic in 1 tablespoon butter for about 2 minutes or until browning starts. Cool. In a small saucepan boil Jack Daniel's for 5 minutes or until the alcohol is reduced. Cool. In a medium bowl, whip butter with an electric mixer for 5 minutes. Whip in salt, pepper, parsley, sugar, Jack Daniel's, and sautéed onion mixture. Form into a long tube on a large sheet of plastic wrap. Roll up. Chill. Slice off pieces as needed.

Chef's Notes
- *If using salted butter do not add any additional salt.*
- *If whipped butter is too soft to form roll, refrigerate for 5 minutes.*
- *While any bourbon will do, Jack Daniel's is a favorite in the South.*
- *This flavored butter may be made up to one week in advance.*
- *Do not freeze.*

Pesto

STEPHEN PERKINS
CHEF GARDE MANGER

The Williamsburg Inn, Colonial Williamsburg, Williamsburg

Chef's Notes
- *Add ¼ cup more olive oil for use on pasta.*
- *Toasting the pine nuts brings out their flavor.*
- *Shredded Parmesan is much more flavorful than the powdered, boxed variety.*

This is a fairly dry pesto perfect for stuffing meats and is used in the Chicken Galantine (page 31).

Complexity ✪   Yield: approximately 2 cups

1 bunch fresh basil
½ cup (2 ounces) pine nuts, toasted
½ cup (1½ ounces) shredded Parmesan
4 cloves garlic, peeled
½ cup (4 ounces) olive oil
¼ teaspoon salt
⅛ teaspoon white pepper

Place all ingredients into food processor. Using pulse and scrape action, process until a paste is formed. Refrigerate until ready for use.

Brandied Mustard Dill Sauce

MICHAEL VOSBURG

EXECUTIVE CHEF

The Salisbury Country Club, Midlothian

This is a medium spicy sauce perfect for smoked fish, gravläx, or freshly cooked seafood such as softshell crabs or steamed shrimp. Try it as a basting sauce before broiling or grilling fresh fish fillets.

Complexity ✪   Yield: about 1½ cups

¾ cup (7 ounces) spicy brown mustard
2 tablespoons (1 ounce) Dijon mustard
3 tablespoons (1½ ounces) white wine vinegar
3 tablespoons (1½ ounces) sugar
  pepper to taste
½ cup fresh dill, chopped
1 tablespoons (½ ounce) brandy
½ cup (4 ounces) peanut oil

In a 1-quart mixing bowl combine all ingredients except peanut oil. Slowly whisk in peanut oil until completely incorporated. Chill.

Chef's Notes
• *Gulden's mustard is recommended.*
• *Without the fresh dill, this sauce can be refrigerated for weeks in a tightly covered container. Add fresh herbs prior to serving.*
• *Lower-fat versions can be prepared by reducing the quantity of oil—even completely eliminating it.*

Chinese Brown Sauce for Stir-Frys

RICHARD IVEY

EXECUTIVE CHEF

**ARAMARK, Campus Dining Services,
Randolph Macon College, Ashland**

Chef's Notes

- *If plum sauce is unavailable use a drained 10-ounce can of whole purple plums. Sauce should be strained before adding cornstarch mixture.*
- *Make extra. Friends always ask to borrow a little.*

While Ivey was executive chef at Virginia Military Academy, some of the Chinese cadets wanted to celebrate Chinese New Year. The owner and chef of a Chinese restaurant in town shared his secret sauce with Ivey. Stir-fry meats and vegetables together and add a little of this spicy sauce. Serve with rice and you have an easy dinner. It makes a bolder, more assertive taste statement than soy sauce alone. The sauce will keep up to one month in the refrigerator.

Complexity ✪   **Yield: one quart**

*1 cup (8 ounces) soy sauce
½ cup (4 ounces) oyster sauce
½ cup (4 ounces) plum sauce
½ cup water
2 tablespoons fresh chopped garlic
2 tablespoons fresh chopped ginger
¾ cup (5 ounces) sugar
¾ cup (6 ounces) white wine or sherry
3 tablespoons cornstarch mixed in ¼ cup water*

In a 2-quart saucepan add all ingredients except cornstarch. Bring to a rolling boil. Reduce heat to low. Add cornstarch dissolved in water. Stir constantly for about 2 minutes or until the sauce is a clear brown color. Store in airtight container in the refrigerator.

Creamy Wine and Dill Sauce for Fish or Chicken

DAVID BRUCE CLARKE

CHEF-INSTRUCTOR

J. Sargeant Reynolds Community College, Richmond

Served with poached salmon or grilled chicken breast, this sauce made of a flavor-intense reduction will become a popular sauce in your repertoire. Chef Clarke suggests using reduced-fat mayonnaise and sour cream for maintaining a healthier profile. Also try with smoked salmon or gravad läx.

Complexity ✪   Yield: about 1¼ cups

2 tablespoons fresh dill
2 shallots (2 ounces), finely chopped
¼ cup (2 ounces) white wine vinegar
¼ cup (2 ounces) white wine (Chablis recommended)
1 teaspoon freshly ground white pepper
½ cup (4 ounces) mayonnaise
¾ cup (6 ounces) sour cream
   salt to taste

In a small saucepan combine dill, shallots, wine vinegar, wine, and pepper. Bring to a boil. Reduce heat to a simmer and reduce just until all liquid is gone. Refrigerate covered until completely chilled. Stir in mayonnaise, sour cream, and salt to taste.

Chef's Notes

- *Reduction, the process of cooking ingredients while reducing the quantity of liquid, creates a very flavor-intense mixture. This particular herb reduction is similar to the one used in making bernaise sauce.*
- *Use a nonreacting, heavy-bottomed saucepan, such as stainless steel.*
- *Low-calorie mayonnaise and sour creams are perfectly acceptable for this recipe.*
- *The herb reduction can be stored for up to 2 weeks refrigerated.*
- *The finished sauce can be held for five days.*

Yogurt, Cucumber, and Mint Sauce

U.S. ARMY CULINARY OLYMPIC TEAM

Fort Lee

Chef's Notes

• *The grated cucumber should be permitted to drain in a small mesh strainer for about 15 minutes. A light sprinkle of salt will speed up the process and help prevent a watery sauce.*

This is the gold medal–winning sauce accompanying the team's incredible showing in the world's Culinary Olympics in Frankfurt. While they served it with their lamb burger (page 130), try it as a refreshing summer salad dressing or drizzle over freshly cooked green peas.

Complexity ✪   **Yield: 6 servings**

½ cup (4 ounces) plain yogurt
1 medium (5 ounces) cucumber, peeled, grated, and drained
1 tablespoon fresh chopped mint
¼ teaspoon ground, roasted cumin seed
2 dashes cayenne pepper
    salt and pepper to taste

Mix all ingredients together in a stainless bowl. Chill.

CHAPTER 9
Passionate Pastries

THE PASTRY CHEF SHOPS THE HARDWARE STORE AND OTHER SECRETS

SAY GOOD-BYE to the traditional rolling pin for rolling all doughs except puff pastry. A more effective device for rolling dough is a ½-inch unpainted dowel or the handles sold for sturdy rakes or brooms. Any unwanted paint can be removed with sandpaper.

For dough uniformity use a combination of wooden or metal yardsticks cut in half at the 18-inch mark. Purchase at the hardware store (or fabric store).

Wooden yardsticks are ⅛-inch thick, metal ones 1/16-inch thick.

For pie crust, place one of the 1/16-inch sticks on either side of the dough to be rolled. Roll dough with roller on top of the sticks. The height of the dough will be perfect.

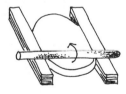

For rolling short dough, sugar cookies, and other rolled cookie dough, place one ⅛-inch stick on either side of the dough.

To roll ¼-inch thick tea biscuits stack 2 wooden sticks on either side of the dough. To roll ½-inch thick scones, breakfast biscuits, and some thicker Christmas cookies—such as Zimetsterne Cinnamon Stars and Brunsli—use stacks of 4 on each side of the dough.—*Chef Marlowe*

OTHER SECRETS

🍍 *While at the* hardware store pick up an inexpensive rubber mallet for pounding meats to any desired thickness and heat resistant screening to use for baking hearth-type rolls and bread.

- *For dusting rolling pins,* pastry boards, and working tables, use a double thickness of cheese cloth or a single thickness of a loose weave fabric about 18 inches square. Place 1 cup flour or confectioners' sugar inside. Draw up ends to make a powder puff. Secure with a rubber band.

- *Also use a powder puff* to dust greased pans, cutters, dough boards, or directly into a pan with butter to make a roux.

- *To clean wooden implements,* scrape off any dough with a pastry scraper and wipe completely with a clean cloth. A putty knife is an inexpensive scraper for rolling dowels. It is not necessary to immerse these in soapy water. Such action causes wood to swell and lose its uniform shape.

- *Purchase paint brushes* in various sizes, ½", 1", 2", and 4" for glazing bread dough with egg, butter, or milk glazes before baking and for royal icings for cookies.

- *Purchase sheets of* heavy plastic to cover counters while working with flours and dough. When finished just shake excess flour into trash and wipe clean with a sponge. These also work beautifully for pounding meats and poultry.

—Chef Marlowe

Torte Japonais Chantilly

OTTO J. BERNET

DIRECTOR OF EUROPEAN SPECIALTIES, C.M.P.C., A.A.C.

Ukrop's Supermarket, Richmond

Ethereal whipped cream between marvelous almond meringues complemented with thin slices of toasted almonds promises an elegant finish to any meal. This conversation-stopping dessert is remarkably rich and light in texture. While the meringues are extremely fragile and crisp, any errors can be hidden with the whipped cream. In the resting stages after filling, the meringues are transformed in texture to the just-chewy stage. Thus, the construction is much more forgiving than it first appears.

Complexity ✪✪✪✪   Yield: 10 to 12 servings

MERINGUE

> 5 egg whites, room temperature
>   pinch salt
> ½ cup (3½ ounces) sugar
> ¼ cup (1 ounce) all-purpose flour
> ⅞ cup (5 ounces) almonds, finely ground with skin

FILLING

> 2 cups (16 ounces) heavy whipping cream
> 1 tablespoon confectioners' sugar
> ½ teaspoon pure vanilla extract

GARNISH

> 1 cup (4 ounces) sliced almonds, toasted

meringue
Cover 3 baking sheets with parchment paper. Draw an 8-inch circle on each. In a large mixing bowl use an electric beater to begin whipping egg whites with salt and 1 tablespoon sugar. Continue to beat until whites are stiff and still shiny. Do not overbeat. In a separate bowl combine the remaining sugar, flour, and almonds. Carefully fold the almond mixture into the egg whites. Using a spatula evenly spread one-third of mixture onto each baking circle. Bake at 325° for 30 to 40 minutes or until light brown and totally dry. Cool. Peel off parchment paper. These will keep in an airtight container for several days if desired.

Chef's Notes
- *It is very important to preheat the oven before starting the meringues. During the preheat stage the broiler unit is activated. The almond slices can be toasted while the meringues are baking.*
- *For economy, whole almonds for the meringues can be purchased in bulk. In food processor grind using a pulsing motion.*
- *A handy template for the meringues is the lid to a large saucepan or an 8-inch cake pan.*

filling
In a cold stainless steel bowl whip cream. Gently fold in sugar and vanilla.

assembly
When layers are cool, spread filling between layers, on top, and on sides. Cover with toasted almonds. Refrigerate for 4 hours, but not overnight. The torte may be frozen and defrosted in the refrigerator for about 6 hours before serving.

Tuxedo Truffle Torte

MARCEL DESAULNIERS
CHEF-OWNER, C.E.C., A.A.C.
The Trellis Restaurant, Williamsburg

This torte, with divine rich chocolate flavor and silky texture, has an effect on the palate that is both lasting and fleeting—a true chocolate dichotomy. The notion of covering the truffle cake with a layer of white chocolate mousse transcends that of flavor synergy. In addition, the mousse serves to mask the dark chocolate with a layer of white that allows no darkness to peek through the subsequent application of white chocolate ganache.

Although the preparation seems daunting due to the four separate recipes, it is actually quite manageable if sufficient time is allowed. To spread the production of this dessert over two days, bake the chocolate truffle cake on day 1. After the cake has cooled to room temperature, cover with plastic wrap and refrigerate until you have made the mousse and ganaches on day 2. For same day preparation of torte, make mousse and ganaches while cake is baking.

Complexity ✪✪✪✪✪   **Yield: 16 serious chocoholic or 32 chocolate devotee servings**

CHOCOLATE TRUFFLE CAKE

1½ pounds semisweet chocolate, broken into 1/2-ounce pieces
¾ pound unsalted butter, cut into 12 pieces
4 large eggs
4 large egg yolks

WHITE CHOCOLATE MOUSSE

6 ounces white chocolate, broken into ½-ounce pieces
2 tablespoons water
1 tablespoon (½ ounce) dark rum
½ cup (4 ounces) heavy cream

WHITE CHOCOLATE GANACHE

¾ cup (6 ounces) heavy cream
1 tablespoon (½ ounce) unsalted butter
12 ounces white chocolate, broken into ½-ounce pieces

Chef's Notes

- *If the heat of the cream for ganaches is not sufficient to melt chocolate or if chocolate does not completely dissolve while stirring, place ganache bowl over very hot, not simmering or boiling, water or put in microwave for 30 seconds on high. Stir to a smooth texture.*

- *When removing cake from springform pan, remove sides only. Allow cake to remain on bottom of springform pan until it has been sliced and served. Alternatively, line the bottom of the pan with parchment.*

- *Depending upon the temperature of your kitchen, it may be necessary to refrigerate the ganache used for the stars if it becomes too soft during the decoration of the torte. Conversely, if the ganache is too firm to pipe from the pastry bag, it may be necessary to warm it by massaging the pastry bag with your hands for a few moments.*

- *It is essential that the torte be refrigerated as directed during the different phases of assembly. Failure to do so will result in a melding of the components and a marked dissipation of the dignified, dressed up look of the torte. (Now you are on to our name for this dessert.)*

DARK CHOCOLATE GANACHE

¾ cup (6 ounces) heavy cream
1 tablespoon (½ ounce) unsalted butter
9 ounces semisweet chocolate, broken into ½-ounce pieces

chocolate truffle cake
In the bottom of a double-boiler heat 1 inch of water over medium-high heat. Place semisweet chocolate and butter in top. Cover. Heat for 15 minutes. Remove from heat. Stir until smooth. Transfer chocolate to large stainless steel bowl using rubber spatula to scrape sides. Keep at room temperature until needed.

In the bottom of a double-boiler heat 1 inch of water over medium-high heat. Place eggs and yolks in top. Whisk for 4 to 6 minutes or until they reach a temperature of 110°. Transfer to large bowl of an electric mixer fitted with a balloon whip (or regular beaters). Whisk on high for about 6 to 7 minutes or until eggs become light and pale in color. By hand fold a third of the eggs into melted chocolate. Add remaining eggs and fold together gently but thoroughly. Pour batter into a 9x3-inch springform pan lightly coated with melted butter. Place on a baking sheet in center of a preheated 300° oven. Bake for 75 to 80 minutes or until the cake interior reaches 170°. (Use an instant-read thermometer). Cool in pan for 45 minutes. Release from the springform pan and remove only the sides. Refrigerate for at least 1 hour.

white chocolate mousse
White chocolate mousse may be prepared while cake is baking. In the bottom of a double-boiler heat 1 inch of water over low heat. When water is hot, but not yet simmering, place white chocolate, water, and rum in top half. Constantly stir with a rubber spatula for about 6 to 7 minutes or until the chocolate is melted and the mixture is smooth. Remove from heat and set aside. Place cream in a well-chilled bowl. With an electric mixer beat for 80 to 95 seconds or until stiff. Using hand whisk, whisk a third of the whipped cream into melted white chocolate. Scrape bowl with rubber spatula and continue to whisk until smooth and thoroughly combined. Add the whisked cream and chocolate to remaining whipped cream using a rubber spatula to fold until smooth. Transfer to a stainless steel bowl. Tightly cover with plastic wrap. Refrigerate for at least 45 minutes.

white chocolate ganache
For the white chocolate ganache, heat cream and butter in a 2½-quart saucepan over medium high heat. Bring to a boil. Place white chocolate in a stainless bowl. Pour boiling cream over chocolate and allow to stand for 5 minutes. Stir until smooth. Refrigerate for 30 minutes.

dark chocolate ganache
For the dark chocolate ganache, heat cream and butter in 2½-quart saucepan over medium high heat. Bring to a boil. Place semisweet chocolate in stainless steel bowl. Pour boiling cream over chocolate

and allow to stand for 5 minutes. Stir until smooth. Refrigerate for at least 30 minutes.

assembly

To assemble, spread the white chocolate mousse evenly over the top and sides of the cake. Place in the freezer for 1 hour. Reserve and refrigerate ¾ cup white chocolate ganache. Pour remainder over top. Use a cake spatula to evenly spread ganache over top and sides. Refrigerate for 30 minutes. Fill a pastry bag fitted with a medium star tip with the reserved white chocolate ganache.

Fill another pastry bag fitted with a medium star tip with the dark chocolate ganache. Score the cake top with 2 parallel lines 1 inch from edge of one side of the cake and 1½ inches apart. Score a third line, intersecting the previous two across the bottom third of the cake. Pipe white chocolate stars (each star touching the next) along the scored lines. Refrigerate the cake for 10 minutes. Pipe dark chocolate stars over the remaining areas on the top of the cake. Refrigerate for at least 1 hour before cutting and serving.

To serve, cut with a serrated slicer heated under hot running water before making each slice. Allow the slices to come to room temperature for 15 to 20 minutes before serving.

Black Beast with Chocolate Ganache Glaze

GORDON ADAMS

ROUNDS CHEF

Stein Erickson Lodge, Park City, Utah

This fudgy single-layer cake is flourless and densely rich with chocolate. More chocolate, in the form of a creamy ganache, should be adequate to assuage the "bete noir," the black beast in the most devoted chocolate lover.

Complexity ✪✪   **Yield: 12 servings**

Chef's Notes
- *Each square of baking chocolate is equivalent to 1 ounce.*
- *To scald cream, heat to just below the boiling point.*
- *When adding sugar to eggs, beating incorporates air, resulting in a lighter cake.*

CAKE

½ cup water
1¼ cups (9 ounces) sugar
7 ounces unsweetened chocolate, chopped
1 cup (8 ounces) unsalted butter, room temperature
5 eggs

CHOCOLATE GANACHE GLAZE

¾ cup (6 ounces) heavy cream
8 ounces semisweet chocolate, chopped

cake
Line 9-inch cake pan with parchment paper. Butter paper. In a small saucepan whisk water with ½ cup sugar. Boil rapidly for 2 minutes. Remove pan from heat and add chopped chocolate. Stir until chocolate is totally melted. Add small pieces of butter, stirring until each is incorporated. In a large bowl beat eggs with electric mixer until foamy. Slowly beat in remaining sugar until mixture is quite pale. Mix in chocolate mixture. Do not overmix. Pour into prepared pan. Place in a water bath in center of oven. Bake 1 hour at 350° or until cake tester comes out clean. Cool in pan for 10 minutes before turning out on wire rack.

chocolate ganache glaze
In a small pan, scald cream. Remove from heat. Add chocolate. Stir until melted. Cool until slightly thickened. Pour glaze over cake. Smooth top and sides with metal spatula.

Pignoli Cake

DAVID BRUCE CLARKE

CHEF-INSTRUCTOR

J. Sargeant Reynolds Community College, Richmond

Rich and elegant, this cake relies on only eggs for rising. There is no bitter taste that comes from the chemicals in baking powder or sodas. Cut into small wedges and garnish with the ripest fruits of the season such as berries, peaches, or citrus slices.

Complexity ❀❀❀ Yield: 8 to 10 servings

½ cup (4 ounces) butter
¾ cup (3½ ounces) pine nuts (pignoli)
6 eggs
1 cup (7 ounces) sugar
2 cups (9 ounces) ground almonds
¾ cup (3 ounces) all-purpose flour
  confectioners' sugar for sprinkling

Melt 3 tablespoons butter in a small skillet. Sauté pine nuts gently stirring until lightly browned. Reserve for later use. Heat remaining butter over double boiler until just soft enough to pour. Using an electric mixer on medium speed beat eggs, sugar, and almonds for about 7 minutes or until thick and ribbonlike. Fold in flour. Fold in butter. Pour into a 9-inch round baking pan. Sprinkle with pine nuts. Bake at 350° for 25 to 30 minutes or until sides shrink from pan and top springs back when pressed with a finger tip. Let cool in pan for 10 minutes. Run knife around edges and unmold onto a cooling rack right side up with nuts on top. Before serving sprinkle with confectioners' sugar.

Chef's Notes
- *Butter cake pan and line with parchment paper on bottom. Dust sides with a small amount of flour. Knock off excess.*
- *When heating butter, any water bath may be used. Do not clarify.*
- *Beating eggs incorporates air, which acts as the leavening for this cake. Fold other ingredients in carefully so as not to "deflate" the eggs.*
- *For a lovely pattern place a paper doily on top of cake. Sprinkle with confectioners' sugar, then remove doily.*

Italian Rum Cake

ROLF HERION

RETIRED HEAD PASTRY CHEF, C.M.P.C., A.A.C.

**The Colonial Williamsburg Commissary,
Williamsburg**

Chef's Notes
- *In place of a vanilla bean, add 1 teaspoon vanilla extract to pastry cream after it has come to room temperature.*
- *Save top of sponge cake for the top layer of the cake.*
- *Use a large bread knife for slicing the cake into layers. Keep blade parallel to counter for even slicing. Do not worry if layers are not perfectly even—an extra bit of pastry cream can compensate.*
- *Toast almonds for 8 to 10 minutes at 350°. Watch carefully to prevent overbrowning.*
- *To keep serving plate tidy, place cut pieces of waxed paper under edge of bottom layer of cake. After assembly remove.*

Make this when in a creative mood—the assembly is almost as enjoyable as is the eating. First a single layer of sponge cake is sliced horizontally making three layers. The first layer is spread with vanilla pastry cream and sprinkled with chocolate pieces. The next layer, after a thorough rum syrup soaking, is covered with more cream and chocolate. The top layer is soaked only on the bottom side so that the top can be dusted with confectioners' sugar. More pastry cream covers the cake's sides, which are then temptingly sprinkled with toasted almond slivers. The cake and pastry cream can be made ahead of time and assembled the day of serving.

Complexity ❂❂❂❂   **Yield: 12 to 16 servings**

SPONGE CAKE

5 egg yolks
1 cup (7 ounces) sugar
2 tablespoons boiling water
1 teaspoon rum extract
1 cup (4 ounces) cake flour
2 teaspoons baking powder
5 egg whites, beaten until stiff but not dry

RUM SYRUP

½ cup water
½ cup (3½ ounces) sugar
½ cup (4 ounces) dark rum

VANILLA PASTRY CREAM

5 egg yolks
½ cup (3½ ounces) sugar
⅓ cup (1½ ounces) cornstarch
2 cups milk
1 vanilla bean

ASSEMBLY GARNISHES

---

3 squares (3 ounces) bittersweet chocolate, cut into small pieces
½ cup (2 ounces) almond slivers, toasted
2 tablespoons confectioners' sugar

---

sponge cake

In a large mixing bowl, beat egg yolks and sugar until light. Beat in hot water. Let cool. Beat in rum flavoring. Sift flour with baking powder. Stir into yolk mixture. Fold egg whites into batter. Place in an ungreased 9-inch cake pan. Bake at 350° for 45 to 50 minutes or until an inserted toothpick comes out clean. Let cool before slicing horizontally into 3 layers.

rum syrup

In a small saucepan, boil water and sugar for 4 minutes. Cool. Stir in rum.

vanilla pastry cream

In a small mixing bowl whisk egg yolks and sugar until well blended. Dissolve cornstarch into ½ cup milk. Whisk into the egg mixture until smooth. In a medium saucepan boil remaining milk with vanilla bean. Slowly whisk in the egg mixture blending well. Bring to a boil. Continue boiling for 2 minutes stirring constantly. Remove vanilla bean. Pour into a bowl and refrigerate until needed.

assembly

Place 1 layer of cake on serving platter. Spread with ¼-inch layer of pastry cream. Sprinkle with half the chocolate pieces. Add second layer. Soak well with rum syrup. Spread with ¼-inch layer of pastry cream and sprinkle with remaining chocolate. On waxed paper, place the last layer of cake with top down. Soak only bottom side of cake. Turn over and place on top of last layer of chocolate. Use remaining pastry cream on sides of cake. Sprinkle sides with almonds. Dust top of cake with confectioners' sugar. Use kitchen knife to make a design. Refrigerate for at least 2 hours before serving.

Frozen Yogurt Génoise with Frangelico

W. KEITH PEARCE

FOOD BROKER

Florida

Chef's Notes
- *Using a hand-held electric beater makes the génoise "easy as cake," but whisking is good for upper body development.*
- *The temperature of the génoise mixture must not exceed just a bit hotter than the hottest tap water, so caution is urged. Remove mixing bowl from heat, if necessary, and continue whisking. Return to heat when in appropriate temperature range.*
- *Lining each cake pan with parchment paper guarantees easy cake removal as does the use of three greased or lined springform pans.*
- *Dip a sturdy serrated knife, such as a bread knife, in hot water between cutting each slice.*
- *Cut this recipe into one-third for serving 8.*

"This is the best cake I have ever eaten. Will you make it for me again?" asked one young man at our tasting. Of French origin, the génoise—which majestically rises with air captured by whipping the egg-and-sugar mixture while it slowly cooks—is truly the queen of cakes. The ground almonds add just the right amount of texture, which holds up royally when frozen. For dinner parties and buffets it can be made ahead, then placed in the refrigerator about 30 minutes prior to service.

Complexity ✪✪✪　　　　　　**Yield: 24 servings**

GÉNOISE

12 eggs
3½ cups (24 ounces) sugar
 2 cups (8 ounces) all-purpose flour
 1 cup (4 ounces) ground almonds

SYRUP

 1 cup (7 ounces) sugar
 1 cup water
 6 tablespoons (3 ounces) Frangelico
1½ tablespoons vanilla extract

FILLING AND TOPPING

½ gallon frozen yogurt, almond or vanilla flavored
½ cup (2 ounces) sliced almonds, toasted

génoise
Preheat oven to 325°. Generously butter or spray with a nonstick spray three 9-inch cake pans. In a large mixing bowl that will fit over a pan of water, mix eggs and sugar. Whisk vigorously over hot water

for about 10 minutes or until doubled in volume. Do not allow the mixture to rise above 120°. Gently fold in flour and almonds. Divide among pans. Bake for 20 to 30 minutes or until toothpick comes out clean and top of cake shows resistance to touch. Cool, wrap in plastic, and refrigerate for 1 hour. Remove from pans.

syrup

In a medium saucepan, bring sugar and water to a boil. Cool for 45 minutes. Mix in Frangelico and vanilla. Remove cake from refrigerator. Drizzle syrup over cakes until absorbed. This may take several minutes.

filling and topping

In the large bowl of an electric mixer, quickly beat frozen yogurt until smooth enough to spread. On cake plate, put in first layer, spread evenly with yogurt. Repeat for second and third layers. Sprinkle top with almonds. Wrap with plastic film and freeze until service.

Apple Nut Cake (I) with Caramel Icing

WILLIAM F. FULTON
C.E.C.
Chester

Chef's Notes
- *This recipe may be doubled or halved.*
- *Each apple slice should be well-coated with dry ingredients to prevent them from sinking to the bottom of the cake.*
- *Icing is rather thin before it sets. Some will run off sides of cake. Rescue with a spatula and use.*
- *For convenience, the cake may be frozen either before or after icing. Thaw at room temperature.*

Locally grown Virginia apples make this a moist and tempting treat. While the flavors improve with a few days' aging, this cake never seems to last that long!

Complexity ✪   **Yield: 16 servings**

CAKE

1½ cups (11 ounces) vegetable oil (canola suggested)
 2 cups (14 ounces) sugar
 3 large eggs
 2 teaspoons vanilla extract
 3 cups (12 ounces) all-purpose flour
 1 teaspoon baking soda
 1 teaspoon salt
 1 cup (4½ ounces) chopped walnuts
 3 cups (about 3 large apples) (1 pound) peeled Virginia apples, thinly sliced

CARAMEL ICING

½ cup (4 ounces) butter
2 cups (1 pound) firmly packed brown sugar (dark or light)
½ cup (4 ounces) milk
½ teaspoon vanilla extract

cake
In a small bowl, combine oil, sugar, eggs, and vanilla. Mix well. In a large mixing bowl lightly mix all remaining ingredients except apples. Stir apples into dry mixture, making sure each slice is coated. Gently combine both mixtures. Pour into a greased and lightly floured 10-inch tube pan. The pan should be about three-fourths full. Bake at 350° for 1 hour or until a toothpick comes out clean. Let cool upside-down.

caramel icing
Melt butter in a medium saucepan. Add sugar and milk. Bring to a boil. Continue at boil for 3 minutes. Let cool. Add vanilla. Beat at medium mixer speed until icing comes to a good spreading consistency. Place cooled cake on a rack over another pan. Spoon icing over cake. Spread evenly with a spatula.

Apple Nut Cake (II)

JUDY PEARCE
PASTRY CHEF, C.W.P.C.

The Colonial Williamsburg Commissary, Williamsburg

Virginians love their apple cakes so much that we are pleased to share this "famous" one of pastry chef Pearce. This one has a bit richer crumb due to the butter. The best way to eat this is while hot, straight from the oven. Even so, Pearce suggests that this luscious, moist, fruity cake adapts well to cream cheese icing or a simple dusting with confectioners' sugar. The mixing is so easy that it can be done by hand.

Complexity ✪   Yield: 12 to 16 servings

4	apples (1 pound), peeled, cored, and chopped
2	cups (14 ounces) sugar
2	eggs
1	cup (8 ounces) butter, melted
3	cups (12 ounces) all-purpose flour
2	teaspoons baking soda
2	teaspoons ground cinnamon
½	teaspoon ground allspice
1	cup (4 ounces) chopped pecans

In a large bowl place chopped apples. Pour sugar over top and allow to sit 10 minutes. Add eggs and melted butter. In a separate bowl mix dry ingredients together. Add dry ingredients to apple mixture. Place batter in a greased and floured 10-inch tube pan. Bake at 350° for 50 to 60 minutes. Test with a toothpick or a knife. It must come out clean.

Chef's Notes
- *Batter may be stiff depending on temperature of ingredients. Room temperature ingredients are preferred.*
- *This cake may be frozen, if you can keep it that long!*
- *Virginia abounds in pick-your-own produce. After all, agriculture is Virginia's largest industry, employing one in every four people. Apples, available July through November, as well as other produce with locations for picking are listed in "Virginia Produce." This free brochure can be obtained by writing the Virginia Department of Agriculture and Consumer Services, Division of Marketing, P.O. Box 1163, Richmond, VA 23209 or by calling (804) 786-5867.*
- *The "Virginia's Finest" trademark is applied to produce meeting the high standards set for blackberries, raspberries, dewberries, apples, peaches, pumpkins, honey, tomatoes, squash, cucumbers, peppers, and other fruits and vegetables.*

Macadamia Fudge Cake

GORDON ADAMS
ROUNDS CHEF
Stein Erickson Lodge, Park City, Utah

Chef's Notes
• *Hazelnuts are an excellent substitute for the Hawaiian macadamia nuts. See tip for removing husks on page 179.*

The single round layer's serving sixteen is a clue to the richness of this cake. Its construction is not complicated, particularly the fudge topping where all ingredients are boiled, cooled, and poured on top of the macadamia nuts scattered over the dense layer.

Complexity ☉   Yield: 16 servings

CAKE

1 cup (4 ounces) all-purpose flour
¾ cup (5 ounces) sugar
¾ cup (6 ounces) sour cream
½ cup (4 ounces) butter, room temperature
¼ cup (¾ ounce) cocoa
2 teaspoons instant coffee
½ teaspoon baking soda
½ teaspoon baking powder
½ teaspoon vanilla extract
¼ teaspoon salt
1 egg

FUDGE TOPPING

1 cup (8 ounces) heavy whipping cream
½ cup (3½ ounces) sugar
2 tablespoons (1 ounce) butter
1 tablespoon (⅔ ounce) corn syrup
4 ounces semisweet chocolate
1 teaspoon vanilla extract
1½ cups (7 ounces) whole macadamia nuts

cake

In large bowl, mix all ingredients with electric mixer at low speed. Scrape down sides with spatula. Continue beating until well blended. Pour batter into a well-buttered 9-inch round cake pan. Bake 30 to 35 minutes at 350° or until cake tester comes out clean. Cool cake in pan for 10 minutes. Remove to a serving plate.

fudge topping

In a medium, heavy-bottomed saucepan heat cream, sugar, butter, corn syrup, and chocolate. Stir until mixture comes to a boil. Reduce heat to medium. Continue stirring for 2 more minutes. Remove from heat. Cool for 5 minutes, then add vanilla. Stir in nuts. Pour over cake.

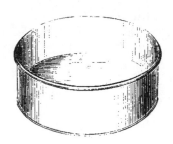

Mom's Forty-five-Minute Chocolate Cake

JOHN LONG
ROUNDS CHEF, C.C.

The Williamsburg Inn, Colonial Williamsburg, Williamsburg

Chef's Notes
- *Mix by hand. Do not use a mixer.*
- *An even easier version is to forget the frosting and give the cake a light dusting of confectioners' sugar.*

From start to finish, the time investment is only 45 minutes. But the payoff is great, as this cake stays moist for a week. And it is easy enough to whip up at 9:00 P.M. when someone says, "Oh, I almost forgot, I need a cake for school (or the office) tomorrow morning."

Complexity ✪✪   **Yield: 16 servings**

CAKE

2	cups (14 ounces) sugar
2	cups (8 ounces) all-purpose flour
1	teaspoon baking soda
½	teaspoon salt
1	cup (8 ounces) butter or margarine
¼	cup (¾ ounce) cocoa powder
1	cup water
2	eggs, beaten
1	teaspoon vanilla extract
½	cup (4 ounces) milk
2	teaspoons vinegar

FROSTING

½	cup (4 ounces) butter or margarine
¼	cup (¾ ounce) cocoa powder
6	tablespoons (3 ounces) milk
1	box (16 ounces) confectioners' sugar
1	teaspoon vanilla extract
1	cup (4 ounces) chopped nuts, optional

In a large mixing bowl, sift together sugar, flour, soda, and salt. In a small saucepan over low heat, melt butter, cocoa powder, and water. Pour melted mixture over sugar mixture. Stir in eggs, vanilla, milk, and vinegar. Pour into a greased 10½x15-inch pan. Bake for 20 minutes at 400°.

While cake is baking, heat butter, cocoa, and milk. Stir in sugar. Add vanilla and nuts. Pour frosting over cake as soon as it comes out of the oven. Cool and cut into squares.

John's Special Cheesecake

JOHN KOGELMAN
HEAD BAKER, C.M.B., C.E.P.C.
The Boca Raton Resort and Club, Florida

Here is a dessert to elevate your cooking reputation to that of a "master." Watch the grandeur of baking as the cake rises high above the pan, proudly puffing until the top is a glorious golden brown. It will shrink back into the pan during cooling. Local Virginia berries, available during the first days of summer and bursting with flavor, make the perfect glaze.

Complexity ❸❸❸   **Yield: 16 to 20 servings**

3¾ pounds cream cheese, softened to room temperature
2 cups (14 ounces) sugar
½ teaspoon salt
1½ teaspoons vanilla
1 cup (4 ounces) all-purpose flour
8 large eggs
3 cups (24 ounces) heavy cream

In a large bowl cream cheese and sugar with an electric mixer on medium speed for 10 minutes. Scrape bowl. Add salt, vanilla, and flour slowly until smooth. Slowly add eggs, mixing until smooth. Scrape bowl. Slowly add cream and mix on low speed until smooth, about 2 or 3 minutes. Grease 10-inch springform pan (3-inch sides) and line with parchment paper on sides and bottom. The side paper needs to be at least 4 inches to form a collar for the cake to rise. Pour batter into prepared pan. Bake in a ½-inch water bath in a preheated 300° oven for approximately 2½ hours until set up. Cake should not jiggle when moved. Cool in pan. Refrigerate overnight. Remove from pan. Place on cake plate or 10-inch cake serving circle. Serve cool.

Chef's Notes

• *The water bath ensures gentle, slow cooking. Starting with cold water in a pan large enough to hold the springform pan will keep the cake from cracking. Try to maintain about ½ inch of water in bottom of pan. Check level. Add more hot water if necessary.*

• *Leave bottom of springform pan under cake for easier manipulation.*

• *For glaze, purée 1 pint of cleaned and hulled strawberries. Force through a sieve to remove seeds. Add to a small saucepan with ½ cup sugar and bring to a boil. Mix 1 tablespoon cornstarch into 2 tablespoons cold water. Stir into saucepan. Bring to a boil. Stir until thickened and clear in color, about 1 minute. Cool.*

• *To decorate cake, place about 1 pint of berries, hulled and sliced in half, on top of cooled cake. Brush with glaze, letting some drip down the sides. Garnish with fresh mint leaves around the sides of the cake plate.*

Blueberry Cheesecake

RENNY PARZIALE

CHEF-OWNER

Virginia Culinary Company, Williamsburg

CHEF-INSTRUCTOR

P. D. Pruden Vo-Tech, Suffolk

Chef's Notes

- *Use 6 whole graham crackers of the finest quality for the crust.*
- *To flavor cheesecake, add sliced strawberries, chocolate in chunks or melted, or liqueur after the cream.*
- *When done, the cheesecake will have a golden brown crust.*
- *A quick crust is made by placing whole grahams and all crust ingredients in a food processor and whirring for about 2 minutes or until small particles are formed.*

For a state and a nation with a passion for this creamy sweet, here is Chef Parziale's incredible tempter featuring summer's tart berries. A touch of cocoa powder makes an unusual crust. The cake may be made several days in advance and kept refrigerated, but add berries just before serving to preserve their integrity.

Complexity ✪✪   Yield: 16 servings

CRUST

1	cup (3 ounces) graham crackers crumbs
1½	tablespoons sugar
1	tablespoon cocoa powder
¼	cup (2 ounces) unsalted butter

FILLING

¼	cup (2 ounces) unsalted butter
1	pound cream cheese
1½	teaspoons vanilla extract
¾	(5 ounces) cup sugar
¼	cup (1 ounce) cornstarch
5	eggs
1	cup (8 ounces) heavy cream
2	tablespoons (1 ounce) lemon juice

TOPPING

1	pint washed and well-drained blueberries

crust
Mix crust ingredients in a buttered 9-inch springform pan. Evenly pack a ¼-inch crust.

filling

In a large bowl of an electric mixer, cream butter and cream cheese. Mix in vanilla, sugar, and cornstarch. Beat in eggs one at a time. Slowly beat in cream and lemon juice. Pour into prepared pan. Bake at 350° for approximately 50 minutes or until cake tester comes out clean. Let cool.

topping

Arrange fresh blueberries on top.

Warm Apple Napoleons with Crème Anglaise

DAVID J. BARRISH
PROGRAM DIRECTOR, C.H.A.
J. Sargeant Reynolds Community College, Richmond

Chef's Notes
- *These should be assembled just prior to serving.*
- *Use a food processor to make fast work of slicing the apples.*

For feeding a crowd, try these elegant warm napoleons. Using frozen puff pastry makes this an easy dessert.

Complexity ✪✪✪   Yield: 30 servings

APPLE NAPOLEONS

> 2 *sheets (2 pounds) puff pastry, thawed*
> 2 *quarts apple cider, unpasteurized*
> 3 *pounds Granny Smith apples, peeled, cored, ⅛-inch slices*
> ½ *pound golden raisins*
> 1 *teaspoon vanilla extract*
> ½ *cup (4 ounces) applejack brandy*
> 1 *tablespoon ground cinnamon*
> ½ *cup (2 ounces) cornstarch*
> 1 *cup cold water*
> ½ *cup (2 ounces) confectioners' sugar*
> 8 *cups (2 quarts) crème Anglaise*
> 1 *pint fresh raspberries, cleaned*
> 1 *pint fresh blueberries, cleaned*

CRÈME ANGLAISE

> 6 *cups (1½ quarts) milk*
> 12 *egg yolks, slightly beaten*
> 1 *cup (7 ounces) sugar*
> ¼ *teaspoon salt*
> 2 *teaspoons vanilla extract*

apple napoleons

Roll each pastry sheet into a 15x12-inch rectangle. Cut each rectangle into 15 rectangles, each measuring 3x4 inches. Place on baking sheets. Bake in a 400° oven for 12 to 15 minutes or until puffed and golden brown. Bring cider to a boil. Stir in apples, raisins, vanilla, brandy, and cinnamon. Simmer until apples are cooked. With a large slotted spoon, remove cooked apples and raisins. Completely mix cornstarch in cold water. Return cider to a boil. Whisk in cornstarch mixture. Reduce heat. Continue to stir for about 3 minutes or until cider is thickened and clear. Remove from heat. Return apples and raisins to cider glaze. Mix well. Slice each pastry rectangle in half lengthwise to form tops and bottoms. Sift confectioners' sugar over top halves.

crème Anglaise
Scald milk in the top of a double boiler. Slowly stir in the egg yolks, sugar, and salt. Continue stirring until thickened to a medium sauce consistency. Remove from heat. Add vanilla. Serve while warm.

assembly
To assemble, lay bottom shelf halves on individual 7-inch plates. Divide apple/raisin/glaze evenly on shells. Pour ¼ cup (2 ounces) of crème Anglaise over each. Put tops in place. Garnish with raspberries and blueberries.

Triple Pie Crusts

ANTHONY CONTE

PASTRY CHEF, C.C.

Country Club of Virginia, Richmond

Chef's Notes

- *Overnight refrigeration gives the gluten time to firm up, which makes the rolling process easier.*
- *Try the new convenient solid shortening sold in sticks.*
- *Faster still is using a food processor, pulsing the flour and shortening until desired size. Pulse in water. Do not overprocess.*
- *For a richer-tasting product, substitute butter for up to half the shortening.*
- *The dough is suitable for 8-, 9-, or 10-inch pies.*
- *If the pie shell is to be prebaked, first line with foil and fill with dried beans (blind baking).*
- *For a herbed crust, surprising with a quiche, add ½ teaspoon dried or 1 tablespoon fresh herbs.*
- *Freeze unbaked shells flat like tortillas for parsimonious freezer storage.*

These shells are easy as pie. Why not make dough for three at a time? Chef Conte uses lower-protein cake flour for a more tender product. Store extra in the freezer baked or just as a ball.

Complexity ✪   Yield: crust for 3 pies

4 cups (1 pound) cake flour
1½ cups (10 ounces) shortening
1 teaspoon salt
1 cup water

Cut shortening into flour and salt with floured hands until the size of walnuts (for flaky crust) or smaller (for softer, crumblike crust). Make a well in the center of the flour, add the water and mix. Be careful not to overmix because this will result in a dough, rather than a crust. Cover with a damp towel and refrigerate overnight in a stainless steel bowl.

Chocolate Silk Pie

RAOUL B. HEBERT

EXECUTIVE CHEF

Bull and Bear Club, Richmond

This intensely chocolatey, silky pie will puff up while baking, mostly around the edges, and will fall in the center when cooling. It is surprisingly light and fast and quick to make—easy as pie.

Complexity ✪   Yield: 8 servings

1 10-inch pie shell, unbaked
1½ cups (10 ounces) sugar
¼ cup (¾ ounce) cocoa
3 eggs
1 cup (8 ounces) evaporated milk
2 teaspoons vanilla extract
¼ cup (2 ounces) melted butter

Whisk all ingredients together or place in blender until completely mixed. Pour into unbaked pie shell. Bake in a 350° oven for 35 to 40 minutes. Even though the center is still soft, it will set up when cooled. Refrigerate.

Chef's Notes

- *Serve plain or dress it up with a flavored cream, Bavarian, or mousse topping.*
- *Scoop ice cream on top—it is like an upside-down fudge sundae pie.*

Mocha Pecan Pie

GORDON ADAMS

ROUNDS CHEF

Stein Erickson Lodge, Park City, Utah

Chef's Notes
- *Chocolate chips may be used in the place of chocolate squares.*
- *Make ahead and freeze. Preslice and place plastic wrap dividers between slices so that single servings can be served when the entire pie is not to be consumed.*
- *Try with walnuts and orange liqueur for a delightful variation.*

With this rich pie, Thanksgiving can come every day of the year. For pecan pie and chocolate lovers, this is heaven. The pie holds up quite well for several days under refrigeration and also freezes beautifully.

Complexity ✪✪   Yield: 8 to 12 servings

PIE

6 ounces semisweet chocolate, chopped
¼ cup (2 ounces) coffee liqueur (Kahlua preferred)
3 eggs, beaten
½ cup (4 ounces) firmly packed dark brown sugar
1 cup (10 ounces) light corn syrup
¼ teaspoon salt
2 teaspoons vanilla extract
½ cup (4 ounces) unsalted butter, melted
1 cup (4 ounces) coarsely chopped pecans
1 unbaked 9-inch pie shell

COFFEE WHIPPED CREAM

1 cup (8 ounces) heavy cream, chilled
1½ tablespoons (¾ ounce) coffee liqueur

pie
In a heavy 3-quart saucepan combine the chocolate and liqueur. Melt over low heat, stirring until smooth. In a large bowl, combine eggs, sugar, corn syrup, salt, and vanilla. Beat until well blended. Stir in melted chocolate mixture, add melted butter and pecans. Mix well. Pour the filling into pie shell. Bake at 350° for 40 to 50 minutes or until the pie is just set in the center. Cool on rack.

coffee whipped cream
Whip cream to soft peaks. Add liqueur. Serve whipped cream on the side.

Sweet Potato Pie

ANTHONY CONTE
PASTRY CHEF, C.C.
Country Club of Virginia, Richmond

Gwen Reid, a talented cook for Colonial Williamsburg, is famous for her rendition of *the* classic southern sweet potato pie. This is an adaptation of the recipe she generously shared with Chef Conte.

Complexity ✪✪	Yield: 6 servings

- 1 9-inch pie crust, baked
- 4 medium (2 pounds) sweet potatoes
- ½ cup (3½ ounces) sugar
- ½ cup (3 ounces) firmly packed light brown sugar
- 1 teaspoon ground cinnamon
- ¼ teaspoon ground nutmeg
  juice of half a lemon
- 1 teaspoon vanilla extract
- 3 eggs
- ½ cup (4 ounces) cream

Peel potatoes. Steam until soft. Mash potatoes. Cool to room temperature. Combine remaining ingredients with potatoes using an electric mixer or food processor. Pour into pie shell. Bake at 350° for approximately 40 minutes.

Chef's Notes

- *The batter consistency should be like a firm milkshake. As potatoes vary to their degree of dryness, more cream may be added if necessary.*
- *Evaporated skim milk may be substituted for the cream.*
- *A faster version, but not quite as flavorful, is to steam potatoes, cool, then peel.*

Coconut Macaroons

OTTO J. BERNET

DIRECTOR OF EUROPEAN SPECIALTIES, C.M.P.C., A.A.C.

Ukrop's Supermarket, Richmond

Chef's Notes

- *Do not even think of making these cookies without parchment paper. The result will be a disaster, with cookies stuck to the sheet.*
- *The cookies are done just as they loosen up from the parchment paper. Patiently wait for them to cool and the backs will pull off with a gentle tug.*
- *Store in an airtight container.*
- *Keep fresh coconuts at room temperature no more than one month. A 1-pound coconut makes 3 cups of grated meat, which can be frozen for up to six months.*
- *Heavy-duty professional baking sheets, in the "half-sheet" size fit home ovens and will revolutionize cookie baking—no more burns. Purchase in a restaurant supply house or in one of the large "club" warehouses. Prices are usually less than $8 per sheet.*

The famous master pastry chef, Bernet, shares his chewy, coconutty, and just-sweet-enough macaroons. It is a flourless cookie using finely grated coconut as the shortening. The mixing procedure is quite unusual—all items are heated in a heavy pot. After cooling they are quickly dropped for baking until golden brown.

Complexity ✪✪✪   Yield: 6 dozen

2½ cups (11 ounces) coconut, finely grated
2⅓ cups (1 pound) sugar
½ cup (2 ounces) cornstarch
8 (8 ounces) egg whites
1 teaspoon vanilla extract

In a heavy pot mix coconut, sugar, and cornstarch with a spoon. Add egg whites and vanilla. Over medium heat, stir mixture constantly for about 5 minutes or until the batter becomes stiffer. Heat to 120° or the point that would almost burn your finger. Remove from heat and cool for about 10 minutes. Cover baking sheets with parchment paper. Drop batter with a teaspoon making small mounds 2 inches apart. Bake at 350° for 15 to 18 minutes or until the ridges become golden brown. Permit to completely cool. Peel off parchment paper.

Scottish Shortbread

OTTO J. BERNET

DIRECTOR OF EUROPEAN SPECIALTIES, C.M.P.C., A.A.C.
Ukrop's Supermarkets, Richmond

Pure sweet butter, flour, sugar, and vanilla never were better married than in this perfect cookie. These "sable vanille" are rich, so serve with tea, coffee, ice cream, or puddings. And when you are in a sinful mood, just eat them all by themselves, making sure to savor every last crumb—sharing only with those you passionately adore. Chocoholics take note, these could redirect your eating passions. And chocolate chip cookie dough-eaters, this dough is even more palatable with the obliquely healthy virtue of containing no raw eggs!

Chef's Notes
- *Use the finest, purest ingredients available for best results.*
- *Cookies may be frozen for future use.*
- *Approximately 10 ounces of dough should be used in each 16-inch roll.*
- *In the United Kingdom shortbreads often were the test of a homemaker's pastry skills.*
- *Halve the recipe if desired.*

Complexity ✪✪   Yield: about 20 dozen (but they are dainty little cookies)

---

  2 *cups (1 pound) unsalted butter, finest quality*
1½ *cups (5½ ounces) confectioners' sugar*
  ½ *teaspoon pure vanilla extract*
  4 *cups (1 pound) all-purpose flour*
  1 *egg white, beaten*
  ⅓ *cup (2 ounces) sugar*

With an electric mixer, work butter until smooth, but not foamy. Add confectioners' sugar. Mix for several turns of the dough. Add vanilla and flour gradually, mixing into a thick dough. Divide dough into four pieces. Form each piece into 16-inch rolls. Refrigerate until firm. Moisten rolls with egg white and roll in granulated sugar. Cut into ¼-inch thick slices. Bake at 350° on sheets covered with parchment paper. Cookies are done in about 8 minutes or when the rims are golden brown. Cool on a rack. Store in airtight containers.

Tuille Biscuit

U.S. ARMY CULINARY OLYMPIC TEAM

Fort Lee

Chef's Notes

- *Dough may be difficult to spread. Try using a large spoon dipped in ice water. Do not worry about holes or small gaps—they add a nice laciness to the cookie.*
- *Tuilles can be made ahead and stored in an airtight container.*
- *Tuille cookies ideally accompany ice cream and fresh fruits.*

In Frankfurt, the culinary team served tuilles propped up between a key lime mousse and a strawberry on a plate flooded with fresh mango sauce bordered with a salpicon of kiwi, pineapple, papaya, strawberries, and red currants in ignited kirsch with a confectioners' sugar dust. Their curves come from a wrap around a rolling pin while still warm and pliable—but do not delay. It is a brief window of opportunity.

Complexity ✪✪   **Yield: 1½ dozen cookies**

½ *cup (4 ounces) butter, unsalted*
2 *egg whites*
½ *cup (4 ounces) confectioners' sugar*
1 *cup (4 ounces) all-purpose flour*
½ *cup (2 ounces) sliced almonds*

Melt butter. Cool. Slowly beat in egg whites. Mix sugar and flour together and beat into butter mixture. Continue beating until batter is the consistency of smooth paste. Let dough rest at room temperature for 30 minutes. Place a lightly greased cookie tray in the refrigerator. Using an oval template, form biscuit on cool tray with the back of a spoon.

Sprinkle with sliced almonds. Bake in a 350° oven until golden brown. While still hot remove from tray and shape lengthwise over a rolling pin. Cool and serve.

Viennese Chocolate Rings

OTTO J. BERNET

DIRECTOR OF EUROPEAN SPECIALTIES, C.M.P.C., A.A.C.

Ukrop's Supermarkets, Richmond

Remember strolling down the cobblestone streets of Old Vienna, listening to the street musicians, peering into the tempting sweet shops, and finally yielding to temptation? Chef Bernet's recipe recreates a sensual butter-and-chocolate-cookie ring filled with rich raspberry preserves.

Chef's Notes
- *Try to find raspberry preserves without seeds.*
- *Melting chocolate is a microwave's forte. Follow directions on package, starting with about 1 minute for the first ounce and 10 seconds for each additional ounce square. Stir midway through. Be careful not to burn; chocolate is very delicate.*

Complexity ❸❸❸   **Yield: 4 dozen**

1½ *cups (12 ounces) unsalted butter, finest quality*
1¼ *cups (5 ounces) confectioners' sugar*
 4 *egg whites, beaten*
 1 *teaspoon pure vanilla extract*
 6 *ounces unsweetened chocolate, melted*
 3 *cups (12 ounces) all-purpose flour*
 1 *cup (12 ounces) raspberry preserves*

With an electric mixer, work butter until smooth. Mix in confectioners' sugar. Gradually add egg whites and vanilla. When lightly foamy, blend in melted, lukewarm chocolate. Slowly add flour, beating until incorporated. Put dough into a pastry bag or a cookie pump fitted with a star tip. Make small rings about 1¼-inches wide on baking sheets covered with parchment paper. Bake at 350° for about 7 minutes or until browning just begins and cookies can be moved freely on paper. Cool. Mount 2 rings together with preserves from a pastry bag. Store in an airtight container.

Wespennester Meringue Cookie

JOHN KOGELMAN
HEAD BAKER, C.M.B.,* C.E.P.C.
The Boca Raton Resort and Club, Florida

Chef's Notes
- *Eggs are easily separated if they are at room temperature. Refrigerated eggs may be placed in a bowl of hot tap water for 5 minutes.*
- *Overmixed egg whites, which are dry, will break down with the addition of other ingredients. Whites should be still glossy to properly incorporate the air bubbles.*
- *Use good quality chocolate for dipping, such as Swiss or Belgian. Melt slowly. The microwave is efficient for this task. For 1 ounce of chocolate melt on high for 1 minute, stirring once at the halfway point.*

This crunchy cookie, with German origins, is enhanced with the Austrian twist of adding caramel and dipping chocolate. Store in an airtight tin, far away from any cookie monsters. Do not freeze.

Complexity ✪✪✪   Yield: 5 dozen

8   ounces caramel squares
6   cups (24 ounces) almond slices
8   large egg whites, room temperature
2½ cups (17 ounces) sugar
2   teaspoons vanilla extract
½   teaspoon ground cinnamon
¼   teaspoon ground cloves
8   ounces chocolate minichips
8   ounces bittersweet chocolate for dipping, optional

Melt caramel squares in double boiler until melted. Cool. Toast almond slices on a baking sheet for 8 minutes in 400° oven until golden brown. Cool at least 15 minutes. In a 2-quart bowl whip egg whites on mixer's high speed for about 1 minute or until foamy. Gradually add sugar to whites, whipping on high for 3 to 5 minutes or until thick and creamy. At medium speed for 30 seconds mix in vanilla and spices. By hand fold in chips, almonds, and caramel until mixed. Drop by teaspoonful on greased baking sheet leaving 1 inch between cookies. Bake in preheated 350° oven for 15 to 18 minutes, until medium brown. Cool on pan for 15 minutes. Optional: Presentation is enhanced by dipping half of cookie in melted chocolate. Wipe bottom of cookie on edge of dish and cool. Serve on silver tray.

* Chef Kogelman is also certified by the National Baking Association as a Certified Master Baker.

Zimetsterne, Cinnamon Star Cookies

OTTO J. BERNET

DIRECTOR OF EUROPEAN SPECIALTIES, C.M.P.C., A.A.C.

Ukrop's Supermarkets, Richmond

Watch faces twinkle like stars on a clear night when presenting these European Christmas cookies. The almondy chewiness with the crisp sweet icing is sure to delight even the grumpiest Scrooge.

Complexity ✪✪✪   Yield: about 2 dozen 2¼-inch stars

3 *egg whites*
3 *cups (12 ounces) confectioners' sugar*
3 *cups (13 ounces) almonds, finely ground*
1 *tablespoon (½ ounce) lemon juice*
1 *tablespoon ground cinnamon*
1 *cup (7 ounces) sugar*

With an electric mixer, beat the egg whites in a large bowl until stiff, but not dry. Add confectioners' sugar and mix for 3 more minutes at medium speed. Retain 1 cup of this mixture for icing. Mix in remaining ingredients until just incorporated. Let stand for 30 minutes. Sprinkle pastry board with a small amount of sugar. Roll dough to ⅜-inch thick. Cut with medium star cutter. Brush icing over cookies. Place on parchment paper–lined cookie sheets. Bake at 325° for 15 minutes. Do not let icing start to brown. Store in an airtight container.

Chef's Notes

- *The dough is very easy to work with. After cutting stars, gather extra pieces together. Roll again and cut more stars.*
- *This is an outstanding base for making petite cookies with a variety of cutters as the dough is robust.*
- *After baking cookies, tilt tray and slide paper with cookies onto counter. Permit to cool.*
- *These are cholesterol free and suitable for those with wheat allergies.*

CHAPTER 10
Desirable Desserts

When cracking a moderate number of eggs for a recipe, crack into a separate bowl, not straight into the other ingredients. Let the eggs sit for 10 minutes undisturbed. Any shell particles will settle to the bottom. Now slowly pour out the eggs leaving all shell pieces behind.—*Chef Conte*

Fresh eggs have a rough, chalky surface. Older eggs have a smooth, shiny surface.
—*Chef Conte*

Before adding honey to a recipe, measure into a plastic cup. Heat for 10 seconds in the microwave. Honey will pour easily.
—*Chef Conte*

When unmolding gelatin or custard first wet the serving plate. It is easy to move it around or center it.—*Chef Conte*

To cleanly cut a baked meringue, coat knife with butter or oil.—*Chef Conte*

To prevent milk solids from sticking to a pot when scalding milk, first rinse the pot with cold water.—*Chef Conte*

To add flour when using an electric mixer, first sift onto a piece of parchment or waxed paper. Pick up two of the edges and you have a chute to slide the flour into the bowl.—*Chef Conte*

For easy and elegant sauce painting on plates, purchase plastic ketchup squirt bottles. Load with chocolate, raspberry, or any other sauce. Draw parallel lines on plate within the circle. Turn plate 90°. Drag the tip of a knife through the lines of sauce in another series of parallel lines.—*Chef Conte*

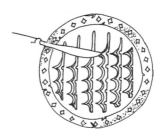

A candy thermometer takes the guess work out of sugar creations. The temperature will rise as the water boils away. The hotter the sugar, the harder it will be when cooled. It only takes a few degrees to change syrups to another stage. Variations may also occur due to altitude and relative humidity. The stages of boiled sugar are:

thread	230°–235°
softball	240°–245°
ball	250°–255°
hardball	260°–265°
little crack	270°–275°
crack	275°–280°
hard crack	285°–315°
caramel	325°–350°

—Chef Clarke

If cream does not whip, add the white of an egg, chill, then whip.—*Chef Fulton*

Set a mixing bowl on a damp cloth while beating to keep bowl steady.—*Chef Fulton*

Mix dry ingredients before liquid or sticky ones. There is less cleanup.—*Chef Fulton*

A teaspoon of honey will give a delicious flavor to whipped cream and it will stay firm longer than when using sugar for sweetening.—*Chef Fulton*

If cream has been whipped too long, add a little cold milk. It will turn smooth again.—*Chef Fulton*

Peaches served at room temperature taste much better than those refrigerated.

—Chef Corliss

Poached Pears with Stilton Cheese

OTTO J. BERNET

DIRECTOR OF EUROPEAN SPECIALTIES, C.M.P.C., A.A.C.

Ukrop's Supermarkets, Richmond

Fresh pears poached and filled with strong English Stilton tempered with cream cheese under raspberry sauce with crispy toasted almonds are, in Chef Bernet's own words, a gourmet's delight! All components can be made ahead of time and quickly assembled for this elegant dessert.

Complexity ✪✪✪✪   **Yield: 8 servings**

4 pears, skinned and poached whole

SHORTBREAD

1¼ cups (5 ounces) all-purpose flour
2 eggs
½ cup (3½ ounces) sugar
½ cup (4 ounces) unsalted butter, room temperature
grated zest of 1 lemon

FILLING

¾ cup (6 ounces) ripe Stilton cheese
¼ cup (2 ounces) cream cheese

RASPBERRY SAUCE

1 cup (4½ ounces) raspberries, fresh or frozen
¼ cup (1¾ ounces) sugar

GARNISH

2 tablespoons (½ ounce) sliced almonds, toasted

shortbread
In a large mixing bowl, make a well in the middle of the flour. Put eggs, sugar, butter, and lemon zest in well. With a pastry blender, stir until well blended. Chill dough until stiff. Roll out dough on a generously floured board. Cut cookies in ovals the size of the pears. Bake on a greased cookie sheet at 350° for 8 minutes or until the edges are golden brown.

Chef's Notes
- *Use pears that are ripe but still firm for poaching. Particularly good choices are Barletts, Red Barletts, Anjou, Red Anjou, and Bosc.*
- *To poach pears, peel with a vegetable peeler. Place in a medium saucepan with 2 quarts of water. Add ½ cup sugar and juice of 1 lemon. Bring to a boil. Stir until sugar is dissolved. Add pear and simmer slowly for about 8 minutes until the fruit is just tender. Let cool in syrup.*
- *Lemon juice is used in the poaching liquid to prevent discoloration.*

filling

In a small bowl or with a food processor combine Stilton and cream cheese until soft and smooth.

raspberry sauce

In a food processor, purée berries and sugar. Remove seeds using a fine mesh strainer, stirring with a rubber spatula.

assembly

Cut pears in half lengthwise. Hollow out seeds. Fill with cheese filling. Refrigerate until ready to serve. Place pear on cookies on dessert plates. Pour raspberry sauce and decorate with toasted almonds.

Figs à la Tulipe

OTTO J. BERNET

DIRECTOR OF EUROPEAN SPECIALTIES, C.M.P.C., A.A.C.

Ukrop's Supermarkets, Richmond

Fresh figs with almond filling on a pool of raspberry sauce is a delightful and unusual dining finisher. Devoid of any cooking, this is the perfect summer treat. Assembly may take place several hours before serving and held under refrigeration.

Complexity ✪✪   Yield: 4 servings

4 large, fresh, ripe figs (1½ pounds)
½ cup (3 ounces) almond paste
½ cup (2 ounces) confectioners' sugar, sifted once
2 tablespoons (1 ounce) cream cheese
8 whole almonds, toasted
¼ cup seedless raspberry sauce

Wash and dry figs. Split from top almost to the base into quarters so that figs hold together like an open tulip. Mix almond paste, sugar, and cream cheese. Place into pastry bag fitted with a medium star tube. Fill center of each tulip with mixture. Top with two almonds. In the center of each plate place one-fourth raspberry sauce in a swirling motion. Place figs in center.

Chef's Notes
- *A very low-calorie variation on this dessert would be to pipe softened low-fat almond or vanilla ice cream into the fig immediately before serving. And if fresh raspberries are available, liberally sprinkle the plate.*

Spun Apples

DAVID BRUCE CLARKE
CHEF-INSTRUCTOR
J. Sargeant Reynolds Community College, Richmond

Chef's Notes
- *A small, very sharp knife makes easy work of apple preparation.*
- *As timing is critical in preparation, have all ingredients arranged near cooking surface before frying apples.*
- *Controlling the temperature of the coating syrup is very important. A candy thermometer should be used. As the water evaporates, the temperature of the sugar increases, resulting in a harder coating when cooled.*
- *When not in use, place thermometer in a nearby jar of very warm to hot water.*
- *Excellent cooking apples are firm or crunchy to the bite and include Winesap, Stayman, Rome, and Chesapeake.*
- *Use a 10-inch skillet as a wok substitute.*
- *Chopsticks also work well for transferring apple pieces.*

Caution: It is impossible to stop eating these apples wrapped in a delicate crunchy candy. Watch the magic when the syrup-coated slices, dropped into the icy bath, instantly harden enclosing the apple in a clear, brilliant glaze. Success is guaranteed by preparing apples and batter, oil for frying, syrup for coating, and ice bath before starting the cooking process. Enjoy immediately as the fragile candy will soften if allowed to stand too long.

Complexity ❸❸❸   **Yield: 4 servings**

BATTERED APPLES

---

1 cup (4 ounces) all-purpose flour
1 egg, lightly beaten with 2 tablespoons cold water
2 medium firm apples (about 10 ounces)

FRYING OIL

---

3 cups (22 ounces) peanut oil

COATING SYRUP

---

1 tablespoon (½ ounce) peanut oil
1 cup (7 ounces) sugar
¼ cup cold water
1 tablespoon black sesame seeds

ICE BATH

---

4 cups water with 12 ice cubes in a large bowl

---

battered apples
Pour flour into large bowl. With a large spoon slowly stir in egg and water mixture to make a smooth batter. With a small sharp knife, cut apples into quarters. Peel off skin. Cut each piece into eighths. Drop 8 apple pieces into batter. Stir with spoon to coat.

frying oil
In a 3-quart saucepan, heat oil to 375° or until a haze forms.

coating syrup
In a 12-inch wok, heat oil with the sugar and cold water. Stir until sugar dissolves. Bring to a boil and cook 10 to 12 minutes to reach 300° or to the hard crack stage. Stir in sesame seeds and reduce heat to lowest point.

assembly
With tongs or slotted spoon, drop battered apple slices into heated oil. Fry for about 1 minute or until light amber. Immediately lift out of oil and put into skillet of hot syrup. Stir wedges to coat thoroughly with syrup. Using tongs or slotted spoon, drop one at a time into the bowl of ice water. Transfer to the lightly greased serving plate and continue with the remaining batches.

Braised Apples, Walnuts, and Honey

M. SCOTT KIZER

The Dining Room, Ford's Colony, Williamsburg

Chef's Notes

- *Dark, local honeys and Virginia apples can often be found at the James City County Farmers Market, 3627 Strawberry Plains Road, Williamsburg (804) 229-2625 or at other specialty produce markets.*
- *Fresh-picked apples from Hill Pleasant Farm, Inc., 7152 Richmond Road, Williamsburg (804) 564-9491 include varieties with approximate earliest date: Lodi—June 1, Rambo—August 5, Jonathan—September 1, Red Delicious—September 10, Golden Delicious, Rome, Stayman, York, Winesap, and Chesapeake—end of September.*
- *Slip a slice of pound cake under these for an even richer dessert.*
- *Try this same recipe with pears when they are in season and use pecans in place of walnuts.*
- *Use any leftovers for pancake or waffle toppings.*

Chef Kiser's rendition of this easy-to-make dessert brings back memories of long-past times. In fact, he uses this dessert as a one-pot dish—more accurately a 2-quart tin boiler—for Civil War reenactments. It is geographically correct for a cookout, especially since much of the war was fought in Virginia's back-yard. Indoor fanatics can make it on their stovetop burners and enjoy other technological developments.

Complexity ○   Yield: 10 servings

12 apples, quartered, seeded, and thickly sliced (4 pounds)
¼ cup (3 ounces) dark honey
1 cup (4½ ounces) coarsely chopped walnuts
  pinch salt
  pinch ground nutmeg or ground cinnamon
2 cups water
1 cup water, optional
1 cup (8 ounces) cream

Combine apples, honey, walnuts, spices, and water in a 2-quart pan. Simmer for 8 to 10 minutes, or until apples are just soft. If the mixture is somewhat dry, add up to 1 cup more water to create a syrup. To serve, spoon apples onto plate and drizzle with cream.

Chocolate Pâté with Melba Swirled Whipped Cream

MICHAEL VOSBURG

EXECUTIVE CHEF

The Salisbury Country Club, Midlothian

Dense dark chocolate pâté paired with a light whipped cream and raspberry sauce is an elegant finale to a dinner. Each plate is sauced with delicate ribbons of melba sauce almost too appealing to eat. But fear not—even the finest connoisseurs of culinary art will find their spoons consuming these creations with a passion.

Complexity ✪✪✪   Yield: 12 servings

PÂTÉ

1¼ pounds semisweet chocolate
1 cup (8 ounces) heavy cream
6 egg yolks
3 tablespoons (1½ ounces) brandy
3 tablespoons (1½ ounces) strong brewed coffee

SAUCE

½ cup (4 ounces) heavy cream
¼ cup (1 ounce) confectioners' sugar
2 tablespoons (1 ounce) melba sauce
1 bunch fresh mint
12 large strawberries (4 ounces), hulled

pâté
Melt chocolate in cream over 2-quart double boiler, stirring occasionally. Remove from heat. When mixture is 120° whisk in egg yolks one at a time. Stir in brandy and coffee. Pour into a buttered 8½x4½x2½-inch mold. Cover with plastic film. Chill until firm.

sauce
Whip cream with sugar just to the point of thickening or sauce consistency. To assemble, ladle whipped cream on plate. Place melba sauce in squeeze bottle with a fine tip. In a circular motion squirt melba on top of cream. With a knife pull sauce through cream to create a spider-web pattern.

Divide pâté into 12 slices. Place on top of sauce. Garnish with mint and fan-sliced strawberry.

Chef's Notes
• For a pâté mold, use a rectangular bread pan.
• Pâté may be prepared one day in advance.
• Melba sauce may be made by placing 1 cup fresh (or frozen, thawed, and drained) raspberries in food processor with 2 tablespoons sugar. Strain.
• Try a mustard squeeze bottle for swirling the melba sauce.
• Chocolate mousse can be made from the basic pâté recipe by whipping 1½ quarts of heavy cream with 6 ounces of confectioners' sugar. Fold whipped cream into cooled chocolate mixture. Pipe into champagne glasses. Chill.

Grand Marnier Caramel Custard

DONALD M. PRITCHARD
Chef-Owner, C.E.C., C.F.B.E.*
Lafayette Mixed Grille, Williamsburg

Chef's Notes
- *The bain marie or water bath guarantees the gentle, even cooking needed for custard. Logistically it is easier to place a shallow pan with individual soufflé cups on the oven rack, then add water.*
- *Bouillon cups, no larger than 8 ounces, make suitable baking containers.*
- *Use a vegetable peeler to remove orange rind. Be sure to avoid all the bitter pith that is in the white lining. Use a large French knife to mince into tiny pieces.*
- *Custard may be served warm or chilled.*
- *In place of Grand Marnier, try 2 teaspoons of natural orange extract.*
- *This is a magnificent dish served with fresh strawberries. Or add paper-thin slices of fresh oranges.*

The classic baked custard is elevated to sensuality with the delicate flavoring of Grand Marnier and orange. While intended for dessert, it makes for a glorious breakfast in the place of traditional egg dishes.

Complexity ❂❂   Yield: 16 servings

4	cups whole milk
1	cup (7 ounces) sugar
1	tablespoon (½ ounce) Grand Marnier
1	teaspoon vanilla extract
2	teaspoons grated orange rind
8	egg yolks
5	whole eggs

Preheat oven to 325°. In medium saucepan scald milk. Do not boil. Add ½ cup sugar, stirring until dissolved. Remove from heat and add Grand Marnier and vanilla. In a small mixing bowl combine whole eggs, yolks, and orange rind until well blended. In a separate saucepan place the remaining ½ cup sugar. Place over low heat until medium brown in color and caramel forms. Remove from fire.

Place 1 tablespoon of caramel mixture in bottom of individual soufflé dishes. Blend milk and egg mixtures thoroughly. Pour ¾ cup of mixture into each dish. Carefully place each dish in *bain marie* or shallow pan half filled with warm water. Bake for 30 to 35 minutes or until the custard is set. Cool custard. For presentation, invert custard on serving plate.

*Certified Food and Beverage Executive

Bread Pudding with Whiskey Butter Sauce

JO OLSON

ACCOUNT EXECUTIVE

Atlantic Food Services, Inc., Richmond

Rich custard envelops clouds of French bread. Prohibition may come back if too many folks learn about the whiskey sauce. Olson frequently doubles the quantity of sauce to satisfy the sweet desires of her diners.

Chef's Notes
• *Evaporated milk may be substituted for the heavy cream.*

Complexity ✪✪   Yield: 6 servings

BREAD PUDDING

1 small apple (4 ounces), diced
¼ cup (1½ ounces) golden raisins
¼ cup (2 ounces) brandy
2 cups (16 ounces) heavy cream
5 eggs
½ cup (3½ ounces) sugar
½ teaspoon vanilla extract
1 tablespoon ground cinnamon
1 tablespoon ground nutmeg
½ pound French bread, cubed

WHISKEY BUTTER SAUCE

¼ cup (2 ounces) bourbon
½ cup (4 ounces) heavy cream
½ cup (4 ounces) butter
1 cup (8 ounces) firmly packed dark brown sugar

bread pudding
Mix together apple, raisins, and brandy in a small bowl. In a large bowl mix cream, eggs, sugar, vanilla, and spices. Add bread cubes to wet mixture. Let soak for 5 minutes. Stir in apple mixture. Mix well. Pour into a 2-quart buttered casserole or a 9-inch soufflé dish. Bake at 350° for 1 hour or until golden brown on top.

whiskey butter sauce
In a medium saucepan heat ingredients until butter is melted. Do not boil. Serve immediately on bread pudding.

Blackberry Soufflé with Chambord Sauce

JEFF BLAND
EXECUTIVE CHEF
Buckhead Steak House, Richmond
CHEF-INSTRUCTOR
J. Sargeant Reynolds Community College

Chef's Notes
- *The egg whites need impeccably clean bowls and utensils for proper whipping.*
- *When separating eggs, use a small dish to collect each white individually. Then pour it into the stainless bowl. Any yolk will be easier to remove in the individual dish. And if a yolk breaks it will not taint the entire set of whites.*
- *The soufflé base may be made ahead of time, then refrigerated. The final product will be better if the base is warm.*
- *See Fat-Free Orange Soufflé (page 262) for more soufflé tricks.*
- *Remember that people wait for soufflés, not vice versa.*

Patience and timing are necessary prerequisites for making perfect soufflés. But the secret to a successful soufflé experience lies in treating the eggs with respect. The eggs' puffing power depends on their purity and temperature. Start with eggs at room temperature—they are easier to separate. Make sure that no yolk slips in with the whites.

Complexity ✪✪✪   Yield: 4 servings

SOUFFLÉS

1 **pint blackberries**
½ **cup (4 ounces) whole milk**
¼ **cup (2 ounces) sugar**
2 **tablespoons (½ ounce) all-purpose flour**
2 **tablespoons (1 ounce) butter, melted**
2 **egg yolks, beaten**
8 **egg whites**

CHAMBORD SAUCE

¾ **cup (6 ounces) heavy whipping cream**
¼ **cup (2 ounces) sugar**
2 **tablespoons (1 ounce) Chambord**
2 **tablespoons (1 ounce) milk**

soufflés

In a small saucepan bring blackberries and milk to a boil. Constantly whisk until the berries are dissolved. Stir in sugar. Using a fine strainer, pour liquid (about 1 cup) out of the berry mixture into another saucepan containing the flour and butter. Boil for 3 minutes or until very thick. Remove from heat. Temper egg yolks, then stir into mixture. With an electric beater whip egg whites in a stainless steel bowl until stiff but not dry. Fold a third of the egg whites into the berry mixture. Gently fold in the remainder. Pour into a butter-and-sugar-lined ramekin to the rim. Bake at 400° for 12 to 15 minutes. Sprinkle with confectioners' sugar.

Chambord sauce

In a medium bowl whip cream until stiff. Add sugar. Stir in Chambord and milk. To serve, cut a cross in the top of the soufflé with a spoon. Pour in sauce.

Fat-Free Orange Soufflé with Yogurt Sauce

JEFF BLAND

EXECUTIVE CHEF

Buckhead Steak House, Richmond

CHEF-INSTRUCTOR

J. Sargeant Reynolds Community College

Chef's Notes
- *Make sure stainless bowl and beaters are scrupulously clean to form the stiff peaks. Note the whites should still be wet.*
- *Sugar substitutes may be used in the place of sugar. However, add the substitute to the orange mixture after the cornstarch mixture. Stir until completely dissolved.*
- *After filling the ramekin, run a knife through the filling to help eliminate large air pockets. Tap the soufflé on the table once gently. Run a clean finger around the outer ramekin edge to seal soufflé.*
- *Make sure that baking temperature is high enough and that your oven is accurate. Otherwise batter may leak from the sides.*
- *Make sure soufflé is on a level baking surface. Try a baking sheet under the dishes.*
- *This recipe is also suitable for a single large soufflé.*
- *Try ½ cup of puréed raspberries, strawberries, or peaches in place of orange juice. If sweetened frozen fruits are used, reduce the sugar in the base by half. Match the yogurt sauce with similarly flavored liqueurs or juices.*
- *Remember that people wait for soufflés, not vice versa.*

A meal without dessert, many believe, is incomplete. In the current movement to reduce fat, new styles of cooking are emerging. On the forefront, Chef Bland has cleverly developed these tangy orange soufflés for diners eschewing fat. Pile the fluffy mixture high in the ramekin—about 4 inches above the rim without additional support—and it will stay that high when baked. The most glorious presentation is immediately after removing it from the oven and sprinkling lightly with sugar. Over the next hour it will slowly begin to shrink, so timing is not as crucial as with traditional soufflés. Any leftover can be refrigerated, which will result in shrinkage down to ramekin level, but the taste and texture will remain delicious.

Complexity ❸❸❸   Yield: 4 servings

ORANGE SOUFFLÉS

½ cup (4 ounces) orange juice, fresh preferred
½ cup (4 ounces) skim milk
  zest from 1 orange, finely minced
¼ cup (2 ounces) sugar
1 tablespoon cornstarch
1 teaspoon water
8 (8 ounces) egg whites
  pinch cream of tartar
1 tablespoon (½ ounce) sugar
1 tablespoon (¼ ounce) confectioners' sugar

YOGURT SAUCE

1 cup (8 ounces) nonfat plain yogurt
¼ cup (2 ounces) orange juice
¼ cup (2 ounces) skim milk
⅓ cup (2 ounces) sugar

orange soufflés

In a medium saucepan bring orange juice, milk, sugar, and zest to a boil. Stir until sugar dissolves. In a small cup completely dissolve cornstarch in water. Stir in cornstarch mixture. Remove from heat immediately. In a medium stainless bowl, use an electric beater to whip egg whites with cream of tartar until stiff peaks form. Fold a third of the egg whites into orange base. Gently fold in the remaining whites. Spray small ramekins or soufflé dishes with vegetable spray. Sprinkle the sides with sugar. Spoon in mixture. Bake at 450° for 10 to 15 minutes. Immediately before serving dust with confectioners' sugar.

yogurt sauce

Mix all ingredients. Cut an "x" in the soufflé and pour in sauce.

Chilled Sherry Soufflé

ROLF HERION

RETIRED HEAD PASTRY CHEF, C.M.P.C., A.A.C.

**The Colonial Williamsburg Commissary,
Williamsburg**

The intense flavor of sherry delightfully permeates these elegant individual soufflés. And there is no fear of falling—air incorporated in both the whipped cream and egg whites creates an ethereally light dessert. Since it is chilled, it can be made ahead. Start this soufflé at least 3 hours before serving.

Complexity ✪✪✪   Yield: 8 servings

SOUFFLÉ

2 ¼-ounce envelopes unflavored gelatin
½ cup cold water
1½ cups (12 ounces) sweet sherry wine
6 egg yolks
¾ cup (5 ounces) sugar, divided
1 cup (8 ounces) heavy cream, whipped
6 egg whites
1 tablespoon (½ ounce) lemon juice

LADYFINGERS

1 dozen ladyfingers, sliced in half lengthwise and crosswise

In the top of a double boiler, soften gelatin in cold water. Place over boiling water. Stir until dissolved. Remove and stir in sherry. Chill for 10 minutes. Beat egg yolks with ¼ cup sugar until thick and light. Add sherry mixture and continue to beat until thoroughly incorporated. With a large spatula gently fold in whipped cream. In a separate bowl beat egg whites until foamy. Gradually add ½ cup sugar beating constantly. Add lemon juice. Fold whites into the sherry and whipped cream mixture. Line soufflé dishes with ladyfingers with the rounded edges on top and flat edges on bottom. Fill with soufflé mixture. Chill at least 3 hours before serving.

Chef's Notes
- *Microwave fresh lemon for 30 seconds to make juicing more effective. A large lemon yields about 2 tablespoons juice.*
- *Chill both beaters and bowl for easier whipping of the cream.*
- *Specialty Bakers, commercial suppliers of ladyfingers, provides a toll-free number with suggestions and treatment of ladyfingers, (800) 755-9890.*

Soufflé Grand Marnier

ROLF HERION

Retired Head Pastry Chef, C.M.P.C., A.A.C.

The Colonial Williamsburg Commissary, Williamsburg

Dissolved gelatin is added to warmed and cooled egg yolks with sugar and Grand Marnier to form the base for this grand soufflé. Whipped cream and egg whites aerate the base, which becomes the filling for a fortress of ladyfingers inside the soufflé dish. Before starting, make sure to have at least 3 mixing bowls and 2 pans that fit over a double boiler.

Complexity ✪✪	Yield: 10 to 12 servings

2 *¼-ounce envelopes unflavored gelatin*
½ *cup cold water*
5 *egg yolks*
½ *cup (3½ ounces) sugar*
1 *cup (8 ounces) Grand Marnier*
5 *egg whites*
2 *tablespoons (1 ounce) sugar*
2 *cups (16 ounces) heavy cream, whipped*
1 *dozen ladyfingers, sliced in half lengthwise*
   candied orange peel for garnish
   whipped cream for garnish

In the top of a double boiler soften gelatin in water. Place over hot water and stir until dissolved. In another pan beat egg yolks and ½ cup sugar with a whisk over hot water until warm and sugar has dissolved. Place egg mixture in a large mixing bowl. Using electric mixer, beat until room temperature. Slowly beat in gelatin mixture and Grand Marnier. In another large bowl, mix egg whites with remaining sugar to a soft foam consistency. Using a large spatula, fold whipped cream and egg whites gently into cooled gelatin mixture. Fill a 10-inch soufflé dish lined with ladyfingers with mixture. Refrigerate for at least 3 hours before serving. Decorate with whipped cream and small slices of candied orange peel.

Chef's Notes

- *Use cream with 40 percent butterfat for whipping.*
- *The egg and gelatin mixture must be cool before folding in whipped cream and egg whites for maximum lifting power.*
- *Invest in a professional rubber spatula, one that has a paddle of 5x4 inches. Folding is extremely efficient with this. Quickly it becomes obvious why in the restaurant business it is called a "money saver."*
- *After soaking, gelatin can be dissolved in a microwave for about 1 minute on high. Check manufacturer's directions.*

Frozen Peach Soufflé

ROBERT D. CORLISS

SOUS CHEF

The Williamsburg Inn, Colonial Williamsburg, Williamsburg

Chef's Notes

- *There should be approximately 1½ cups of prepared fruit.*
- *Other pretty garnishes are a dusting of confectioners' sugar and scattered berries.*
- *Try with blackberries, plums, blueberries, and strawberries.*
- *If fruits are out of season, frozen ones can be used. For those packed in syrup, use the concentrated syrup and reduce the quantity of sugar added to the purée.*

With this frozen mousse towering an inch above the individual soufflé dish, you will hear "How did you make that?" Chef Corliss extends the height of the dish with foil, crimps the foil, spoons in this low-calorie fruit and egg-white filling and slowly bakes in a gentle water bath. After 24 hours in the freezer and an artful decoration with more fresh fruit, this dessert has the perfect profile—a culinary delight and preserver of the figure. It is parsimonious on equipment—1 saucepan and 2 small bowls.

Complexity ❂❂   Yield: 4 servings

1	**tablespoon (½ ounce) sugar**
¼	**cup water**
5	**peaches (1¼ pounds), peeled and cut into small slivers**
1	**teaspoon peach schnapps**
¼	**teaspoon cream of tartar**
3	**to 4 egg whites**
1	**tablespoon (½ ounce) sugar**

Prepare 4-ounce soufflé dishes by wrapping foil an inch high around the top to form a collar. Crimp foil to hold into place.

In a small saucepan make a simple syrup by dissolving sugar in water. Add peaches. Cook until soft. Stir in schnapps. Purée with cream of tartar. Cool. In a separate bowl whip egg whites to medium peak. Add sugar gradually while whipping to a stiff meringue. Fold into cooled peach mixture. Spoon into prepared cups. Bake in a water bath for 30 minutes at 250°. Place in freezer for at least 24 hours. To serve, unwrap foil and decorate with a peach fan and garnish with mint sprigs. Serve in the dish.

Pineapple and Mango Mousse with Rum Custard

DOMINADOR VALEROS
SUPERVISOR LEAD CHEF, C.C.

Shields Tavern, Colonial Williamsburg, Williamsburg

Fresh tropical fruits lining individual soufflé dishes are topped with a creamy mousse and frozen. Do not be surprised if your guests start native dances when it is served with its rum custard. Do not be overly fussy with lining the molds as the mousse will hold the fruit in place. If in a hurry, simply place fruit slices in the dish, then fill with mousse and serve with fresh raspberries in place of the sauce.

Complexity ✪✪✪   **Yield: 6 servings**

MOUSSE

1 *mango (8 ounces), peeled, cut into thin strips, and trimmed to the height of the serving dish*
1 *small pineapple (2 pounds), peeled, cored, cut into thin strips, and trimmed to the height of the serving dish*
3 *egg yolks*
2 *tablespoons cold water*
¼ *cup water*
¼ *cup coconut milk*
2 *tablespoons (1 ounce) sugar*
1 *teaspoon vanilla extract*
1 *tablespoon (½ ounce) Malibu liqueur or other tropical fruit liqueur or rum*
⅔ *cup (6 ounces) heavy cream*

CUSTARD

3 *egg yolks*
3 *tablespoons (1½ ounces) sugar*
1¼ *cups (10 ounces) milk*
2 *tablespoons (1 ounce) rum*
1 *teaspoon vanilla extract*

GARNISH

diced mango and pineapple pieces
fresh mint leaves

Chef's Notes

• *Vanilla pods can be used in the place of extract in the custard. Use one pod split lengthwise in the boiling milk. Remove before pouring into eggs.*
• *If sauce happens to curdle, put into food processor and whirl about any lumps for a truly amazing recovery.*
• *Use a mango that is ripe but still firm.*
• *Dice any unused fruit for garnish.*
• *Try 1 tablespoon toasted coconut as garnish.*
• *Serve with a well-chilled Sauterne.*

mousse

In individual soufflé dishes or ramekins, line sides with vertically alternating pieces of mango and pineapple. In a large mixing bowl with an electric mixer, beat egg yolks with 2 tablespoons cold water for 5 minutes or until 4 times the original volume. In a small saucepan, boil for 2 minutes ¼ cup water, coconut milk, and sugar. With electric mixer on low, gradually pour sugar mixture into egg yolk mixture. Scrape down sides. Increase speed to high and continue mixing until the mixture is cool. Stir in vanilla and liqueur. In another large mixing bowl, beat cream to a light peak. Fold in egg and sugar mixture carefully. Pour into individual dishes over fruit. Smooth tops with a spatula. Freeze for 6 to 8 hours.

custard

In a small mixing bowl, use electric beaters to beat egg yolks with sugar for 4 minutes or until a pale straw color. In a medium saucepan bring milk and rum to a boil. Reduce heat and simmer for 5 minutes. With electric beater on, slowly mix milk into egg mixture. Mix in vanilla. Return the custard to saucepan over medium heat. Stir and cook until thickened enough to coat the back of a spoon. Refrigerate to cool.

assembly

Let mousse sit at room temperature for about 15 minutes, then run a knife around the interior edges. Unmold mousse onto serving plate. Spoon custard around base. Scatter diced fruits around. Top with mint leaf.

Grapefruit Champagne Granite

ANTHONY CONTE
PASTRY CHEF, C.C.
Country Club of Virginia, Richmond

This Italian-style sorbet needs no ice cream maker. It also is a delightful intermezzo or between-course palate cleanser. A moderately priced Spanish champagne, such as Codorniu, Brut class, is suggested. It is moderately priced but has excellent flavor.

Complexity ✪   Yield: 10 servings (use ⅓ cup portions)

- 1 cup (7 ounces) sugar
- ⅔ cup water
- 3 grapefruits (3 pounds)
- ¾ cup (6 ounces) champagne

Combine sugar and water in a small saucepan. Stir and bring to a boil over moderate heat. Cook and stir until sugar is dissolved. Remove any scum. Cool. Juice grapefruits. Combine all ingredients, mixing well, and place in a stainless steel shallow dish or bowl. Place in freezer. Stir occasionally while it is setting up so it does not become a solid mass.

Chef's Notes
- *The simple syrup solution can be made in advance and stored in a covered container.*
- *A little pulp from the grapefruit is acceptable. Remove any seeds.*
- *There should be about 2 cups of juice.*
- *Less expensive champagnes can be used. Avoid sweeter styles like extra dry and sec.*
- *Grapefruits from Florida from October through May will be the most flavorful. A ruby grapefruit, which is pink, adds a nice pink color to this ice and has an interesting taste variation.*

Homemade Maple Ice Cream

JOHN LONG
ROUNDS CHEF, C.C.

The Williamsburg Inn, Colonial Williamsburg, Williamsburg

Chef's Notes
- *Since this is the ultimate in rich ice cream, serve with a tiny scoop into your finest crystal dishes or glasses.*
- *Try as the à la mode part of a freshly baked apple pie.*
- *It is important to strain mixture before freezing so that any egg particles can be removed.*

Nothing is more old-fashioned than hand-cranking ice cream made with fresh dairy cream, milk, and egg yolks on a hot summer day. Chef Long's version has another natural component, pure maple syrup, to enhance its beautiful flavors.

Complexity ✪✪✪   Yield: 1 quart

¾ cup (8 ounces) maple syrup
2 cups (16 ounces) fresh cream
2 cups (16 ounces) milk
8 egg yolks

Reduce maple syrup by a third in a medium saucepan over medium heat. Add cream and milk. Bring just to a boil. In a stainless bowl mix egg yolks. Add milk mixture slowly to eggs, stirring constantly. Return mixture to saucepan. Cook over very low heat, stirring constantly with a wooden spoon. Continue to cook for about 4 minutes until it is thick, or when it leaves a trail on the spoon when you run your finger across. Strain through a fine mesh strainer into a stainless bowl. Set bowl in ice water. Stir until cooled. When completely cooled pour into an ice cream freezer and turn until frozen.

Chocolate Pecan Microwave Toffee

JOHN LONG

ROUNDS CHEF, C.C.

The Williamsburg Inn, Colonial Williamsburg, Williamsburg

Loaded with nuts, chocolate, and buttery toffee crunch, this candy is incredibly easy and fast to make. Preparation time is less than 15 minutes. Try other nuts, such as walnuts, sliced almonds, pistachios, and hazelnuts, solo or in combination.

Complexity ✪   **Yield: 1 pound**

½ cup (2 ounces) finely chopped pecans
½ cup (4 ounces) butter or margarine
1 cup (7 ounces) sugar
1 teaspoon salt
¼ cup water
¾ cup (5 ounces) semisweet chocolate morsels
¼ cup (1 ounce) finely chopped pecans

Sprinkle ½ cup pecans in a 9-inch circle on a greased cookie sheet or piece of waxed paper. Set aside. Coat the top 2 inches of a 2½-quart glass bowl with butter. Place remaining butter in bowl. Add sugar, salt, and water. Do not stir. Microwave on high for 11 minutes or until mixture just begins to turn light brown. Pour sugar mixture over pecans on cookie sheet. Let stand 1 minute. Sprinkle with chocolate morsels. Top with ¼ cup chopped pecans. Chill until firm. Break into bite-size pieces.

Chef's Notes
- *Store in an airtight container.*
- *Make this for an unusual and easy gift.*
- *This was tested using a 700-watt microwave oven. Check the power of your oven and make appropriate timing adjustments.*
- *Substitute butterscotch pieces for the chocolate as a variation.*

Truffles

DAVID BRUCE CLARKE

CHEF-INSTRUCTOR

J. Sargeant Reynolds Community College, Richmond

Chef's Notes

- *Purchase a #60 or #70 scoop for easy formation of balls. Look for one with a spring-action release that makes production speedy. These scoops are readily available at restaurant supply houses or gourmet cooking stores.*

- *Finished balls may also be coated with couverture chocolate or finely chopped nuts.*

- *Raspberry truffles can be made by adding 1 cup seedless raspberry purée and 2 tablespoons framboise (raspberry liqueur) after the incorporation of the cream and sugar.*

- *For longer term storage, freeze. Let sit at room temperature for several hours before serving.*

The first bite into this decadent creaminess will positively ruin the desire for store-bought truffles. For consumption in the next few days, store in the refrigerator. Test your patience to see if you can wait until they come to room temperature before indulging.

Complexity ✪✪✪　　　　　　　**Yield: approximately 90 pieces**

1 *pound bittersweet chocolate, cut into ¼-inch pieces*
¼ *cup (2 ounces) butter, cut into small pieces*
⅞ *cup (7 ounces) cream*
3 *tablespoons (¾ ounce) confectioners' sugar*
2 *tablespoons (1 ounce) amaretto or cognac*
　chocolate wafers, finely grated
　cocoa powder

In double boiler, melt chocolate. Remove from heat. Stir in butter. Cool 8 minutes. Stir in cream and sugar. Add liquor. Pour into a clean bowl. Refrigerate at least 1 hour. With 2 spoons or a small scoop, form rough balls on a baking sheet covered with waxed paper. Chill again for 1 hour. With hands, quickly roll into smooth balls. Roll half in chocolate wafers and half in cocoa powder.

Black and White Truffles

JO OLSON
ACCOUNT EXECUTIVE
Atlantic Food Services, Inc., Richmond

The heavy cream is first melted slowly in a saucepan. Then chocolate and butter are stirred in with raspberry for the dark chocolate or orange for the white chocolate truffles. After chilling, the mixture is formed into truffles using 2 teaspoons. Pass these intense truffles with coffee and liqueurs.

Chef's Notes
- Be sure to use quality chocolate and not imitations.
- Toast pecans for 15 to 20 minutes on a baking sheet in a 325° oven.
- Try a small action release scoop, similar to an ice cream scoop, to form truffles.

chocolate raspberry truffles

Complexity ❂❂❂   Yield: 40 servings

½ cup (4 ounces) heavy cream
14 ounces semisweet chocolate, chopped fine
¼ cup (2 ounces) butter, unsalted, cut into pieces
½ cup (6 ounces) seedless raspberry jam
½ cup (2 ounces) sifted cocoa powder

In a heavy-bottomed 2-quart pan bring cream to a boil over moderate heat. Remove from heat. Stir in chocolate until it is completely melted and smooth. Let sit 10 minutes. Add butter a bit at a time, stirring until smooth. Stir in jam. Transfer mixture to a baking pan and chill for about 5 hours or until firm. Form heaping teaspoons into balls. Roll in cocoa powder. Chill until very firm. Store in an airtight container.

white chocolate truffles

Complexity ❂❂❂   Yield: 30 servings

¼ cup (2 ounces) heavy cream
6 ounces white chocolate, chopped fine
2 teaspoons unsalted butter
2 tablespoons (1 ounce) orange juice concentrate
1½ cups (6 ounces) chopped pecans, toasted and cooled

In a heavy-bottomed 2-quart pan bring cream to a boil over moderate heat. Remove from heat. Stir in chocolate until it is completely melted and smooth. Add butter. Stir until melted. Stir in orange juice. Chill until mixture is firm. Form heaping teaspoons into balls. Roll in chopped pecans. Chill for 1 hour or until firm. Store in an airtight container.

CHAPTER 11
Beautiful Breakfasts

🍍 *For sweeter pancakes,* add vanilla to the batter.—*Chef Fulton*

🍍 *Fresh orange juice* should be just that! Squeeze just before serving for full vitamin C value.—*Chef Fulton*

🍍 *For less greasy* and more tender sausage start in a cold frying pan; do not add fat. Always place ham and bacon to be fried into pan before turning on heat.
—*Chef Fulton*

🍍 *To prevent sausage links* from bursting, prick them thoroughly or boil prior to frying.—*Chef Fulton*

🍍 *When poaching eggs,* add a teaspoon of vinegar to cooking water. This prevents whites from spreading.—*Chef Fulton*

🍍 *For larger, lighter omelets,* add warm milk to the beaten eggs.—*Chef Fulton*

🍍 *Do not salt eggs* before beating; it makes them watery causing omelets to stick.
—*Chef Fulton*

🍍 *Cover pan while cooking* to develop white film over the yolk of fried eggs. It will not toughen egg.—*Chef Fulton*

🍍 *For an unusual breakfast,* fill a custard cup half full with sweet cream and drop 1 egg in each cup. Add breadcrumbs and a little grated cheese. Brown in a 350° oven for 10 minutes.—*Chef Fulton*

🍍 *Eggs do not come* in the perfect package. The shell, in addition to being very fragile, is porous. Eggs must be in a closed container to prevent the loss of interior moisture and to avoid picking up flavors and odors from other foods. The open egg containers in refrigerators are a true mystery—solve this one by asking friends what they do with them.

🍍 *Eggs are graded* for freshness—AA, A, and B. The freshest egg, AA, has the most height when cracked and permitted to sit and has the best taste. As the egg ages it loose moisture and height. Most retail eggs are graded A while B eggs are usually sold to commercial baking operations.

🍍 *Most recipes call* for large eggs that weigh 24 ounces per dozen or 2 ounces each. In each egg one-third of the weight is the yolk, which is high in fat and protein, while the rest is the white that is mostly albumen protein. Feel free to substitute egg sizes. The following lists the number of eggs required to make 1 cup: 4 extra-large, 5 large, 6 mediums, or 7 smalls. For 1 cup of egg whites use 6 extra-large or 7 large or 8 medium or 10 small.

🍍 *Never boil eggs* or cook on high heat. They will toughen and become rubbery.

🍍 *Scrambled eggs that sit* too long or hard-cooked eggs that have been overcooked develop a greenish cast or ring caused by the chemical reaction between the sulfur in the egg with the iron in the yolk, which yields iron sulfide.

🍍 *Use eggs that are* several days old for hard-cooked (never hard-boiled) eggs as they will be easier to peel.

🍍 *Pancake and waffle batters* can be made the night before and stored in the refrigerator if made with baking powder. Those made with baking soda will loose their leavening power. Note that baking soda is used with acidic ingredients such as buttermilk, sour cream, chocolate, and molasses.

🍍 *Cook bacon and sausage* at low temperatures to prevent shrinkage.

🍍 *Coffee is best* when the beans are freshly ground. Store coffee in a tightly sealed container in a cool, dry place for less than one week. If storage is longer, freeze whole beans and use when needed.

🍍 *Brewing coffee* should be done between 195° and 200°.

🍍 *Brewed, percolated, or drip coffee* should never be kept on a heating unit for more than 30 minutes as it becomes bitter. The preferred holding temperatures are between 185 and 190°.

🍍 *Fresh, cold water* containing dissolved air makes the best coffee or tea.

🍍 *A pound of coffee* makes 40 servings while a pound of fermented tea makes 200 servings.

🍍 *Keep lemon drops* on hand for hot tea.
—*Chef Fulton*

🍍 *Try brown sugar* to sweeten tea—a delightfully different flavor.—*Chef Fulton*

🍍 *Use 1 tea bag* or 1 teaspoon of loose tea to brew one 6-ounce cup of tea. Pour briskly boiling water made from fresh, cold source over bag or loose tea in cup. Steeping should be leisurely, allowing from 3 to 5 minutes.

🍍 *Be creative* in selection of items for breakfast. Leftovers from dinner might be the perfect way to start the day.

Spinach and Bacon Quiche

TED KRISTENSEN
CHEF-OWNER, C.E.C., A.A.C.

The Willows Bed and Breakfast, Gloucester

Pine nuts accent the sharp Cheddar and spinach variation on this supreme breakfast pie. Bake it ahead of time and then reheat.

Complexity ❂❂   **Yield: 8 servings**

6 slices bacon (6 ounces), julienned
1 medium (4 ounces) onion, minced
2 cloves garlic, minced
1 pound fresh spinach, chopped, discard stems
½ cup (4 ounces) cream
10 eggs
    pinch nutmeg
⅓ cup (1½ ounces) pine nuts, toasted
4 ounces New York Cheddar cheese, grated
    10-inch pie shell, baked

In a 10-inch skillet sauté bacon until light brown. Remove pieces from pan. Sauté minced onions, garlic, and spinach in bacon fat until tender. In 3-quart mixing bowl, completely mix cream, eggs, and nutmeg. Stir in bacon, onion, spinach mixture, pine nuts, and cheese. Pour into pie shell. Bake 45 minutes in a preheated 350° oven until filling is firm in the center.

Chef's Notes
- *A slice of this savory quiche with a couple of cranberry muffins and a cup of good, hot coffee will start your morning in good fashion.*
- *For good color and nutritional blend, try to garnish breakfast plates with fresh fruit such as a cluster of seedless grapes or orange sections.*

Æggekage, Danish Omelet

TED KRISTENSEN
CHEF-OWNER, C.E.C., A.A.C.
The Willows Bed and Breakfast, Gloucester

Chef's Notes

- *Filleted smoked herrings may be used instead of bacon. Use about 2 tablespoons of butter to fry the omelet.*
- *Whole-grain breads, including rye and pumpernickel, are original farm country favorites.*
- *For a lower-calorie version, substitute low-fat bacon and milk in the place of cream. While the resulting product is not as rich, it is still delicious.*

At the Willows, guests are treated to this hearty late morning weekend breakfast after a night of relaxation in the well-appointed Gloucester inn. In Denmark since the early 1700s, these omelets would be the just reward for dairy farmers who rose at 4:00 A.M. for milking and chores. In the dairy country, this healthy breakfast fueled the body and warmed the soul after hours of work.

Complexity ✪✪   Yield: 4 to 6 servings

16 slices bacon (1 pound)
2½ teaspoons cornstarch
 1 cup (8 ounces) heavy cream
 ½ teaspoon salt
 ½ teaspoon finely ground pepper
 8 eggs
   chives, finely chopped, garnish

Fry bacon until crisp in a large fry pan. Save fat and wipe pan clean. Mix cornstarch with cream, salt, and pepper. Be miserly with salt as the omelet is to be fried in bacon fat. Beat eggs into cornstarch mixture. Pour a small amount of bacon fat into the pan and add egg mixture. Over gentle heat, permit mixture to set, raising edges occasionally allowing liquid mixture to contact hot pan surface. When nearly set decorate with bacon and sprinkle with chives. Cut into quarters. Serve directly from pan with whole-meal rye bread and mustard.

Austrian Poached Eggs on Potato Pancakes

TED KRISTENSEN
CHEF-OWNER, C.E.C., A.A.C.
The Willows Bed and Breakfast, Gloucester

Since Columbus's voyage and the subsequent introduction of the potato to the Old World, the spud has played a daily starring role in European cuisine. Adding the potato to this Austrian-style pancake makes a wholesome country-style breakfast.

Complexity ✪✪　　　　　**Yield: 6 servings**

- ¼ cup (1 ounce) all-purpose flour
- ¾ cup (6 ounces) milk
- 1 egg
- ½ teaspoon salt
- ¼ cup (2 ounces) butter
- 4 large potatoes (1½ pounds), grated
- 6 eggs, poached
- 6 ounces thinly sliced ham
- 6 slices brioche
- jam of choice

Mix flour and milk in 3-quart mixing bowl. Beat in egg and salt. Mix in grated potatoes. Heat butter in 10-inch cast-iron skillet. Portion a heaping ¼ cup for each pancake. Spread the mixture thinly and fry 2 to 3 minutes on each side or until golden brown. Place 2 pancakes on each plate with poached egg on slice of ham. Place warmed, fresh brioche on side.

Chef's Notes
- *The breakfast plate should include some fruit. A special treat is the addition of old-fashioned applesauce or apple butter.*
- *Bacon or lean turkey ham may be substituted for the ham.*
- *Cook potato pancakes on a nonstick griddle sprayed with vegetable spray for a lower-calorie rendition.*

Eggs Chesapeake

TED KRISTENSEN

CHEF-OWNER, C.E.C., A.A.C.

The Willows Bed and Breakfast, Gloucester

Chef's Notes

• *Do not add any salt when making Hollandaise sauce as the Smithfield ham is extremely high in salt.*

• *Try the packaged Hollandaise mixes for a quick sauce.*

Two famous Virginia products—the distinguished, well-smoked Smithfield ham and the delicious crabmeat from the Chesapeake Bay—team-up, creating a distinguished and unforgettable breakfast or brunch experience. Generous slices of grapefruit and orange finish these lovely plates. An easier version is to substitute a pat of butter for the Hollandaise sauce.

Complexity ✪✪   Yield: 4 to 6 servings

4 English muffins, cut in half and toasted
8 eggs, poached
8 slices (1 ounce each) Smithfield ham
1 pound backfin crab, picked over and lightly sautéed in butter
½ cup (4 ounces) Hollandaise sauce
1 grapefruit, ½-inch thick slices
1 orange, ½-inch thick slices

On plate place 2 halves of toasted muffin. Add slice of ham on each. Place egg on top, then cover with crabmeat. Finish with 1 tablespoon Hollandaise sauce on each. Garnish plates with citrus slices.

Cotswold Country House Breakfast with Cumberland Sausage

TED KRISTENSEN
CHEF-OWNER, C.E.C., A.A.C.

The Willows Bed and Breakfast, Gloucester

Give your day a wonderful start with a good English country breakfast that dates back to the days of Sir Francis Bacon. Many claim that breakfast is the finest part of English cuisine.

Complexity ❂❂❂   **Yield: 2 servings**

THE COTSWOLD MENU

2   *eggs, fried sunny-side up*
2   *Cumberland sausages*
3   *ounces fresh mushrooms, sliced and sautéed*
2   *small tomatoes (8 ounces), sliced and sautéed*
2   *strips bacon (2 ounces), cut thick and cooked*
2   *croissants*
2   *slices toast*
4   *Parmesan cheese straws*
    marmalade
    honey

CUMBERLAND SAUSAGE

Yield: 12 servings

3   *pounds lean pork shoulder*
4   *to 5 ounces pork fat, reserved from shoulder trimmings*
1   *slice bacon (1 ounce)*
2   *ounces breadcrumbs, fresh*
1   *teaspoon salt*
½   *teaspoon pepper*
    large pinch ground mace
    large pinch grated nutmeg

Grind pork with fat and bacon on medium grinder blade. Mix breadcrumbs and seasonings. Roll into a 1-inch thick roll. Bake on a sheet pan for 35 to 40 minutes in a 350° oven until cooked through and golden brown. Remove from oven. Cool for at least 5 minutes. Cut into 3-inch portions and serve.

Chef's Notes
- *Before grinding for sausage, place meat, fat, and grinder blade in freezer for 30 minutes. This will create a more desirable texture and prevent the fat's melting from the friction of grinding.*
- *Roll sausage on a long piece of plastic wrap. Remove film before baking.*
- *Try this sausage with ground turkey in the place of the pork shoulder and fat.*
- *Freeze portions for future use.*
- *To make Parmesan cheese straws, roll puff pastry (available in most frozen food sections) to a ¼-inch thickness. Cut into 5-inch lengths. Roll in freshly grated Parmesan cheese. Twist. Bake for 5 minutes in a 400° oven.*

French Toast, Provence Style

TED KRISTENSEN
CHEF-OWNER, C.E.C., A.A.C.
The Willows Bed and Breakfast, Gloucester

Chef's Notes
- *A vegetable peeler can remove orange peel without the bitter white part. To finely chop, place peel with sugar in a small food processor.*
- *Serve with ham or sausages and a cluster of seedless grapes.*

French toast originally used up leftover, fat-free bread with no keeping power. After tasting this version of French toast, one may be wont to forgo fresh bread and wait for breakfast. The French people lead the world in per capita consumption of bread, but with this recipe revealed we may soon be catching up.

Complexity ✪✪   **Yield: 4 servings**

6 eggs
⅔ cup (7 ounces) orange juice
⅓ cup (2½ ounces) Grand Marnier (or other orange liqueur)
⅓ cup (2½ ounces) milk
3 tablespoons (1½ ounces) sugar
¼ teaspoon vanilla extract
¼ teaspoon salt
zest of 1 orange, finely grated
8 slices French bread, ¾-inch thick
¼ cup (2 ounces) butter
orange slices, garnish
confectioners' sugar
maple syrup

Beat eggs in a 3-quart bowl. Add orange juice, Grand Marnier, milk, sugar, vanilla, salt, and zest. Mix well. Dip bread into mixture and coat all surfaces. Transfer to a buttered 3-quart baking dish in a single layer. Pour remaining mixture into baking dish. Cover and refrigerate overnight. Melt butter in a 12-inch skillet. Over medium heat cook toast for about 4 minutes on each side or until golden brown. Place orange slices diagonally on plates with toast. Sprinkle with confectioners' sugar. Serve with a fine maple syrup.

Lemon Coffee Cake

RAOUL B. HEBERT
EXECUTIVE CHEF
Bull and Bear Club, Richmond

Egg whites and baking powder puff up this lemon cake. Serve with lots of strong black coffee or a spirited Earl Grey tea that is spiked with bergamot (the essential oil from a delightfully acidic orange).

Complexity ✪✪   **Yield: 12 to 16 servings**

CAKE

3 cups (12 ounces) all-purpose flour
1½ cups (10½ ounces) sugar
5 teaspoons baking powder
½ teaspoon salt
½ cup (4 ounces) butter, softened
1½ cups (12 ounces) evaporated milk
1 tablespoon grated lemon rind, zest only
4 egg whites

GLAZE

¾ cup (3 ounces) confectioners' sugar
1½ tablespoons lemon juice

Mix flour, sugar, baking powder, and salt in a large mixing bowl. Add butter, milk, and lemon rind. Beat until smooth. Beat egg whites separately until stiff peaks form. Fold into cake batter. Pour into a 10-inch greased and floured bundt pan. Bake at 375° for 35 to 40 minutes or until done. Cool. Remove from pan. Mix powdered sugar and lemon juice. Pour over cake.

Chef's Notes
- *Try as a dessert with mixed berries.*
- *Batter may be processed either in a blender or electric mixer.*
- *The cake may be prepared one day in advance.*
- *Try this with orange rind and juice as a variation, then serve with fresh orange slices.*

Sour Cream Coffee Cake

JOHN KOGELMAN
HEAD BAKER, C.M.B., C.E.P.C.
The Boca Raton Resort and Club, Florida

Chef's Notes
- *The batter is quite thick. Spread with spoon in pan. After adding fillings, spoon remaining batter on top and gently spread. Variations create a beautiful swirl in the filling that is vastly appreciated when slicing.*
- *Serve with freshly brewed coffee or tea.*
- *An easy apple filling is made by finely chopping 2 apples to mix with the sugar and cinnamon.*
- *This may be baked ahead, tightly wrapped, and frozen.*
- *Make other varieties by changing the fillings and flavorings or by adding different spices to the batter.*

The aroma of cinnamony coffee cake is sure to get even the sleepiest person up and into the kitchen. The baker will be rewarded with appreciative smiles while the eater revels in the even texture, delicate taste, and light sweetness. Preparation time is minimal for this special treat.

Complexity ✪✪   **Yield: 24 servings**

CAKE

½ cup (4 ounces) butter
2 cups (14 ounces) sugar
4 large eggs
2 cups (16 ounces) sour cream
½ teaspoon vanilla extract
5 cups (1¼ pounds) all-purpose flour
2½ teaspoons baking powder
1¼ teaspoons baking soda

FILLING

1 cup (7 ounces) sugar
1 tablespoon ground cinnamon

TOPPING

confectioners' sugar

With a mixer fitted with paddle or heavy beaters, cream butter and sugar on medium for 1 minute. Slowly add eggs 1 at a time until incorporated. Add sour cream until blended, about 1 minute. Add vanilla, flour, baking powder, and soda. Mix on slow speed for 1 minute. Increase speed to medium-high until smooth. Put half of the batter into a 10-inch greased and floured bundt pan with center tube. Sprinkle mixed sugar and cinnamon on top. Cover with remaining half of batter. Bake at 325° for 50 to 60 minutes or until toothpick or silver cake probe comes out clean. Cool 15 minutes and remove from pan. Sprinkle with confectioners' sugar.

Vetebröd, Swedish Coffee Bread

KAREN SHERWOOD
CHEF-OWNER
Sherwood Consulting, Richmond

This is a fragrant cardamom sweet bread gloriously destined to accompany coffee. Chef Sherwood says, "My fondest memories growing up were when my Swedish grandmother and mother would bake this type of bread." Later when Karen traveled through Sweden she understood "why there was always a plentiful presentation of Vetebröd on every breakfast Smorgasbord."

Complexity ❁❁❁   **Yield: 2 braided loaves**

1¼ cups (10 ounces) whole milk, 100°
2 teaspoons active dry yeast
1 teaspoon sugar
4 cups (1 pound) bread flour
1 teaspoon ground cardamom
1 teaspoon salt
⅓ cup (2½ ounces) sugar
1 egg
1 egg yolk
½ cup (4 ounces) butter, melted and cooled
1 teaspoon cardamom mixed with 2 tablespoons sugar

Warm milk in small saucepan. Whisk in yeast and sugar. Proof for 5 minutes. In a 5-quart mixing bowl combine flour, cardamom, salt, and sugar. Beat eggs and butter into yeast mixture. Add liquid mixture to flour mixture. Knead dough until smooth and elastic (about 7 minutes with electric mixer with dough hooks or paddle). Let rise in a warm place for 1 hour. Punch down. Let rise for another hour. Evenly divide dough into 6 pieces. On a floured pastry board, roll each piece into a 4x10-inch rectangle. Sprinkle cardamom sugar over rectangles. Roll each lengthwise into a rope. Braid 3 ropes to form each loaf. Transfer each to a greased baking sheet. Let rise 1 hour. Sprinkle tops with a small amount of sugar. Bake at 350° for about 45 minutes or until golden brown. Cool on rack.

Chef's Notes
- *Cardamom is a very pricey spice. Buy in the smallest quantity. Like all ground spices, store away from light and heat and use in less than 6 months.*
- *For a shiny, professional-looking top, brush braided loaves with a mixture of 1 egg yolk in 1 tablespoon of water.*
- *For the holidays sprinkle chopped nuts and candied fruits on each rectangle before rolling.*
- *Cinnamon may be substituted for the cardamom mixed with sugar for filling.*
- *This dough should be sticky and stiff and pale golden yellow. Use only a small amount of flour when rolling.*

Sourdough Hot Cakes and Syrup

WILLIAM F. FULTON
C.E.C.
Chester

Chef's Notes
- *A small round sauté or crêpe pan can be used, or try free-form on a griddle.*
- *To avoid contaminating the starter, scald utensils to be used. Do not use metal containers or spoons. Use either a 2-quart pitcher, a glass jar, or a stone crock that is large enough to allow for the expansion of the dough.*
- *For syrup flavoring, use any natural extracts such as vanilla, cherry, lemon, butter rum, or maple.*
- *Waffles may be made with this batter. Beat eggs separately to make an especially light waffle. Place strips of fried bacon across the waffle.*

Sourdough cakes are not like other hot cakes—they are deceptively light and crêpelike, more breadlike than eggy. In fact the dissimilarity of these hot cakes to other cakes becomes a delightful topic of conversation. Yeast is used instead of baking powder, and soda is used to neutralize the acidity of the yeast and make the batter light. A yeast starter may be kept going for years if it contains nothing but flour, water, and yeast, and if it is kept cool and used once a week or more often. If the starter must be kept longer, it should be refrigerated or dried. Why not make extra starter to share with friends?

Complexity ✪✪   Yield: 4 to 6 servings

STARTER

2½ teaspoons (¼ ounce) active dry yeast (or ¼ cup starter reserved from previous batch)
¼ cup lukewarm water (110°)
2 cups lukewarm water (110°)
2½ cups (10 ounces) all-purpose or bread flour

FOR HOT CAKES THE NEXT MORNING

Starter (save ¼ cup of the bubbling starter in a scalded pint jar, cover, and keep in refrigerator to use in place of yeast for the next hot cakes)
2 eggs
1 teaspoon baking soda
1 teaspoon salt
1 tablespoon sugar
2 tablespoons (1 ounce) vegetable oil
2 to 4 tablespoons (1 to 2 ounces) milk (optional: if batter is too thick to pour)

SYRUP

1 cup (8 ounces) firmly packed brown sugar
1 cup (7 ounces) sugar
1 cup water
1 teaspoon flavoring

starter

Soften yeast in ¼ cup water. Add remaining ingredients. Mix well and set in a cupboard free from drafts. Cover lightly and let stand overnight. This batter should be rather thin.

for hot cakes the next morning

Mix all ingredients into starter. The batter should be the consistency of cream, no heavier. If the batter is too thick to pour, add milk. Never add more flour to the raised batter. Use it even if it seems thin. For each pancake pour ¼ cup of batter on a greased, medium hot griddle. When small bubbles form after about 2 minutes, flip. Continue to cook for 2 more minutes. Serve hot.

syrup

Place sugars and water into a medium saucepan. Boil for 2 minutes. Let cool slightly and stir in flavoring. Yields about 1½ cups.

Grits Soufflé

MARCEL DESAULNIERS

Chef-Owner, C.E.C., A.A.C.

The Trellis Restaurant, Williamsburg

Chef's Notes

- *This soufflé is very easy to prepare. Once begun, it must be completed. All ingredients should be gathered before beginning assembly.*
- *Salt-cured Virginia ham can be processed in a food processor fitted with a metal blade in about 1 minute. Some supermarkets offer ground ham, usually made of the unsliceable end pieces, which is ideal for this recipe.*
- *If you are lucky enough to get fresh ramps (a wild onion found in forested regions of the eastern United States), discard the leaves and substitute ¼ cup of the sliced pinkish-white portion for the scallions.*

Chef Desaulniers's first taste of grits was, unfortunately, at Marine Corps boot camp. He remembers, "Whatever was placed on your mess tray had to be consumed no matter your opinion of its culinary validity." Years later, he greedily and happily eats every bite of the delicious and lovingly cooked grits prepared by his wife's Grandmother Shaw of Wilmington, North Carolina. She would not approve of this recipe; it is not made with stone-ground grits and its form and embellishment go far beyond the mound of grits with a large pat of butter that she so dearly enjoys.

Complexity ❂❂   Yield: 8 servings

¼ *cup (2 ounces) unsalted butter, softened*
4 *cups whole milk (3½% butterfat)*
1 *cup instant grits*
1 *cup (4 ounces) grated Tillamook Cheddar cheese*
¼ *cup (¾ ounce) freshly grated Parmesan cheese*
2 *teaspoons salt*
1 *teaspoon baking powder*
1 *teaspoon sugar*
½ *cup (3 ounces) ground country ham*
4 *scallions, thinly sliced*
6 *large eggs, separated*

Lightly coat insides of 8 ceramic crocks with butter. Place on baking sheet. Melt butter in a small nonstick sauté pan over low heat. Set aside.

Heat milk in a 2½-quart saucepan until almost boiling (bubbles should begin to form around the edges) over medium heat. Add grits, stirring constantly. Cook until slightly thickened, about 1 minute. Add cheeses and cook until thick, stirring constantly, about 2 minutes. Remove from heat, transfer to a stainless steel bowl. Add salt, baking powder, melted butter, and sugar to grits mixture and mix well. Fold in ham and scallions. Beat egg yolks until well mixed. Add to grits. Whip egg whites until they hold soft peaks, about 3 minutes. Gently fold whites into grits mixture. Divide mixture among crocks. Bake in a preheated 375° oven for 20 minutes, until risen, set, and browned. Serve immediately!

Summer Breakfast

PHILIP LADD
EXECUTIVE CHEF
Holiday Inn Executive Center, Chesterfield

During the warm summer months, here is a welcome, no-cooking-required breakfast that has added virtues—economy, taste, and health. Vary the fruits during their seasons. Serve also for buffets and coffee breaks.

Complexity ✪   Yield: 8 servings

2 cups (6 ounces) raw oats
1 cup (8 ounces) milk (low-fat or 2 percent)
1 peach (4 ounces), peeled and chopped
1 plum (3 ounces), peeled and chopped
½ cup (4 ounces) white seedless grapes, sliced
¼ cup (2 ounces) raisins
2 tablespoons (½ ounce) chopped walnuts
2 tablespoons (1½ ounces) honey
   fresh mint, garnish
   fresh berries, garnish

Soak oats in milk for about 6 hours. Add remaining ingredients, except garnishes. Stir. Refrigerate. Serve with fresh mint and berries as garnishes.

Chef's Notes
- *This healthy breakfast can be prepared several days in advance and consumed as desired.*
- *For a special and rich treat, add ½ cup whipped cream just before serving.*
- *And there is really no reason not to have this whatever the season by matching with the appropriate fresh fruits. Or when extravagance is needed, splurge on an exotic fruit out of season!*

Appendix

SANITATION SECRETS

THE SAFETY of food is not always visually apparent except to a microbiologist. Food-borne illness is caused by bacteria. Pathogens may taint food, often causing illnesses, particularly in the elderly and the young. General symptoms are nausea, cramps, diarrhea, and pain. Harmful bacteria happily thrive with moisture at room temperature. High salt, sugar, or acid contents are not friendly environments for bacteria.

Certified chefs are well-trained in proper sanitation procedures. The Virginia Chefs Association provides classes on current procedures for continuing education. Participation is mandatory for recertification.

Food left at room temperature for more than 1 hour is the perfect medium for growing bacteria. As such all foods should be stored at the proper temperatures. The danger zone for foods is between 40° and 140°. That means that foods should be chilled to less than 40° and hot foods kept at temperatures higher than 140° for safety.

As a guide for leftover foods, chill in small batches, wrap tightly.

If holding foods heated, bring to the boiling point first.

Thaw frozen foods in the refrigerator or follow microwave instructions. Do not thaw foods at room temperature.

If any foods are the slightest bit questionable, discard them. The price of fresh ingredients is minuscule compared to the grief from a food-borne illness.

Wash hands before touching any foods. Wash hands after touching any raw meat products.

Tasting a dish requires a clean spoon for each taste. Never taste from a stirring spoon.

Keep all raw and cooked foods separate. Keep a separate cutting board for meats. Current research suggests that wooden cutting boards may be more sanitary for meats. But be sure to clean and disinfect all boards. Small plastic ones that fit into a dishwasher are particularly safe.

Carefully follow temperature doneness guides for potentially dangerous foods such as meats, fish, poultry, eggs, and dairy products. Instant read thermometers are particularly useful for this purpose. And remember to clean thermometers after each use to avoid cross-contamination.

When purchasing foods, keep raw meats and poultry products away from other foods. If any meat juices leak onto the checkout conveyor belt, have the checker clean it immediately. For your own safety, place meat products on belt last. Have them bagged separately. And insist that the belt be cleaned if there is any indication that a previous order had any leakage problems.

Date all foods in the pantry. Use before expiration dates, then toss. If anything appears questionable, throw it away.

Chef Contributors

OTTO BERNET, CMPC, AAC, *Director of European Specialties, Ukrop's Supermarket, Richmond*, is responsible for menu, production, training, and quality control in the 22 Ukrop's markets for their pastries. Chef Bernet has attained the ultimate level of certification that of Certified Master Pastry Chef. At this time there are only seventeen such master pastry chefs in the United States. After three days of practical and one day of written examinations, at twenty-four years old, he became one of the youngest chefs to receive this demanding designation. He began at a young age working in his father's pastry shop. Later he apprenticed with a very famous chef—"a master who taught me everything." Next he worked with Europe's most prestigious chefs. He is a founding member of the National Guild of Pastry and Baking Professionals. He has won gold medals at the Culinary Olympics in Frankfurt and in the *Hospes* International Culinary Competition in Switzerland. Born and trained in Switzerland, he, his wife, and son emigrated to the United States in 1959. A few years later "we were happy to have a second son." He was formerly with Chef Otto's Bakery and La Petite France Pastry Shop. He is active in the community, participating at the Taste of the Nation, The Chocolate Lovers Weekend for the Kidney Foundation, Horizons 2000 dinners, and teaching high school students at career days about the trade and how to become a chef. He is the Virginia Chef's past president and treasurer and was honored as Chef of the Year 1980.

JEFF BLAND, *Buckhead Steak House, Richmond, Sous Chef,* and an instructor at J. Sargeant Reynolds Community College, teaches Introduction to Food Preparation, Food Purchasing, Commercial Food, and Garde Mange. He formerly worked at the Downtown Club and Pillars, served an externship at Walt Disney's Empress Lily, and worked in New York as chef and baker in a private school. At fourteen years old he began as a dishwasher in a Richmond Italian restaurant. In his spare time he began to make salads, then advanced to pizza making. He graduated from Johnson and Wales, Providence, Rhode Island, with an associates degree in occupational science. He was so hungry for cooking knowledge that he offered to work without pay for three months with Chef Paul Ebling. Known as Chef Jeff to many, he spends considerable time with high school students spreading the joy of cooking as a career. On a totally volunteer basis he widely travels Virginia sharing with young people the totally satisfying career he found. He is creating a newsletter for Virginia food occupation teachers with information and ideas to teach better. His hobbies include cooking (naturally), chess, and reading novels.

DON BLEAU, *Minnesota,* manages restaurant chains, formerly the Executive Chef at The Butlery, Ltd., Richmond.

DAVID BRUCE CLARKE, *Chef-Instructor, J. Sargeant Reynolds Community College, Chesterfield,* where he teaches Introductions to Culinary Arts and Commercial Foods, Advanced Food Preparation, and Garde Mange, Food Purchasing. Originally from Maryland, Clarke received special cooks and bakers training at the U.S. Army Quartermasters School (honor graduate, second in class of 800), U.S. Air Force Food Safety and Sanitation Management, and Baltimore International Culinary Arts Institute. He received the International Food Services Executive Association Award for Culinary Excellence. Former positions include the Jefferson Lakeside Club, Creative Catering by Conner, Ltd., Country Club of Virginia, Sheratons Park South and Airport Inn, Le Bistro Francois and Chef-Instructor at the Baltimore Culinary Arts Institute. Clarke spends considerable time with students as adviser to VCA apprentice

program, member of Allied Hospitality careers tech preproject action team, curriculum writing team coordinator and in fundraising activities such as SOS Taste of the Nation and the International Food Festival Gourmet Theatre.

DENNIS CONNELL, *Pittsburgh, Pennsylvania,* formerly with Lafayette Mixed Grille, Kingsmill Resort, and Newport, Rhode Island, waterfront restaurants. From a large family in Pennsylvania, Dennis started cooking at a young age and proceeded with his culinary education until he graduated from the Culinary Institute of America, Hyde Park.

ANTHONY CONTE, CC, *Assistant Pastry Chef, Country Club of Virginia, Richmond,* formerly at the Williamsburg Inn, Hotel Jefferson, Ford's Colony, Lafayette Mixed Grille. Conte began cooking in tiny seafood places during summer vacations. After earning a bachelor's degree in management at Hampden Sydney he was General Manager of the historic Michie Tavern, Charlottesville. With partners he started the bistro in The Blue Ridge Brewing Co. Wanting to learn more about the technology/culinary side of food, he spent the next four years at the Williamsburg Inn and took classes at J. Sargeant Reynolds Community College. He was a contributing writer for the ACF Apprentice Manual: *The Art and Science of Culinary Preparations* on "How Foods Are Flavored and Seasoned." He earned both gold and silver medals at the VCA ACF Culinary Salons. A devoted computer buff, he teaches Hospitality Computers at the college level and writes recipes in the wee morning hours.

ROBERT CORLISS, *Sous Chef, Williamsburg Inn, Williamsburg,* graduated cum laude from Johnson and Wales, Providence, with an associates degree in occupation science. As a junior in high school Robert became intrigued with foods. He began working as a prep cook at a local country club, then moved to Hershey Lodge and Convention Center. He has become a first-class chef, meticulous in his work, presentation, and teaching. Serving as the cookbook liaison, he made this book possible by acquiring recipes from the chefs, contributing many recipes, generously adding secrets for the chef's notes, reading various versions, and organizing promotional activities. As a member of the Williamsburg Inn Culinary Team, he has earned numerous awards in sanctioned culinary competitions. He serves as the editor and writer for *The Stockpot,* a monthly newsletter for the VCA. Chef Corliss was honored as Chef of the Year in 1993 and also received the President's Award.

EDWARD DAGGERS, CEC, *Country Club, Memphis, Tennessee,* is originally from Pennsylvania and a graduate of the Culinary Institute of America. Formerly with Kingsmill Resort, Sky Top Lodge and Resort, Innisbrook Resort. Daggers has recipes in Marcel Desaulniers's *The Burgermeisters* and in *The Flavors of Kingsmill* (Norfolk: J&B Editions, 1991). Daggers has won many medals at culinary salons including Best of Show. His bread and salt dough sculptures are outstanding.

MARCEL DESAULNIERS, CEC, AAC, *Chef-Owner of The Trellis Restaurant, Williamsburg.* He has written *The Trellis Cookbook, Death by Chocolate: The Last Word on a Consuming Passion, The Burgermeisters,* and *Desserts to Die For* (forthcoming). Chef Desaulniers is an avid runner and avoider of cholesterol. He graduated from The Culinary Institute of America. A Marine veteran of Vietnam, he was a chef at Hotel Pierre in New York and a food broker for Colonial Williamsburg. VCA Chef of the Year in 1985, he has also received a James Beard Award for best dessert cookbook and in 1994 was named Regional Chef of the Year.

STUART DEUTSCH, *Executive Chef, The American Tobacco Company, Chester.* He was formerly with Stonehenge Country Club, Chardonnay's, and Oscar's Restaurant. Born in Munich, Germany, his parents came to the United States when he was two years old. Six years later he was flipping eggs with his dad making Sunday brunch at home. Following his passion for food, he graduated from Johnson and Wales, Providence, Rhode Island, then spent five years at the Sheraton in Washington, D.C. Today he operates a large-scale food service during the day so he can enjoy evenings and weekends with his family.

WILLIAM FULTON, CEC, *Retired, Chester.* A native of Wytheville, Virginia, Fulton spent his career with the military service with both the Army and Navy. He started the U.S. Army Culinary Program at Fort Lee, laying the course for the outstanding training and show teams (the 1992 team is of course well-represented in this book). He started and coordinated for twelve years the culinary program at Richmond Technical Center. This same program progressed to Mark Kimmel, who set up the apprentice program that today is operated by David Barrish at J. Sargeant Reynolds Community College.

WINSLOW GOODIER, CEC, *Executive Chef, Hermitage Country Club, Richmond,* is a graduate of Johnson and Wales University with an associates degree in culinary arts and bachelors in food service management. He has worked at Colonial Williamsburg, the Chamberlain Hotel, and the Richmond Airport Hilton. Goodier served as president of the VCA during the second year of this cookbook project.

RICHARD GOODWIN, *Chef-Owner, Delaney's Cafe and Grill, Richmond.* After ten years with the Hyatt Corporation at six different locations (including the executive chef position at the Richmond property), Chef Goodwin opened his own restaurant in the West End in May 1992. Delaney's, with a seasonally driven regional American cuisine, enjoys a three-and-a-half star rating. Goodwin was named by *Richmond Magazine* as one of the top chefs of Richmond.

RAOUL HEBERT, *Executive Chef, Bull and Bear Club, Richmond.* Raoul was born and raised in Virginia. Chef Hebert has worked his way up from head line cook, through the brigade system, to his ultimate position. His training was through the VCA apprenticeship program along with continuing education classes at the Culinary Institute of America. Former positions include L'Italia and Holiday Inn, Richmond.

ROLF HERION, CEPC, AAC, *Retired Executive Pastry Chef and Manager of Bakery Colonial Williamsburg, Williamsburg.* Rolf hails from the idyllic town of Bad Sackingen in Germany, a stone's throw from Switzerland. He came to North Carolina in 1959 after an European apprenticeship. Herion ran the bakery for Colonial Williamsburg and had the responsibility of supplying baked goods to all the taverns, the inn, and the lodge. He is a charter member of the Virginia Chefs Association, and was named Chef of the Year in 1978.

RICHARD IVEY, ARAMARK, *Executive Chef Campus Dining, Randolph Macon College, Ashland,* formerly at Virginia Commonwealth University in Richmond, has a wide clientele from high-calorie on-the-run students to the extremely refined tastes of the faculty.

MARK KIMMEL, CEC, AAC, *Executive Chef, The Tobacco Company Restaurant, Richmond,* also developed the menu and trained and developed the staff at T. C. West Steakhouse in Richmond. A certified ice carver from Findlay, Ohio, Kimmel turned down a college football scholarship to attend The Culinary Institute of America, where he earned an associates degree in occupational studies. He has

been the director of the apprenticeship program since 1987 and was honored as Chef of the Year in 1981 and 1990.

M. SCOTT KIZER, *The Dining Room, Ford's Colony, Williamsburg.* Scott was graduated from the Culinary Institute of America in 1986 with an associates degree in culinary arts. His career began in 1985 at Pennsylvania's largest winery—the Bucks Country Winery in New Hope. He then worked the at Hotel Thayer at West Point Military Academy, Hawks Bay, Williamsburg Inn, Berkeley Plantation, and the Downtown Shortstop Cafe. Active in Civil War reenactments, he cooks for two local infantry units.

JOHN KOGELMAN, Certified Master Baker, *Head Baker, The Boca Raton Resort and Club, Florida,* formerly executive head baker with Colonial Williamsburg Bakery, received his education through Walters State Community College, Control Data Institute, Michigan State University, Camden College, the Culinary Institute of America, and apprenticed in bakery with Krogers Bakery. Former positions were held with Bread and Company, John Wanamakers, Hilton Hotel, German Bakery, Michigan State University Faculty, Hyatt Regency, and the Noshia Bakery. Kogelman was highly active with the VCA apprenticeship program and the Virginia Culinary Salon sponsored by Carmine Foods.

TED KRISTENSEN, CEC, AAC, *proprietor of the Willows Bed and Breakfast in Gloucester and food services director of Williamsburg Landing, Williamsburg.* As the second son of a Danish dairy farmer, he apprenticed at the Hotel and Restaurant School in Sweden at the Grand Hotel. His schooling was interrupted for obligatory military duty as a palace guard and as part of a United Nations unit in the Gaza Strip. Early glimmers of adventure on the high seas perhaps were responsible for his signing on with a

Danish shipping line. Later he became a chef in the British protectorate of Malay at a remote rubber plantation, forty miles southwest from Kuala Lumpur. At American Airlines' Sky Chef facility at La Guardia Airport, he oversaw a system that served thirty-six thousand meals a day, half of which were hot. Kristensen came to Colonial Williamsburg in 1978 to manage the Williamsburg Lodge and three taverns. In 1991 he opened a bed and breakfast and continued to operate several institutional food operations. He was named Chef of the Year in 1982.

PHILIP LADD, *Executive Chef, Holiday Inn Executive Conference Center, Chesterfield.* Chef Ladd worked at Richmond-area restaurants while in high school. He attended the Culinary Institute of America, Hyde Park, and completed his externship in Washington, D.C., at Blackie's House of Beef. Ladd has cheffed at some unusual locations, including the Pegasus Restaurant and the Meadowlands Race Track, and some prestigious properties— Hyatt Regency on Capitol Hill, Chicago's Palmer House, and New York's Hemsley Palace. He runs the Court Cafe restaurant, numerous banquets, and the Chesapeake Bay Buffet two days per week.

GRACE LIU, *Chef-Owner, The Dynasty, Williamsburg,* is from the Hunan province of China. Her family fled to Taiwan during the revolution. A former specialist with NASA, she has master's degrees both in mathematics and computer science. With her astrophysicist husband, Eddie, Grace opened their first restaurant in Newport News. Now in a palatial restaurant designed after Eddie's grandfather's home in China, they have created a center of Chinese food and culture in Williamsburg. Their knowledge about Chinese cuisine by province is unsurpassed, making their restaurant *the* place to celebrate Chinese New Year.

JOHN LONG, CC, *Rounds Chef, Williamsburg Inn, Colonial Williamsburg,* is an adviser to the Long Catering, Out-of-Town Club, Cape Charles, and an ice sculptor. He earned an associate of arts at Johnson and Wales University, Norfolk, Virginia, in 1988. Long was formerly with the Trellis, Keystone Resort, Colorado. He is a member of the Team Food Show Competition gold medal winners.

REGINA LOWERY, *Apprentice, The Tobacco Company Restaurant, Richmond,* is a student at J. Sergant Reynolds Community College.

LIZ McCANN, CC, *Coyote's management team,* formerly with The Tobacco Company, Richmond, is also a full-time mother with two children.

JIM MAKINSON, CEC, *Executive Chef, Kingsmill Resort, Williamsburg,* is a Londoner by birth and has been employed around the world. His former position at Bishop's Lodge in Santa Fe was a delightful regional "hot cuisine" counterpoint to that of the California cuisine he served at the Regent Beverly Wilshire in Beverly Hills. Other positions include the Boulders Resort in Carefree, Arizona, the Maui Prince, Kapalua Bay Hotel, and other properties in Switzerland, London, Bermuda, and the Virgin Islands. Makinson is also a member of the Resorts Chef Association.

JOHN MARLOWE, CPC, *Pastry Cook and Pastry Chef of Production in Store, European Specialties, Ukrop's Bakery, Richmond,* spent his early days in drawing and painting. From Danville, Virginia, his talent led him to a three-year apprenticeship under the famous Master Pastry Chef Otto Bernet at Ukrop's. While he is widely adept in pastry, he finds wedding cakes to be his favorite medium, particularly enjoying the subtle and precise details for such special cakes—marzipan figures, rolled fondant, and hazelnut fillings.

JOHN MAXWELL, CEC, *Executive Chef-Owner, Chef Maxwell's Catering Company, Richmond,* formerly executive chef with ARA at NationsBank, Richmond, and Pierce's Catering, Richmond. He was instrumental in moving the apprentice program from Richmond Vo-Tech to J. Sargeant Reynolds Community College. He has expended considerable efforts for SOS Taste of the Nation and other charitable causes.

BRAD OZERDEM, *Executive Chef, Hyatt Richmond at Brookfield, Richmond.* Born in Philadelphia, he was a chemistry major at Drexel University working part-time and summers cooking. Ultimately he found the art and chemistry of food more compelling than college and became a full-time chef. Coming up through the school of hard knocks, he rotated through all the kitchens at the Dearborne Hyatt and the Hyatt properties in San Antonio and Crystal City. He was appointed in 1992 to the Executive Chef's position at the Richmond Hyatt. But his scientific methodology comes in handy as he assembles computers and creates programs for the machines.

MATT PARTRIDGE, CWC, *Executive Chef, Willow Oaks Country Club, Richmond.* Chef Partridge was trained in the VCA apprenticeship program through Richmond Vo-Tech College under Chefs Mark Kimmel and Mitford Simms. He began at Willow Oaks in 1983 as their Sous Chef. His tenacity and outstanding abilities were appropriately appreciated with his promotion to Executive Chef in 1991. Seafood is his specialty, particularly smoked salmon.

RENNY PARZIALE, *Chef-Owner, Virginia Culinary Company, Williamsburg, and Chef-Instructor, P. D. Pruden Vo-Tech, Suffolk.* Chef Parziale's company caters with a heavy nouvelle influence and markets a line of fine oils, vinegars, and mustards. One of his first entrepreneurial ventures was the

Raw Bar Bay in Norfolk. A native of Alexandria, Virginia, he began as a dishwasher at the age of fifteen, then worked his way up to Sous Chef at the Westin Hotel in Washington, D.C. Former positions include the Williamsburg Inn and Lodge, the Coach House at Berkeley Plantation, the Powhatan Plantation, the Masters, and Chez Pierre. In recent culinary salons he has been awarded a bronze in 1989, a gold in 1992, and best of the show in 1993 for his native American theme.

JUDY PEARCE, CWPC, *Pastry Chef, The Colonial Williamsburg Commissary, Williamsburg.* Chef Pearce has been in her current position since 1984. During the Christmas season she can frequently be seen with sugar glue repairing the many beautiful gingerbread houses in Colonial Williamsburg. She started decorating cakes for her children, enrolled in classes, then made cakes for friends, and finally at the Quality Bake Shop, Richmond. Pearce is a member of the National Guild of Pastry and Baking Professionals and is active in their annual Learning Weekend, which brings renowned international pastry stars to Williamsburg.

W. KEITH PEARCE, *an independent food broker in Florida,* was formerly with ARA Services in Richmond and a student in J. Sargeant Reynolds Community College apprenticeship program. His supervisor, John Maxwell, at ARA facilities in Richmond and Charlottesville describes Pearce as an incredibly creative chef. Pearce, a native of Richmond, was introduced early to the food profession as his father (now an international food consultant) operated his own catering company, CaterCorpa.

STEPHEN PERKINS, *Chef Garde Manger, Williamsburg Inn, Colonial Williamsburg, Williamsburg.* After graduating from the Culinary Institute of America, Hyde Park, New

York, he decided that the place of the country's founding was also an excellent place to begin a career. For a brief time he worked at the Kingsmill Hilton, then moved to the five-star inn. In recent culinary salons he has been a member of the Williamsburg Inn team, winning two gold meals and a bronze.

LISA PITTMAN, *Chef-Proprietor, Lisa's Elegant Edibles, Williamsburg,* enjoys grilling expensive items. Formerly with Colonial Williamsburg at the Lodge, Inn, and Golden Horseshoe Clubhouse Grill, The Trellis, and the Inn at Urbanna. Pittman is a member of the Peninsula Caged Bird Association, sometimes working at the Feathered Nest Pet Shop, where duties include cheffing for the birds—mixing beans and rice.

DON PRITCHARD, CEC, *Executive Chef, The Sanderling Inn, North Carolina,* formerly chef-owner of the Lafayette Mixed Grille and food and beverage manager at the Kingsmill Resort. Pritchard, originally from Pennsylvania, is a high-energy, entrepreneurial chef with vast experience in most aspects of the food-related hospitality industry. His ventures have provided great opportunities for many chefs. The Lafayette Mixed Grille was acclaimed for its creative yet highly approachable food.

BILLIE RAPER, *Chef Production Manager, ARAMARK, Bell Atlantic, Richmond,* is active in the junior chapter and formerly apprenticed with the Kingsmill Resort, Williamsburg, while a student in the J. Sargeant Reynold's Apprenticeship Program. He served as president of the junior chef's chapter. Now finished with his apprenticeship, he hopes eventually to earn the ultimate certification of master chef. He particularly enjoys creating pasta dishes and desserts.

MANFRED ROEHR, CEC, AAC, *Chownings and Christiana Campbell's Taverns,*

Williamsburg, originally from Neukirch, East Prussia, has traveled the world with the merchant marine before becoming a U.S. citizen. Manfred intended to be a mechanic in the U.S. Army, but he was instead assigned as a cook. When he joined the staff at Colonial Williamsburg, he moved from administration to the kitchen. He opened Shields Tavern, the only restaurant serving authentic eighteenth-century foods, then back to managing two of the famous Colonial Williamsburg taverns. Manfred has managed the financial concerns for the VCA. His recipes are always prize winners in chef's competitions. He was named Chef of the Year in 1982 and 1995.

HANS SCHADLER, CEC, AAC, *Executive Chef and Director Food Operations, Williamsburg Inn, Lodge, and Conference Center, Williamsburg.* Originally from Hanau am Main, Germany, Schadler began his apprenticeships with the M. Junghans Chain, Inc., graduating in 1961. He worked in all brigade positions from Commis de Cuisine to Sous Chef in hotels in Germany, Switzerland, and Norway. He served as the executive chef for the Norwegian-American Line. In 1968 he joined Rockresorts at Caneel Bay Plantation. Schadler joined Colonial Williamsburg Hotel properties in 1982, where he heads a staff of sixty. His leadership positions for both the VCA and ACF are legendary, culminating in award, medals, and honors, including the ACF Presidential Medallion, the Southeastern Region Chef Professionalism Award, and Chef of the Year in 1989. He is a founding member of the Resort Food Executive Committee, German Chefs Association, Order of the Golden Toque, and Les Amis d'Escoffier Society. He lectures at Johnson and Wales, Norfolk campus, from which he received an honorary doctorate in culinary arts in 1994.

KAREN SHERWOOD, *Chef-Owner, Sherwood Consulting, Richmond,* consults with restaurant and food service groups and substitutes for executive chefs. Her first career was as a research chemist for Philip Morris. After sixteen years she pursued her lifelong ambition to attend the prestigious L'Academie de Cuisine, Bethesda, Maryland. Her scientific background is invaluable for the technical side of food consulting.

EDWARD SWAN, *Chef, Shields Tavern, Colonial Williamsburg, Williamsburg,* trained in the Colonial Williamsburg's apprenticeship program, is chef at the only tavern serving genuine eighteenth-century fare. In his modern, underground kitchen he roasts chickens, serves up Indian pudding, pastries, and the tipsy syllabubs. Edward came to Williamsburg at the age of fourteen to live with his brother, Chef William Swan. While he ultimately followed the same career path, neither overshadows the other. Given his effusive outgoing personality and movie-quality smile, Edward is a frequent chef in the Parade of Homes and serving as a spokesperson at food shows promoting Virginia products.

WILLIAM SWAN, *Executive Sous Chef, Williamsburg Lodge, Colonial Williamsburg, Williamsburg,* trained in Colonial Williamsburg's apprenticeship program and is still with them twenty-eight years later. Swan, a Surry, Virginia, native, is a well-seasoned master at directing the frequent banquets in the lodge's ballroom and other conference rooms.

DOMINADOR VALEROS, *Supervisor Lead Chef, Shields Tavern, Colonial Williamsburg, Williamsburg,* former chef of the Virginia Beach Yacht Club, he studied baking in the U.S. Navy and attended the Navy Mess Management School, Tidewater Community College, and the Culinary Institute of America. He is originally from the Philippines and develops outstanding creative desserts.

MICHAEL VOSBURG, *Executive Chef, The Salisbury Country Club, Midlothian,* in

addition to his regular chef responsibilities, uses ice carving as one of his artistic outlets. Vosburg serves on the apprenticeship and membership committees and has volunteered for the International Food Festival and other charitable events. In 1992 he was named Chef of the Year.

THE U.S. ARMY CULINARY OLYMPIC TEAM is led by Maj. John C. Miller, chief of the Culinary Skills Training Division at the U.S. Army Quartermaster Center and School, Fort Lee. Thirty nations competed at the 1992 International Kochkunst-Ausstellung. The team won a gold medal with distinction in the hot-food-displayed-cold category and a gold medal for the three-course cooking event for two hundred people.

HOSNI ZEID, *Executive Chef, Indian Creek Yacht and Country Club, Kilmarnock,* is originally from Egypt, formerly with the Kitchen at Powhatan Plantation, and classically trained as a French chef.

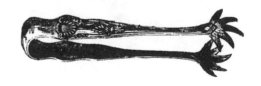

ASSOCIATE CONTRIBUTORS

BRUCE BAKER, *President, Baker Brothers Produce, Richmond,* now runs the family restaurant-supply business specializing in produce.

DAVID BARRISH, CHA, *Program Director, Hospitality-Restaurant-Institutional Management, J. Sargeant Reynolds Community College, Richmond,* as a youth in Cleveland, Ohio, considered being a fireman. Now a well-respected academician, he ensures that his graduates know both how to avoid and extinguish fires.

COBY FITZHUGH, *Carmine Foods, Division of the Virginia Food Service Group, Richmond.* This organization sponsors the prestigious regional culinary competition, an ACF-sanctioned event in Richmond. Carmine received the 1993 Purveyor of the Year Award.

JO OLSON, *Account Executive, Atlantic Food Services, Inc., Richmond,* formerly executive chef at The Butlery, Richmond, earned her degree in culinary arts in Des Moines, Iowa. Atlantic Food Services supplies local restaurants. For 1993 she was named Associate of the Year.

AMERICAN CULINARY FEDERATION THE AUTHORITY ON AMERICAN CUISINE

IT IS AMAZING that people eat in establishments where total strangers prepare the foods. Why? The public has trust in restaurants. Consuming foods is an extremely intimate action, with enormous impact on one's well-being and entertainment. But why leave it up to fate?

Diners who are more discriminating want to know the answers to these questions. Who is the chef managing the back of the house?

What are his or her credentials, education, experience, and creativity? Can the chef present quality foods within the price structure? Does the chef subscribe to the high level of professionalism established by the American Culinary Federation (ACF)?

Member chefs subscribe to a formal code of ethics of which the first line is "I pledge my professional knowledge and skill to the advancement of our profession and to pass it on to those who are to follow."

The ACF, more than sixty-five years old, is the largest U.S. professional culinary organization with more than twenty-one thousand chef and cook members. The ACF Educational Institute, registered with the Department of Labor for its National Apprenticeship Program, was established in 1963. Their mission—"set professional standards for culinary education and assist in career development of individuals interested in the culinary profession."

The ACF is *the* authority on the United States' cuisine. The ACF sponsors more than sixty culinary salons per year and selection of the U.S. Culinary team which competes every four years in the Culinary Olympics against thirty or so national teams in Frankfurt, Germany. The National Restaurant Association cosponsors the team.

The Virginia Chefs Association (VCA) is the regional chapter from Williamsburg to north of Richmond with more than one hundred members. They are *the* authorities on Virginia's regional cuisine.

Monthly the VCA meets in members' hotels, resorts, restaurants, private clubs, or at the premises of an associate member. After the business meeting, which often concentrates on an upcoming event where chefs work together donating their time, efforts, and supplies for charitable causes (Boys and Girls Club, Share our Strength, Horizons 2000, Chef and the Child), an education program commences.

Continuing education is crucial for chefs. They must be abreast of the latest developments in nutrition, sanitation, ingredients, and culinary trends. Industry experts in seafood, meats, produce, and dairy deliver excellent programs often with demonstrations, videos, and tastings. As the industry changes, so do the chefs. As their cuisine changes so does the diet of the American populace.

More intensive classes frequently are held, especially in sanitation and nutrition, that are partial requirements for certification. Chefs must also have formal training, on-the-job experience, and contributions to the profession.

Annually, the VCA sponsors a seminar with the College of William and Mary's Virginia Institute of Marine Science (VIMS). More than two hundred chefs attend this popular forum, which includes the latest information on seafood.

The certification titles after chefs' names indicate the professional levels established by the American Culinary Federation Education Institute (ACFEI). More than seven thousand members have qualified based on written examinations, education, experience, and professional association activities. Certifications must be renewed every five years.

Levels of professional certification are Master Chef (CMC), Master Pastry Chef (CMPC), Executive Chef (CEC), Executive Pastry Chef (CEPC), Working Chef (CWC), Pastry Cook (CPC), and Cook (CC).

In the coming years the certification levels will change slightly with the following designations: Executive Chef (CEC), Sous Chef (CSC), Chef de Cuisine (CCC), Working Chef (CWC). New designations in the pastry field include: Culinary Educator (CCE) and Pastry Chef (CPC).

Meetings are also social, giving chefs an opportunity to meet with peers, exchange ideas, and get help with issues in a friendly forum. The member host always provides food and beverages in the same elegant manner provided for their guests.

The claim to regional Virginia cuisine authority is strengthened by the number of Virginia chefs holding the honor of membership in the Academy of Chefs (AAC), the most prestigious chefs' organization. To be eligible the chef must have a high-level ACF certification, fifteen years in the profession, and have made significant contributions to professionalism and the organization.

Virginia Chef members are also active in two special and active ACF groups—the Resorts Chefs and The National Guild of Pastry and Baking Professionals.

Index